Pillars of E

Pillars of Evolution

Fundamental principles of the eco-evolutionary process

DOUGLAS W. MORRIS
Professor of Biology and Lakehead University Research
Chair in Northern Studies, Lakehead University, Canada

PER LUNDBERG
Professor of Theoretical Ecology, Department of Biology,
Ecology Building, Lund University, Sweden

OXFORD
UNIVERSITY PRESS

OXFORD

UNIVERSITY PRESS

Great Clarendon Street, Oxford OX2 6DP

Oxford University Press is a department of the University of Oxford.
It furthers the University's objective of excellence in research, scholarship,
and education by publishing worldwide in

Oxford New York

Auckland Cape Town Dar es Salaam Hong Kong Karachi
Kuala Lumpur Madrid Melbourne Mexico City Nairobi
New Delhi Shanghai Taipei Toronto

With offices in

Argentina Austria Brazil Chile Czech Republic France Greece
Guatemala Hungary Italy Japan Poland Portugal Singapore
South Korea Switzerland Thailand Turkey Ukraine Vietnam

Oxford is a registered trade mark of Oxford University Press
in the UK and in certain other countries

Published in the United States
by Oxford University Press Inc., New York

© Oxford University Press 2011

British Library Cataloguing in Publication Data
Data available

Library of Congress Cataloging in Publication Data
Data available

Typeset by SPI Publisher Services, Pondicherry, India
Printed in Great Britain
on acid-free paper by
CPI Antony Rowe, Chippenham, Wiltshire

ISBN 978–0–19–856879–7 (Hbk.)
978–0–19–856880–3 (Pbk.)

1 3 5 7 9 10 8 6 4 2

Preface

Six years ago, in this very room and in the good company of friends and students, we shared the kernel of an idea. 'Wouldn't it be grand', we mused, 'to write a book that transforms the way that we and others think about the union between evolution and ecology'. So began our personal odyssey toward the *Pillars of Evolution.*

What we call and understand as evolution by natural selection depends only on its three postulates, each of which is a repeatedly verified fact. Wherever those facts apply, so too does adaptive evolution. Life is self-replicating with error. More offspring are produced than can survive. The survival of (future) offspring depends on heritable characters that effect demography.

Thus, the fabric of life, with its interwoven patterns and textures, emerges only through evolution. Biology is a subset of evolution, not the other way around. Our intent is to take this message to senior undergraduates and graduate students while they are developing their worldview. But we also attempt a style and content that makes our book attractive to practising scientists who may be provoked to follow, or challenge, our approach.

We take no credit for the majority of ideas covered in this book. Indeed, they have been shaped and honed over many enjoyable hours contemplating life with friends and colleagues. We have space to name but a few of the most influential and inspiring: Joel Brown, Robert Holt, and Jörgen Ripa. Kelly Morris and Lena Lundberg Magnusson made it possible for us to write with heart, and not just a scientist's impartial mind. The ideas in our little book were improved by the comments from sage and sincere anonymous reviewers, and through the wise counsel of Ian Sherman and Helen Eaton.

We are thankful for the financial support provided to DWM by Canada's Natural Sciences and Engineering Research Council, and to PL by the Swedish Research Council. Most of all, we are grateful for the opportunity to share our ideas and perspectives on a discipline that we consider more important than any other. We believe that our approach to those ideas is somewhat unique, and that it hopefully has some potential to alter the ways that future scientists understand, study, and teach biology. We are saddened that the shortness of human lifetimes will let us see but a tiny fragment of that future. But we are heartened that, because of evolution, we can visualize possible future worlds, and savour, surreptitiously, the ways that our descendants may enjoy them.

Our text begins with 'Imagine . . .'. Yes, imagine!

Kakabeka Falls, Canada
All Hallow's Eve 2010

Contents

1

Introduction

Why study evolution?

Imagine that you are walking through your favourite woodland. Perhaps you visualize trees of different forms and types. Some are tall, some short. Some have smooth bark, some rough. Some have large single leaves, others compound. Perhaps you imagine songbirds flitting about in the shrubs. They serenade you with song. Their iridescent plumage sparkles as it catches a shaft of yellow light gently filtered through a patchwork of fluttering foliage. Others, cloaked shabbily in tattered feathers, scratch in the litter near your feet. Perhaps you see yourself stooping to peer intently into the golden, ivory, or indigo corolla of a wildflower. You inhale its fragrant perfume. You marvel at bees hovering, momentarily, beside one inflorescence before buzzing to the next. You pause, look up, and like a desert gazelle slaking its thirst, drink deeply from the diversity that flows around you. Life embraces you like an old and cherished friend.

'Evolution is the ultimate field-guide to biodiversity'

You are not alone. All naturalists are enthralled with life, which from shared and humble beginnings yields such splendour, diversity, and superb fit between form and function. We know that all of these features are products of evolution. Descendants differ from their ancestors. No matter how large or small the difference, it is caused by processes that link one generation to the next.

'Evolution explains human origins and portends our collective future'

Human culture and religion are centred on finding (or defining) humanity's place and context in life, time, and space. Evolution provides the most parsimonious and elegant answer. Each year we cumulate irrevocable evidence of our primate origins. We, like all other species on this planet, are a product of evolution. No educated human can deny that adaptive evolution is as much a part of the human experience as are our great religions, cultures, literature, and music. That experience, like all of the others, is deserving of respect and nurture. Moreover, it is our only collective long-term salvation.

Yes, our populations continue to adapt to change that confronts us. But they do so at an incredibly slow rate in comparison to the vast numbers of species that profit from the opportunities presented by ourselves and our plant and animal symbionts. If we are to keep pace with our pests and pathogens, then we need to know the rules that govern their evolution. And we need to know how human activities are likely to shape our shared evolutionary futures.

'Evolution has pragmatic value'

Life is filled with peril. The struggle for existence mercilessly casts off the losers in its endless parade of diversity. Losers come in two forms: the handicapped, who begin life with reduced expectations, and the unlucky, who end life without reaching their promise. Most humans view each option as neither necessary nor desirable. Indeed, one of our most cherished traits is elimination of human suffering. Yet each day, tens of thousands of our kind die 'needless' deaths through disease, strife, and starvation. Each day, our enemies, whether they be the myriads of parasites that plague human health or invaders from distant shores, undergo adaptive evolution. Microbes and pests evolve resistance to our superdrugs and pesticides. Genetically modified organisms are groomed and flourish in our laboratories and fields. Invasive species decimate natives. Hundreds of thousands of other species are threatened with imminent extinction.

We have a desperate need to understand the rules explaining why some species are so imperilled by our activities while others are so successful at exploiting us. And we similarly need to understand the implications of the massive global extinction of biodiversity. Those answers lie in evolution.

'Evolution is the cornerstone of all biological disciplines'

For some characteristics, given enough time and energy, we should be able to trace change between generations to its adaptive advantage and, ultimately, to its nucleotide roots. But for many other characteristics, rules of inheritance operate in hazy, stochastic environments that let us reconstruct the past, but with little ability to forecast the future.

We believe that these differences emerge from fundamental limits on our ability to understand evolution's manifold processes and patterns. The way that biologists have partitioned the elements of evolution into disciplines of genetics, development, systematics, and ecology reflect those limits. But the partitions constrain synthesis. Most molecular geneticists work on different mechanisms than do ecologists. Systematists (and ecologists) use molecular tools, but often are interested in different problems and patterns than are the geneticists and molecular biologists who share the tool kit. And while biologists in different disciplines subscribe to the same grand idea that life can be understood only by knowing evolution, they often ask different questions or try to answer them at different scales. So our collective approach to evolution can be likened to planning a long trip with detailed maps of each destination, but with few or no directions on how to move from one place to another. How can we conduct the business of evolution with such a map?

The year is 1815. Scottish gentlemen from the head office of the North West Company in Montreal have travelled west with 14 *mangeurs du lard* in 10-m long birchbark *canots du maitre*. In only eight weeks they have paddled 2000 km, and crossed 38 portages, to arrive at the western end of Lake Superior for the great rendezvous of the company's employees.

The gentlemen directors and partners conduct business within the palisade of Fort William. Their decisions are guided by reference to a huge map hung in the great hall. The map covers an area of five million square kilometres and includes the locations of each of the company's fur-trading posts. The map was drawn by the careful hand of the world's premier land cartographer, David Thompson. It summarizes 22 years and 88,000 kilometres of painstaking surveys (Gottfred and Gottfred 1995)[1] and gives the gentlemen the spatial and legal context of their empire.

Contemporary geographers are amazed by the accuracy and detail in Thompson's maps and journals. Modern-day 'explorers', guided by their global positioning systems, can find easily the bends in the rivers, the points and heights of land, that Thompson surveyed on foot 200 years before. The accuracy of each point allowed Thompson to summarize the vast lands controlled by the North West Company. Although he could have mapped the local geography of each post, he ignored it so that his map would reveal the large-scale pattern of the company's lands. Small-scale details, so essential to find one's way through a maze of rivers, creeks, and footpaths, would have produced a map of dizzying and unnecessary complexity.

The map of evolution

Thompson's map was a caricature of a huge and gloriously wild land, a simplified model of nature. It defined the area controlled by the North West Company and gave context to its posts. Can we say something similar about the 'map' of evolution? Browse the pages of your favourite evolution text. Think of it as an atlas. Is the sequence of maps complete? Can you move easily among them, or do wonderfully explicit small-scale maps of such things as phylogeny, variation, genetics, development, and ecology leave you wondering about how they relate to one another?

Your answer will depend as much on your worldview as it does on the text's organization. Perhaps you believe that the road to understanding evolution is best travelled

[1] In 1815, Thompson, hobbled by a leg broken 27 years earlier, blind in one eye, and with failing vision in the other, lived 'comfortably' in the Upper Canada community of Williamstown. He died penniless in 1857 at the age of 86. A small recreation of Thompson's great map, given to DWM in the reconstructed great hall by the Board of Trustees of the Canadian Museum of Nature, hangs proudly in the office of the Lakehead University Habitron.

through its mechanics; that you must know how heredity, movement, and survival influence gene frequencies. But if this is your perspective, then you must explain how changes in gene frequencies translate into nature's patterns. Perhaps you will argue instead that the dynamics of ecology are key to evolutionary understanding; that we need to know how density and frequency-dependence change the values of traits from one generation to the next. Even so, you may wonder what processes and rules connect ecology with genetics and molecular biology. Others will realize, regardless of perspective, that the best we can ever do is to generate a caricature of evolution. But if that caricature is to be valuable, it must account for the diversity and history of life, the evolution from simple to more complicated forms, the distribution and abundance of organisms, and the fit of form with function.

'Our understanding of evolution often reflects a reductionist worldview'

Evolutionary understanding, like life itself, is a compromise. It hangs us on the horns of a dilemma. If we attempt to describe large patterns, then we may be forced to ignore the underlying detailed mechanisms responsible for those patterns. But if we dedicate our interest towards mechanism, then we may be unable to foresee its potential to create pattern. To make sense out of the world around us, we are taught to stand one perspective, like a pillar, alongside others. We decide which questions pique our interest, then balance our worldview precariously on whichever pillar seems best able to provide the answers. When seen from a distance, the pillars define a treasury of knowledge centred on evolutionary understanding like the Parthenon on the apex of Athen's acropolis.

To the Parthenon's architects,[2] no pillar was independent from the others. True, the columns vary subtly in size, form, spacing, and orientation. These slight deviations were unnecessary for the pillars' primary function as a collective colonnade supporting the temple's tiled marble roof. But they were essential for the secondary aesthetic function of correcting parallax and optical illusions that can cause long and parallel straight lines to appeared bowed.[3] Architects and teachers of evolutionary thought have much to learn from this example. Typically, we expose students to such topics as the molecular basis of inheritance, rules of gene expression and development, population and quantitative genetics, interactions with the environment, movement of individuals, and the dynamics of populations. We sculpt each with illustrations, equations, and cogent case studies, then move on to the next. The progression reflects the way that we practise our science. But the topics represent separate scopes of interest and fields of inquiry so distant that their practitioners interact rarely, if at all. There must be a better way.

---

[2] Although Iktinos and Kallikrates served as the Parthenon's architects, the sculptor Phidias appears to have been responsible for its decoration.

[3] We discuss the issue of primary versus secondary function of biological traits in Chapter 7.

Pillars of evolution

If we think of evolution as a single body of knowledge supported by its pillars, what would the pillars be? Would we stand the evolution of sex alongside speciation? Would we place the evolution of life histories on equal footing with quantitative genetics? And from what material would we make them? Would we pour concrete examples into a mould reinforced with theory? Would we carve the pillars from the sedimentary sandstone of ideas layered through a century of evolutionary thinking? Or would we send our evolutionary stonemasons to the marble and granite quarries of logic and mathematics?

'Evolutionary understanding is centred in logic and mathematics'

We believe that there is no alternative to logic and mathematics, and that we should let students of evolution construct their temples by standing each pillar in sequence. Subsequent chapters of this book represent how we would choose and place those pillars. Question their assumptions as you stand them next to one another. Chip away imperfections. Polish each one with new and emerging ideas. You may want to rearrange them or change their orientation. When you are finished, stand back, admire your craftsmanship, and reflect on your worldview.

Students new to evolution may find that some pillars are not plumb with their prior assumptions or background knowledge. Some students may worry that their mathematical foundation is too uneven, or that the bedrock of their pre-conceived ideas is so tilted that not even a single pillar can stand firmly on top of it. Do not fret. We provide mathematical and conceptual shims that can help you place each pillar upright, straight, and, we hope, parallel with the others.

Mechanics—Chapter 2

We begin with the pillar called 'Mechanics'. Readers familiar with genetic models of evolution might wish to scan the italicized *'principles'* in order to evaluate which sections are new to them and which would benefit from more careful study. Although Mechanics is more of a review than our other pillars, it is no less essential nor independent. A firm grasp of mechanics is as crucial to our understanding of evolution as is the appreciation of function or the emerging theories of adaptive dynamics.

We begin by reviewing the stochastic processes of mutation, drift, and migration that underlie the genetic and non-genetic variation essential for evolutionary change. We then move on to systematic changes reflected in the rules of Mendelian inheritance. We review models based on one locus and two alleles to examine the population consequences of simple inheritance. We use these models to reveal the four laws of adaptation. Here, our map of evolution has a clear and unambiguous genetic origin. There is a direct link between the frequency of alleles in populations, genetics, and the traits we study.

However, many of the traits that define organisms and allow them to do the work of converting resources into descendants are not inherited locus by locus. Most are linked to their underlying genetic architecture through complex rules of development, interactions with other genes, and interactions with their environment. These interactions produce emergent, continuously varying traits that require us to summarize the basics of quantitative inheritance. We review how interacting genes (epistasis), and the ability of single genes to have multiple effects (pleiotropy), limit the heritability of traits. We then show how the constraints of epistasis, pleiotropy, and genotype × environment interactions limit our ability to predict how adaptation will alter allelic frequencies, and dash the hopes of those seeking a simple lock-step progression from genes→trait→fitness and back to genes.

We illustrate how the expression of polygenic traits is shackled by pleiotropy and non-random associations among genes (linkage disequilibrium). There is no perfect organism. Yet many shed their genetic shackles through phenotypic and behavioural plasticity. Flexible development and plastic behaviour provide another sobering perspective on the ability to move from genes to trait frequencies in populations. Individuals with exactly the same genomes can express different trait values, and possess substantially different mappings of those traits onto fitness.

'Adaptive evolution occurs through inheritance of genes and through inheritance of environment'

All students of evolution know that the phenotypes we observe at any instant in time depend on the success of their genetic ancestors. Fewer students appreciate the important role that exposure to environmental variability can play in phenotypic expression. We attempt to clarify the environmental contribution by introducing non-genetic inheritance through the concept of environmental pedigrees. Such a pedigree traces an individual's 'inheritance' of different environments in much the same way that a genetic pedigree traces one's ancestors.

Adaptive evolution does not occur within single individuals,[4] but is instead a collective property operating within and among populations. The mechanics of population growth and decline are thus as essential to our understanding of evolution as are the mechanics of genetics and development.

No matter how thorough our understanding of the mechanistic basis of inheritance and its transmission through populations, we would be unable to predict the future of evolutionary change knowing only about mechanism. Genetics and development gain evolutionary context through the functions of traits created from the genetic-developmental process. Fitness cumulates the relative differences among individuals in the abilities of their traits to function in real working organisms.

---

[4] Organisms living within or on others, such as bacterial and viral populations, often do evolve within a single host, but do so as populations, not as individuals.

Function—Chapter 3

Traits and strategies meet the environment through function in two different ways. First, we can think of the function of each trait or strategy. In order to make evolutionary predictions from those functions we need to understand how they map onto the traits and strategies that we study. And we also need to know their relationship to fitness. The fitness of many traits at low population density will be different from their fitness at high density. So our mappings must include density dependence. Finally, the adaptive value of many traits will also depend on their frequency in the population and on the frequency of different environments experienced by the population.

Interactions between the environment, traits, and their constituent genes demonstrate that it is impossible to predict evolutionary change in anything but the simplest environments. Even then, we can predict the expected course of evolution only by mapping the traits' values onto fitness (the fitness-mapping function). If individuals exploit more than a single environment (or habitat), then we can use the set of fitness values in each one to help explore whether evolution will favour specialized or generalized phenotypes. The solution requires more than the fitness-mapping function. We need to also generate an adaptive function that determines the average adaptive value of each trait in the mix of environments that it exploits. One of the interesting lessons to be learned from this approach is that density changes the fitness-mapping function while the frequency of physical and biological environments alters its adaptive value.

Most models of trait evolution assume that each trait evolves separately from others. These models teach us valuable evolutionary lessons, but they will often be incapable of predicting the distribution of trait values. This caveat applies to any trait that has a complex mapping onto fitness. The problem becomes much more acute when we attempt to predict the evolutionary dynamics of multiple interacting traits.

We suspect that you are becoming uneasy with the complexities of evolution. Single-locus models fail because many traits are polygenic with complex structures. Direct models of function fail because different traits can perform the same function in different types of organisms. Trait models fail because traits interact with one another, the environment, population size, the frequency of trait values, and the frequency of different environments.

'Understanding of adaptive evolution depends on thorough mappings of inheritance onto traits, traits onto function, and function onto fitness'

Although we agree that evolutionary models are often gross simplifications of evolutionary processes, we would argue that none has failed. Each deepens our understanding of evolution, directs us towards new research questions, and reveals where we might most profitably invest our research effort. Those who are disappointed with the models' predictive ability need to reassess whether or not they are asking the correct question. Too many of us aim to predict how the mechanics of evolution produce distributions of trait values in real populations, and then expect to use the fitness of individuals possessing those values to predict genetic change. This perspective imagines that evolution can be written as a series of recursive equations looping back onto one another in a perfectly predictable manner. And there are good reasons to think so. Genes map onto traits, traits onto function, function onto fitness, fitness onto its adaptive value, and adaptive value onto the next generation of genes. If we know these mappings, as complex as they may be, then surely we can build completely predictable models of evolution. And if we can do this, then the doors are wide open for humans to manipulate evolution to their own ends.

This seductively reductionist worldview also fails on at least four counts:

1. The mappings of most traits and strategies are likely to be sufficiently complex such that no single model can encapsulate their evolutionary dynamics.
2. Many of the functional relationships will include non-linear terms that, depending on starting conditions, can yield multiple alternative outcomes.
3. Stochastic variability in the mechanics and dynamics of evolution means that any prediction is only an approximation of what is possible.
4. If evolutionary predictions must be represented as probability distributions, then our predictions of evolutionary change will drift in unpredictable directions through time.

Structure—Chapter 4

Within these constraints, our ability to predict the dynamics of evolution depends critically on its underlying genetic and environmental structure. The structure is defined by the ways that traits map onto fitness. The mapping is seldom direct because traits are linked to fitness only through their function. The mapping is complicated by the state of the individual because function often differs with age, size, body condition, social status, and a myriad of other variables. And, as we have seen, the mapping depends on correlations among traits, trade-offs between them, and a host of genetic and other options and constraints.

> *'The rules that determine how genes map onto traits, traits onto function, and function onto fitness represent the structure of adaptive evolution'*

We encapsulate these concerns in the elements of a structure matrix. The matrix defines the linkages among environments, genotypes, function, and the traits that perform those functions. The structure matrix is bulky and burdensome to use, but it can serve as a useful heuristic model summarizing the complex interactions that join genes, environment, and function with the traits we measure. The matrix helps to clarify why, when we attempt to map fitness onto traits, that it is nevertheless difficult to predict future evolution. Traits map onto fitness through their function, so only the simplest of traits will yield direct and repeatable relationships with fitness. And traits that are tightly bound to a given function will evolve more rapidly than traits with more variable effects on the same function. We suspect that these sorts of differences will create repeated patterns in the structure matrices of different populations and species. It should then be possible to use the patterns to help direct future research.

Trait values emerge through a rather complex maze of constraints that limit expression of genetic variation, plastic responses to varying conditions, and optimization amongst trade-offs. Developmental processes operating at different rates and times yield a wide variety of trait and organism types through relatively simple patterns of allometric growth. These differences among individuals gain their evolutionary traction through the spatio-temporal structure of populations.

Scale—Chapter 5

Space and time represent two of the many dimensions specifying the scale of evolutionary change. Thus scale adds yet another intimidating level to our attempts to thoroughly understand evolution, and even more so when merged with the complications associated with mechanics, function, and structure. Fortunately, we can use abstract shortcuts to account for scale when we model evolution. One effective way is to build so-called fitness-generating functions that implicitly incorporate many of the complex mappings embedded in the structure matrix. Fitness-generating functions (also called G-functions) are one solution to the problem of scale. If one is interested in micro-evolution,[5] construct a G-function to model the fitness of different alleles. If the interest is macro-evolution, expand the G-function to include suites of strategy sets. Allow your evolutionary interest to be a sliding scale where the assumptions and simplifications you make to answer one question are different from those necessary to solve another.

'Many problems of scale can be addressed through the "grain" of the environment'

We provide an example by assessing the evolution of habitat preference. All organisms live in a world where they use some habitats in proportion to availability (fine-grained generalists) and other habitats selectively (coarse-grained specialists). To understand the evolution of habitat preference we must map habitat use in these sorts of spatial landscapes onto its fitness consequences in adaptive landscapes. When we do that, we learn that subtly different generalist phenotypes are favoured in different fine-grained mixtures of habitat patches. Each habitat is likely to have its own specialist at the larger

---

[5] Micro-evolution refers to cumulative changes accruing to allelic and trait frequencies within populations. Macro-evolution refers to the (usually) longer-term branching that separates one lineage from others.

coarse-grained scale, so each species is both a specialist at large scales and a generalist at smaller ones.

The important sub-theme is that few models and few model constructs actually deal with scale. There is a notable exception: allometric growth tackles scale head on. Although often viewed as constraints, we present the alternative perspective that allometric relationships represent evolutionary solutions, the reaction norms, of how body proportions and functions scale with body size.

Other models explore different components of the structure matrix and different subsets of the gene→trait→function→fitness map. The strategies studied by behavioural ecologists have a genetic basis but that does not mean that evolutionary models of optimal behaviour must include the mechanics of genetics. Changes in allelic frequencies are the consequences of births, deaths, and dispersal, but that does not mean that genetic models need to be explicit about the ecological mechanisms causing death or the demography of populations. Let the scale of your interest determine the scale of your inquiry. Know precisely what question you are asking. Then assess at what scale you might find its answers.

Dynamics—Chapter 6

So we must constantly ask what it is that we expect our evolutionary models to achieve. Do we really aim to build models that predict the future course of evolution? Or do we want our models to give insight into the evolution of biodiversity, the fit of form and function, progression from simple to more complex forms, and the distribution and abundance of organisms?

Fortunately, we can often solve these more general questions by simplifying the complexities of evolution. One promising method subsumes adaptive value within the fitness-mapping function. It then imagines that it can map the fitness of all competing trait values or strategies as a function of population size. This simplification makes it possible to use the resulting fitness-generating function to predict which, if any, trait values and strategies are evolutionarily stable.

'The mechanics, function, structure, and scale of evolution gain their adaptive context through the dynamics of populations'

Although adaptive evolution is built with the mechanical nuts and bolts of inheritance, it occurs through changes in the population frequencies of traits, strategies, trait values, and alleles in time and space. These values depend at least as much on the dynamics of populations as they do on the mechanics of inheritance. And it is in dynamics that we discover the crucial roles of ecology on evolutionary change.

There are actually two major types of dynamics that are essential to model evolution. We develop the principles of strategy dynamics to examine the processes responsible for the success and failure of some traits and trait values over others. Different traits and their values represent competing strategies to be tested by adaptive evolution. The success of each strategy depends on the spatial and temporal dynamics of populations.

We merge strategy and population dynamics to evaluate the evolutionary stability of competing strategies. The fitness of alternative strategies changes with variation in population density. Therefore, a winning strategy must be able to invade when rare, resist invasion from other mutant strategies when common, converge on a steady state when population densities vary or when new strategies are tested against those currently available, and attain a stable pattern in population size. We summarize the mathematical rules that allow us to find the optimum strategy, to assess whether it is stable or not, and to forecast future evolution. Strategies may converge toward a single optimum at an evolutionarily stable attractor, or diverge towards new species at evolutionary branching points. A third possibility that we save for our final chapter is that existing strategies remain separated by unattainable strategies called evolutionary repellors.

The search for evolutionarily stable strategies is hinged on the mathematics of equations. The mathematics presumes that evolution can attain a stable endpoint. And should it do so, evolution stops. Astute students will quickly realize that this is a somewhat misleading caricature of adaptation. There are no winners in the race of adaptation, only leaders, trailers, and losers. Leaders are those strategies currently most fit. Trailers are strategies of lower fitness pursuing the leaders. They may be gaining evolutionary ground, maintaining their position, or falling behind. Losers are those strategies that have been eliminated from the race.

On one hand we thus have a perspective and body of theory evaluating evolution as a single race to be won by those most fit. Their prize is perpetual equilibrium, and the end of evolution. The alternative perspective is that evolution is endless. Leading strategies attain a disproportionate share of resources, like marathon runners who replenish themselves from the food and fluid stations along the course. If a straggling runner falls too far behind, then the stations will be closed when she arrives. Unable to continue without nourishment, she will be forced to exit the race.

So victory, in this race of evolution, is not to win, but simply to keep running. Our models of adaptation, should we choose to build them, would identify the runners. We would want to know what characteristics differentiate runners from those unable to enter, or stay in, the race. Once we determined the runners, we would monitor their speed and position and, perhaps, even to try to predict the leaders and trailers at different points in space and time. But we would have no interest in predicting the winner, because no runner can finish the race.

You may wish to assess these distinctions when you think about evolution and evolutionary stability. Models seeking evolutionarily stable strategies provide deep insights into evolution. But they do so by imagining an ending that, thankfully, is undefined and unattainable.

Much of our understanding of dynamics can be gained from Sewall Wright's metaphor of adaptive landscapes. We use the metaphor to map the contours of mean fitness among competing strategies. In the classical view of adaptation, strategies climb up fitness hills lying on a static and rigid adaptive landscape. We show how this static view changes when connected to the density and frequency dependence of populations. Adaptive landscapes sink as populations increase; they become fluid with changes in frequency. Populations whose strategies might be marooned near the summit of peaks in a static, rigid landscape can evolve many different options when the 'landscape' is fluid.

Adaptation—Chapter 7

One of the beauties of the evolutionary perspective is that it provides all biologists, regardless of their specific interest, with a common theme to guide their work. For most of us, that theme is adaptation. Adaptation provides the answer to our questions about the fit (and occasional lack of fit) of form with function, the diversity and progression of life, and the distribution and abundance of organisms. Moreover, the rules we learn about adaptation are universally applicable to any system where there is heritable variation, a struggle for existence, and an interaction between them. To a large extent, then, the study of evolution is the study of adaptation. Viewed in this light, we can begin to ask whether or not other adaptive systems obey the same sorts of rules as biological evolution. We suspect that they do.

Adaptation, in any form, will require mechanisms that create heritable variation. There must be structural links between that variation and its function. Function must have fitness consequences. Those consequences depend on scale, and the frequency and dynamics of alternative strategies.

One can study evolution, and do so effectively, within any one of the six pillars. Each is represented by multiple biological disciplines built on the insights of brilliant thinkers: Huxley, Mendel, Fisher, Haldane, Wright, Dobzhansky, Mayr, MacArthur, Watson, Maynard Smith, and, of course, Darwin. But to do so gives but a glimpse of the wonder and realm of evolution in the process of life. Evolutionary insights are most likely to emerge when we embrace them all, give each a fair hearing, and only then decide on how our worldview fits among them.

2

Mechanics

HOW CHANCE, MOVEMENT, REPRODUCTION, SURVIVAL, DEVELOPMENT, HEREDITY, AND BEHAVIOUR EFFECT EVOLUTIONARY CHANGE

Overview

Evolutionary theory is an abstract discipline. Our models typically imagine a process of adaptation whereby some genetic variants yield greater probabilities of survival and reproduction than do others, and subsequently increase in frequency. This adaptive process is limited (or enhanced) by the amount of heritable variation available, the underlying genetic and phenotypic architecture of the variants, and by a variety of non-genetic and stochastic processes. In order to appreciate and model their possible synergistic effects on evolution, we must first understand the mechanistic basis of each process.

We begin by surveying purely stochastic or probabilistic changes in genetics. Internal stochasticity (mutation) is complemented by a variety of external sampling and dynamic effects that alter the frequencies of alleles, traits, and strategies in the population. The consequence of random changes in genetics on traits and strategies is similarly influenced by the stochasticity inherent in development.

We then move on to the systematic changes induced by adaptation. We review abstractions based on classical Mendelian inheritance to build simple models of natural selection. Most ecologically relevant traits are the products of numerous interacting genes, so we will explore how the algebra of quantitative genetics expands our understanding of adaptive evolution. We emphasize models that reveal fundamental principles of evolution.

Genetic models are complicated by numerous mechanisms that reduce the direct translation of genetics into traits and strategies with adaptive value. We explore these complicating trade-offs and constraints then demonstrate how one mechanism, phenotypic plasticity, can help solve otherwise intractable solutions for adaptation to variable environments. We complete our discussion of genetic mechanisms by evaluating a new developmental perspective that challenges the lock-step gene-to-trait perspective of genetics. This exciting *Weltanschauung* argues that much of the eventually adaptive phenotypic variance in populations emerges through development and only subsequently is incorporated into the genetic makeup of the population.

The mechanics of evolution are not restricted to genetics and development. A variety of non-genetic mechanisms yield heritable variation that can have rather dramatic consequences for adaptation. Ultimately, whether of genetic or non-genetic origin, the value of traits is expressed through their function and the relationships among function and fitness. Fitness, measured by changes in the frequencies of different trait values or strategies through time, is determined by the mechanics of population growth and decline. We briefly review the processes responsible for population dynamics, then conclude with a reminder that mechanics, though essential, provides an incomplete map for evolution.

Introduction: the scale of mechanism

One can make a very good case that the prototypical North American mammal is the deer mouse (*Peromyscus maniculatus*). It is easy to find these diminutive and curious rodents in virtually any of the continent's terrestrial habitats. They appear equally well-adapted to the scorching desert scrub in Mexico and the southwestern United States as they are to the windblown prairies in the great plains west of the Mississippi River. You will find them in the deep shadows of Carolinian forests in the east, in the sodden temperate rain forests along the Pacific coast, and in the snow-covered evergreen taiga and frozen tundra through northern Canada and Alaska. The diversity encapsulated in nearly 60 described subspecies (some authors suggest more) is rivalled only by the 50 or more identified species within the genus.

Each subspecies is different from all others. They vary in such characters as the length of their tails (short in prairies, long in forests), the hue and tone of their bicoloured pelage (dark silky brown dorsal fur in forests, washed tan in dry habitats), and their restriction to certain types of habitat. It is easy to imagine that deer mice, like their parent genus, have set a course toward ever-expanding diversity. But their winding path towards eventual speciation has numerous twists, turns, and dead ends. Divergence depends on whether deterministic processes of inheritance can win out in a stochastic world of mutation, dispersal, survival, and reproduction.

Each of these processes depends, in turn, on its own underlying mechanics. Inheritance and mutation depend, for example, on the rules associated with chemical bonding and the genetics of translation, transcription, and recombination (as well as transformation, transduction, and conjugation in microbes). The differences that we recognize among individuals are built on such mechanisms as protein synthesis, cell division, differentiation, apoptosis, and tissue formation guided by principles of metabolism, active transport, hormone production and regulation, and innumerable others. Consequently, evolutionary patterns emerge from mechanics operating across many scales in time, space, and organization.[1] Many of these processes include a major

---

[1] Scale is one of the most vexing problems faced by any biologist. Each pattern that we observe is the consequence of mechanisms operating at other scales (usually these scales are smaller than the one of

element of stochasticity. A reasonably comprehensive knowledge of evolution and ecology must be grounded, therefore, in understanding random processes that create and maintain genetic variation, and that restrict or enhance gene flow.

Random change

'Random' is, perhaps, the most misunderstood word in evolution. Opponents to evolution (why should there should be any?) frequently misinterpret (or, worse, misrepresent) random to correspond with the spontaneous origin of genetic variants (mutations) that subsequently combine probabilistically to create heritable traits subject to differential survival and reproduction. They then argue that the probability of generating even one complex trait through this doubly random process is exceedingly small, hence what we perceive as evolution cannot occur except through some form of (usually divine) intervention.

> *'A random mutation is a new genetic variant created independently from the prospects of its future function and fitness'*

There are numerous flaws in this argument,[2] but for our purposes the most important lesson to be learned and retained is that when evolutionary biologists refer to random mutation, they mean that mutation, a heritable change in the genetics of a single genome, occurs independent of its future function and fitness. Whether a mutation occurs in a particular part of the genome, in particular individuals, or specific environments is also stochastic in the sense that we can calculate the probability of it happening, but not when, where, or in which individuals.[3] The reason for this uncertainty is that mutations occur through a variety of 'accidents' such as errors in base-pair substitutions, insertions and deletions (indels) of nucleotides in DNA sequences, recombination, transposable elements, and various chromosomal modifications.[4]

Most mutations, particularly those involving base-pair substitutions, either cause loss of function, or have little phenotypic effect. Deleterious loss-of-function

---

interest, but we provide a remarkably important reversal in the short section on the mechanics of population growth and decline). Each pattern also constitutes part of the mechanics creating different patterns at (usually) larger scales. We can do little more than advise readers to identify the scale of their interest, then experiment to reveal and understand the mechanisms that create patterns at that scale, as well as to treat those patterns as mechanisms causing emergent patterns at other scales.

[2] Bell (2008) provides a wonderfully clear counter-argument demonstrating how replacement of old variants with new improved ones yields rapid evolutionary change.

[3] The insertion/deletion of DNA in genetically modified organisms represents a combination of directed (the gene of interest) and random (linked and epistatic components) mutation.

[4] We assume that readers are familiar with the genetic basis of inheritance and have at least a rudimentary understanding of DNA replication and molecular genetics. Readers who wish to review the molecular biology of evolution, including the mechanisms of mutation, will find an excellent and readable account in Barton *et al.* (2007).

mutations, particularly if dominant, will tend to be cleaved from the gene pool because their carriers produce few descendants. Occasionally, however, single mutations can cause substantial phenotypic changes that lead to rapid divergence within and among populations. Polyploidy, the duplication of the entire genome, is a prime example of this form of macromutation. Numerous plant species, including many agricultural crops, possess two or more copies of all chromosomes. Successful reproduction between polyploids and their ancestral types is usually impossible because chromosome numbers become unbalanced during meiosis. It is thus possible for a mutation that increases ploidy level to simultaneously create phenotypic change and reproductive isolation, and thus near-instantaneous speciation. Regardless of these 'exceptions', and the discreteness of most genetic mutations, most have marginal influence on phenotypes.

Even so, each mutation, whether random or not, has the potential to modify a trait's value and the emergent function that helps to determine evolutionary success and failure. Hence, mutation rate is central to most theories in population and quantitative genetics as well as some of those that summarize the joint consequences of ecological and evolutionary dynamics (Chapter 6).

> '*Although mutations provide the raw genetic variation for evolution,*
> *their translation into phenotypes is also influenced by chance*'

The reason why we hedge on 'evolutionary success' is twofold. First, many mutations appear neutral in their effect. Neutral mutations are necessarily independent of any component of the genome that influences function and fitness. The frequency of such mutations is thus subject only to chance. Second, mutation is but one of many stochastic processes that influence evolutionary change. Numerous stochastic events operating at many different levels influence the interactions among genes, genotypes, gene expression, development, and trait values. Much of the variation among phenotypes depends, for example, on the timing, location, and rate of development (heterochrony). Rather complex interactions among genetic regulatory mechanisms that dictate gene expression and protein synthesis, as well as among numerous internal (e.g. hormonal) and external (environmental) influences, guarantee that chance will play a substantial role in creating non-heritable variation among phenotypes.[5] Although much of evolutionary developmental biology (evo-devo) evaluates mechanisms responsible for the presence versus absence of traits (Klingenberg 2010), there is expanding interest in underlying stochastic events that cause continuous variation in trait expression.

McGill University's Maria Kilfoil and her colleagues (Kilfoil *et al.* 2009) demonstrate that stochastic influences on evolution occur at multiple scales of biological

---

[5] We will soon learn that adaptation operates on the additive component of genetic variance because it 'breeds true'.

organization. At the molecular level, where chemical processes dominate mechanism, noise is introduced through the stochastic interactions amongst molecules. Such chance variation in gene expression creates substantial variation among cells in protein concentrations, which can have dramatic phenotypic consequences. The fate of individual cells during development is similarly subject to chance, whereby only one of many candidate cells may differentiate and inhibit the options of its neighbours. Similar events occur at much higher levels of biological organization. Reproductive inhibition by dominant individuals is common in social species, but the identity of the actual individual achieving dominance will often include a substantial component of luck.[6]

'Numerous mechanisms influence the chance survival of alleles
from one generation to the next'

Even if we know the function, fitness, and heritability of a particular trait value, it is increasingly clear that numerous additional stochastic events modify the course of evolution. Stochastic events can be thought of as sampling exercises. What is the probability, for example, that a particular allele will be transmitted from one generation to the next? This probability will depend on whether the allele contributes to a function with fitness consequences (whether or not it is adaptive), and numerous additional events involving the joint dynamics of populations and environments. Unfortunately, all of these additional mechanisms tend to be categorized together under the single heading of 'genetic drift'.

One common heuristic way of understanding and modelling drift is to think of it as binomial sampling (such as tossing a coin). The 'ideal' probability of outcome A versus outcome B during a single event is equal (0.5), and the joint probability of a sequence of either A or B is the product of their separate and independent probabilities (0.5^n, where n is the length of the sequence of events). This simplistic example nevertheless demonstrates that the likelihood of change in the frequency of outcomes from a purely random process depends on the number of events. Thus, the probability of observing a change in the frequencies of neutral alleles through time depends on how many copies of the alleles are present (population size) and the length of time (generations). For any interval of time, genetic drift is more likely in small populations than in large ones.

This purely neutral and random sampling process is often mistakenly represented as 'the mechanism of genetic drift in small populations' that instead emerges from other stochastic influences also associated with population size. The probability that an allele is transmitted from one generation to the next depends on many probabilistic events,

---

[6] We are drawn to the insight of the oft-quoted phrase, 'I'd rather be lucky than good', attributed to the New York Yankees' Hall of Fame pitcher Vernon 'Lefty' Gomez.

including random variation in mating opportunities for sexually-reproducing individuals, variation in offspring viability, and variation in parental survival.

The size of the population, in turn, depends on the proportion of successfully reproducing individuals, its spatial and temporal structure (Chapter 4), the area or volume available to it (Chapter 5), and its dynamics (including immigration and emigration; Chapter 6). Each of these 'mechanisms' includes numerous additional sources of stochasticity, varying from probabilities of survival and recruitment by individuals to the vicissitudes of the environment in which the population is located. The main point to keep in mind is that these many random events working in concert influence random variation in allelic (and trait) frequencies. They do not give direction to evolutionary change. For that, we require a different type of process.

'The distribution of alleles, traits, and strategies in a local population depends on the rate of migration from and to other populations'

When individuals move from one population to another, they carry their genetics with them. If these individuals reproduce successfully after immigrating, they can change the frequency of alleles, and the products coded for by genetics and development, in future generations of their newly adopted population. Whether the frequency actually changes as a consequence of migration depends on the adaptive values of different alleles, the initial frequencies in the two populations, the net rate of dispersal between them, whether dispersal is passive or varies with phenotype and condition, and on the consequences of migration to subsequent population growth. Classical treatments of migration assume that all genotypes possess the same rate of dispersal. These models are most easily understood in the context of migration from large mainland to small island populations. The models demonstrate, for genes with similar mutation rates and fitness in both populations, that migration homogenizes genetic variance. This statement is easily proven with a simple model.[7]

'Migration between populations, when acting alone, tends to homogenize genetic variation'

Let p_i represent the frequency of a particular allele in the small island population, and let p_m be the frequency in the large mainland population. We imagine that a fraction of the island's population, m, arrives from the mainland each generation. The new frequency of the allele after one generation is given by

$$p_i' = (1 - m)p_i + (m)p_m \tag{2.1}$$

---

[7] We follow the presentation given by Freeman and Herron (2007).

where the prime indicates the new frequency following one generation of migration. The first right-hand term is the frequency on the island before a proportion m migrate, and the second term is the frequency of the allele contributed by new immigrants from the mainland. The change in allelic frequency is directly proportional to the migration rate. In order to see this, define the change in allelic frequency on the island as $\Delta p_i = p'_i - p_i$, and substitute the values for p'_i and p_i into this expression to yield $\Delta p_i = m(p_m - p_i)$. Thus the frequency of the allele on the island converges on that of the mainland each generation. This process will continue until the equilibrium condition, $p_i = p_m$, is reached. Migration, in the absence of other mechanisms, acts to homogenize genetic variation.

This simple genetic treatment assumes, however, that migration is passive. All individuals have an equal probability of dispersal. It is more likely that dispersal represents a form of bet-hedging that allows individuals to escape areas of low fitness advantage and to occupy areas with more ecological opportunity. We return to this important point in our treatments of habitat selection (Chapter 5) and dynamic evolution (Chapter 6). For now, we caution readers that it is best to think of migration as a process that includes both stochastic and systematic elements.

> *'In sexually reproducing species, mate choice can alter the frequencies of genotypes, but by itself, not allelic frequencies'*

Basic (one might better call them null) models of genetics assume independent assortment of alleles each generation, an assumption that leads to a simple binomial expectation of genotypes (see page 22). This assumption can be violated in sexually reproducing species whenever mating is non-random. Non-random mating, either by design (mate choice) or chance (a non-random sample of mates available), will tend to increase (positive assortment) or reduce (negative assortment) the frequency of homozygotes in the subsequent generation. If all genotypes yield similar fitness, and if the genotypic identities of individuals have no influence on the other processes influencing allelic frequencies, then assortative mating alone will not alter the course of evolution. This conclusion holds even though assortative mating can inhibit gene flow between populations and act in concert with disruptive selection in the formation of new species. Inhibited gene flow implies a non-random population structure (Chapter 4) that violates the assumption of independent assortment in the population as a whole.

Systematic change

Adaptation: the key process of evolution

We have explored how mutation can create genetic variation, how various forms of chance (especially drift and random migration) alter genetic frequencies, and how the variation in genotypic frequencies can be modified by mate choice. None of these processes, acting alone, can cause predictably repeated patterns in nature (other than changes associated with homozygosity). Yet when we observe nature we see pattern, and not just any pattern, but patterns repeated through time, patterns repeated from place to place, and patterns repeated among different taxa. We observe a tight fit between form and function. Organisms appear designed for the work that they do. We observe a huge diversity of lifestyles and lifeforms that nevertheless possess discontinuities that we recognize as different species and taxa. We note that organisms are not everywhere abundant and that certain types of organisms are more abundant in some places than they are in others. And we observe a diversity of life that corresponds to a procession through time from less complex to more complex forms and designs of biological organization. What process can cause these repeated features of biotic diversity?

Charles Darwin (1859) gave us the answer with a vision of adaptive evolution. Suppose that:

- the traits of offspring resemble those of their parents (there is heritable variation);
- resources are limited and organisms are capable, at least some of the time, of producing more offspring than there are resources to support them (there is a struggle for existence);
- the fit of some traits and their values with the environment (their ability to do the work of life) exceeds that of others (the expected survival and reproduction of individuals with particular traits and trait values is greater than that of others with different values—the outcome of the 'struggle' depends on heritable variation in traits).

Then, the frequency of individuals possessing the most 'favourable' traits and combinations of values will increase through time.

Most authors recognize these three points as Darwin's key postulates for natural selection. Darwin chose the term 'natural selection' because he contrasted it with the artificial selection of plant and animal breeders. This choice of terms is unfortunate for two reasons. First, it tends to emphasize differential survival (the form of 'selection' practiced by most breeders—note that we do not call them 'selectors') over differential reproduction.[8] Second, it suggests that the 'selection' imposed by humans somehow violates 'natural' evolution. It does not. Domesticated organisms possess certain values and combinations of traits for exactly the same reason that 'wild' organisms do. The frequency of individuals possessing the most 'favourable' traits increases through time. Domesticated organisms are adapted to their environment in the same sense that wild organisms are adapted to theirs. Plant and animal breeders bend the rules of evolution

---

[8] Kingsolver and colleagues (2001) reviewed estimates of the 'strength of selection' for components of fitness associated with mating success, fecundity, and survival. 'Selection' in the 14-year data set was stronger on mating success and fecundity than it was on survival.

(for example by intensifying mortality on individuals with extreme 'undesirable' trait values), but they certainly do not break them.

Because of this, we will frequently use the term 'adaptive evolution' (or simply 'adaptation') in place of 'natural selection'. Thus, 'to adapt' means to evolve according to rules specified by the three key postulates of adaptive evolution. Adaptive evolution produces adaptations: traits, or values of traits,[9] that cause individuals to produce more descendants than individuals with other traits or trait values. And because adaptations represent traits that match their function with the environment, the emergent patterns themselves appear 'adaptive'. Some occur far more frequently than do others.

Mutation, drift, and migration can also cause the frequency of traits and their values to change, but they are not adaptive. They do not produce repeated patterns any more frequently than expected by chance alone.

Let's make certain that we understand adaptation by formalizing a model for the adaptive evolution of a single trait. To make our model as clear as possible, we imagine a single genetic locus with Mendelian inheritance (additive effects and independent assortment) of two alleles and a one-to-one correspondence between the gene and its function. We will also assume a one-to-one correspondence between function and the expected number of future descendants (some measure of what Darwin called 'fitness'). Thus we can imagine that one allele is better able to carry out the gene's function than is the other, and that it will thereby convey higher fitness. How should adaptation proceed?[10]

'Adaptation operates through function, and only indirectly on traits'

Our assumptions allow us to easily derive each allele's fitness relative to others. Relative fitness measures the trait's contribution to its function(s). So when we imagine that we can understand adaptation with simple one-gene models, we assume implicitly that the gene is responsible for all of the functions performed by the organism. And when we assume that each allele has a particular fitness relative to all others we assume that function maps directly onto fitness. A simple trait-value-to-function-to-fitness mapping is unlikely for any trait. We cannot overemphasize this crucial point. Adaptation operates on function, not on traits, and not on their values.[11] Some functions influence the ability to survive and reproduce more than others, and so some traits (and trait values) also are more exposed to adaptation than are others. Any feature that tends to separate function from survival and reproduction, or that separates function from inheritance, will weaken the ability of adaptation to yield a population of individuals

---

[9] Our use of 'trait' at this point implicitly includes 'strategy'.

[10] Readers may wish to contemplate how frequently such simple caricatures of evolution are actually implied by the way that we study and manipulate genomes.

[11] Our emphasis on function does not detract from the view that insights into adaptation can be gained from a gene-centred view (Williams 1966, Cronin 2005).

possessing the same value for that trait. So when we ignore those features, as we will with our single-gene models, the solutions represent a very special case for adaptive evolution. The map of evolution that we draw in this book will be explicit on the relationship between traits and fitness. But for now we use a simplified model of nature by assuming that different trait values vary in function with direct effects on fitness. Please keep this assumption in mind as we explore adaptation.

> *'Whenever allelic frequencies are maintained in a steady state,*
> *genetic evolution is impossible'*

Shortly after the turn of the 19th century, Godfrey Hardy and Wilhelm Weinberg used the binomial expansion to demonstrate that genotypic frequencies will always attain a stable (Hardy–Weinberg) equilibrium in the absence of mutation, drift, migration, adaptation, and assortative mating. Thus, if we imagine a single-locus autosomal gene[12] with two alleles in frequencies p and q (i.e. $p + q = 1$), then in a sexually reproducing diploid population, the frequency of homozygous and heterozygous genotypes in the next generation will be given by $(p + q)^2 = p^2 + q^2 + 2pq$.[13] The original allelic frequencies will also be preserved. So if, in a population of interest, we observe a frequency other than that predicted by the Hardy–Weinberg equilibrium, then we can be assured that one or more of its fundamental assumptions has been violated. We *may* have observed evolution. But, if the genotype frequencies have not changed from one generation to the next, then no evolution will have occurred *at that locus in that generation*.

> *'Genetic evolution occurs only when there is a change in the distribution*
> *of traits and in the underlying genetics'*

Some readers will wonder, if we observe a change in genotype frequencies from one generation to the next, then why we cannot always claim evolution. Surely a change in the distribution of genotypes will almost certainly involve a concomitant change in the distribution of traits that we observe. The solution to this paradox lies in the assumption that a Hardy–Weinberg equilibrium can be attained only through random mating in large populations. The assumption corresponds to a scenario where allelic frequencies of mating individuals are unbiased through common ancestry (the gene pool is completely mixed every generation). Since the probability of mating between any two individuals is independent of their genetic makeup, the joint probability of mating

---

[12]   An autosomal gene is one that is found on normal chromosomes shared by both males and females and is thus subject to Mendelian inheritance.

[13]   The Hardy–Weinberg equilibrium also applies to loci with more than two alleles. The equilibrium frequencies of genotypes homozygous for the ith allele is given by p_i^2; the frequency of heterozygotes for any pair of alleles i and j is $2p_ip_j$ where p_i and p_j correspond to the respective allelic frequencies. Readers interested in more complicated scenarios of inheritance can find useful overviews in Bell (2008).

between two individuals sharing the same allele is the product of the allele's frequency (Hardy–Weinberg equilibrium). But if mixing is incomplete, then there is an increased probability that mates might be related to one another (inbreeding). What is the expected distribution of genotype frequencies?

Imagine a single offspring whose mother had two types of 'suitors': males who were unrelated to the female and males who shared a common ancestry.[14] We define the proportion of males sharing the same allele at an autosomal locus *and* unrelated to the female as $(1 - F)$. The proportion of related males is (F).[15] Imagine that there are only two alleles, A_1 and A_2, in frequencies p and q, respectively. The probability that the offspring is homozygous for A_1A_1 and that it received its alleles from unrelated parents is given by the probability that it is homozygous (p^2) multiplied by the probability that the parents were unrelated $(1-F)$. We calculate the probability that the individual's alleles share common ancestry by first imagining that individuals are capable of self-fertilization. In this instance, $F = 1$, all individuals are autozygous,[16] and the probability that the individual is autozygous for a given allele is necessarily equal to the allele's frequency in the population, $(pF$; there are no heterozygotes). The same will be true when heterozygotes are produced $(F < 1)$, so the new frequency of A_1 homozygotes following one generation of inbreeding is thus equal to

$$p^2(1 - F) + pF = p^2 + F(p - p^2). \tag{2.2}$$

Substituting $1-q = p$ for the left-hand term in Equation 2.2 we can show, after a few lines of algebra, that Equation 2.2 is equivalent to $p^2 + Fpq$. Thus, with inbreeding, the expected frequency of homozyotes has been increased by Fpq. Similar logic applies to allele A_2. Heterozygotes cannot share common alleles, so their frequency is given by the probability of being heterozygous and unrelated $(2\ pq[1-F])$. And if related and unrelated parents produce equal numbers of surviving offspring, then there will be no change in allelic frequencies from one generation to the next. Inbreeding has created an excess of homozygotes but no genetic evolution.

We can detect the degree of inbreeding by comparing the observed frequency of heterozygotes, H, across several different loci with that expected by random mating. We need to include multiple loci to minimize the probability that a reduced frequency of heterozygotes could be produced by a different violation of the Hardy–Weinberg equilibrium. We recall that the frequency of heterozygotes produced through inbreeding, H, is

---

[14] Our treatment of single-locus models for inbreeding and adaptation follow those in leading evolution texts by Freeman and Herron (2004) and Futuyma (1998, 2005).

[15] Population geneticists refer to F as the inbreeding coefficient. $F = 0$ only if all individuals are unrelated to one another.

[16] Genotypes with two identical alleles sharing a common line of descent are 'autozygous'. All autozygous individuals are also homozygous (heterozygotes receive two different alleles).

$$H = 2pq(1 - F) \qquad (2.3)$$

and thus we can estimate the inbreeding coefficient as

$$F = \frac{(2pq - H)}{2pq} \qquad (2.4)$$

where H is measured on the population of interest and $2pq$ (the expected number of heterozygotes if there is no inbreeding) is calculated from our knowledge of the initial allelic frequencies occurring in the population.

'Inbreeding depression alters the frequency of alleles, and can thereby lead to adaptive mate choice'

So with inbreeding, we observe an increase in the frequency of homozygotes and not necessarily a change in allelic frequencies. But recessive deleterious alleles are expressed only in homozygotes. Often, therefore, inbreeding causes a reduction in survival or fecundity (called inbreeding depression). These changes in fitness alter the values of different alleles, change their frequencies in the population, and cause subsequent adaptation.

Imagine, for example, that a mutation arises in a population with inbreeding depression, causing individuals to preferentially mate with non-relatives (or at least with distantly related individuals). Individuals possessing the mutation will produce more descendants, on average, than will those lacking the mutation. Avoidance of inbreeding, in this example, leads to adaptive mate choice. Based on our general understanding of adaptation, we predict that this and other beneficial mutations will increase in frequency. We need, nevertheless, explicit models of the adaptive process to guide us towards a thorough comprehension of adaptive evolution.

'Adaptive evolution depends on relative, not absolute, differences in fitness'

Models of adaptation often begin by defining absolute fitness of genotype i as the per capita growth rate of that genotype (roughly equal to the number of descendants in the next generation, R_i). The mean value of absolute fitness for all genotypes in the population yields the population's growth rate. Adaptation of a given genotype depends only on its success relative to other genotypes, not on its absolute fitness. So we need to calculate a measure of relative fitness. We can do this by standardizing our fitness estimates relative to the genotype with the highest R (there are instances, such as heterosis—heterozygotes possess higher fitness than do homozygotes—when it may be appropriate to select an alternative genotype as the reference). If we denote this genotype as A, then its relative fitness will be $W_A = R_A/R_A = 1$. Similarly, the relative fitness of genotype B will be given by $W_B = R_B / R_A$. We will now use these basic relations to derive a general model of adaptation for a single autosomal diploid locus (one allele each from two homologous chromosomes) with alleles A_1 and A_2 in frequencies p and q, respectively.

'Models of adaptive evolution for simple Mendelian traits reveal four "laws of adaptation"'

We imagine random mating so that the expected frequencies of zygotes obey the Hardy–Weinberg distribution. We then invoke differences in relative fitness by imagining that different genotypes have different probabilities of surviving to become reproductive adults (survival rates for A_1A_1 homozygotes $= W_{11}$, for A_2A_2 homozygotes $= W_{22}$, and for A_1A_2 heterozygotes $= W_{12}$). The mean fitness of the population is thus the summed product of the proportion of each different genotype multiplied by its survival rate

$$\overline{w} = p^2 w_{11} + 2pq w_{12} + q^2 w_{22} \tag{2.5}$$

The final frequencies of adults belonging to each genotype will thereby be the product of their initial frequency multiplied by their survival rate, divided by mean fitness (to re-standardize the sum of frequencies to equal 1). The genotype frequencies of adults belonging to the different genotypes are

$$A_1A_1 = \frac{p^2 w_{11}}{\overline{w}}; A_1A_2 = \frac{2pq w_{12}}{\overline{w}}; A_2A_2 = \frac{q^2 w_{22}}{\overline{w}}$$

respectively. To calculate the new allelic frequencies, we add the proportion of alleles contributed by homozygotes plus one-half of the alleles contributed by heterozygotes. Thus the frequency of allele A_1 in the adult population is given by

$$p' = \frac{p^2 w_{11} + pq w_{12}}{\overline{w}}$$

and that of A_2 by

$$q' = \frac{pq w_{12} + q^2 w_{22}}{\overline{w}}$$

We can now proceed to determine the degree of evolutionary divergence after one generation by calculating the change in allelic frequency as

$$\Delta p = p' - p$$

Substituting the value for p' that we calculated above, we can show that

$$\Delta p = \frac{p}{\overline{w}}(pw_{11} + qw_{12} - \overline{w}) \tag{2.6}$$

An alternative version of Equation 2.6 can be derived by substituting Equation 2.5 in place of w to yield

$$\Delta p = \frac{pq([p\{w_{11} - w_{12}\}] + q[w_{12} - w_{22}])}{\overline{w}} \tag{2.7}$$

Equations 2.5 to 2.7 reveal four important adaptive 'laws':

1. Under the conditions of adaptation alone (no drift, migration, or mutation), the allele with the highest relative fitness will, unless at equilibrium, always increase in frequency (Equation 2.7 is always positive when $w_{11} > w_{22}$).
2. Under the conditions of adaptation acting alone, the rate of evolutionary change is proportional to the initial allelic frequencies and the difference in fitness among alternative genotypes.
3. The rate of evolutionary change caused by adaptation is inversely proportional to mean fitness.
4. Whenever $\Delta p \neq 0$, adaptive evolution acting alone will increase mean fitness—refer to Equation 2.5.

Although Equation 2.6 represents a general expression for the adaptive evolution of a single allele, it is often rewritten in a somewhat different form. Imagine, for example, that the fitness of the heterozygote exceeds that of both homozygotes ($w_{11} < w_{12} > w_{22}$). If we substitute $1-s$ for w_{11}, $1 = w_{12}$, and $1 - t$ for w_{22}, and substitute these values for mean fitness in Equation 2.5 (recall that $p^2 + 2pq + q^2 = 1$), we can rewrite Equation 2.6 as

$$\Delta p = \frac{pq(tq - sp)}{1 - sp^2 - tq^2} \tag{2.8}$$

where s and t are the so-called 'selection coefficients' of the two respective homozygotes (we prefer the term 'adaptive coefficients'). An adaptive coefficient represents the difference in fitness between the genotype of interest and the reference genotype. Equation 2.8 illustrates that, if adaptation is acting alone, a rare allele A_1 will always increase in frequency when heterozygotes have the highest fitness. Moreover, if we set $\Delta p = 0$, then we can calculate the equilibrium frequency of the A_1 allele to be

$$\hat{p} = \frac{tq}{s}$$

and substituting $1-p$ for q,

$$\hat{p} = \frac{t}{s+t}$$

Similar equations can be constructed for any combination of adaptive coefficients for the three genotypes. Thus, if we know the initial allelic frequencies and the adaptive coefficients, then we can iteratively predict the future frequency of each allele.

'A thorough analysis of adaptation must include models for traits with polygenic inheritance and a complex mapping onto genetics and development'

Many of the traits that interest us are unlikely to have the simple Mendelian inheritance and one-to-one correspondence between genotypes and traits assumed by our models. Before we begin to assess these more realistic scenarios, let us comment briefly on why we chose to review the single-locus approach for adaptation, and its unrealistic assumptions.

Scientific models tend to fall into two divergent camps.[17] One set is composed of highly simplified theories that pack on assumptions so that a single process (or set of processes) can be examined logically for general principles. Such are the single-locus models of adaptation. The other set of theories, though still simplified, cleave off those assumptions in an attempt to help us explore, and ultimately predict, outcomes from natural experiments. Both types of models can help us understand trait evolution in real populations.

Quantitative inheritance: a full understanding of mechanics must include an assessment of polygenic traits

Polygenic traits (such as body size) require a treatment different from that of discrete genotypes because most vary continuously. Quantitative genetics, the discipline associated with polygenic inheritance, arose from agriculturalists interested in predicting the evolutionary consequences of plant and animal breeding. We shall see that much of the terminology, and many of the simplifying assumptions, reflect that applied focus. But adaptation obeys general rules, so the insights revealed by quantitative genetics are as applicable to our general understanding of evolution as they are to those who wish to 'improve' agricultural species and their numerous varieties. There is, however, a rather substantial difference between applied and 'theoretical' quantitative genetics. Plant and animal breeders typically control environmental influences on the traits they are aiming to improve. In completely natural systems, environmental effects are much more variable, and play a substantially more significant role in evolution.

'Models of adaptation of quantitative traits must be based on the values of the traits themselves, not on the underlying genotypes'

---

[17] We refer interested readers to a limpid discussion of model building by Rice (2004). We also recommend Rice's book as required reading for anyone interested in the mathematics of evolution.

Our treatment of adaptation earlier in this chapter assumed that we actually knew the genetic structure of the trait. The trait was the single-locus genotype. The complex genetic control of quantitative traits is unknown.[18] So instead of modelling adaptation in terms of genetics, we are forced to model it in terms of the traits themselves. Quantitative traits emerge not only from the genotype (denoted by G), but also from environmental influences (E), and from interactions between the genotype and the environment, ($G \times E$, we develop the underlying structure more completely in Chapter 4).[19] Thus, for any specific trait of interest we can write

$$T_{ij} = G_i + E_j + (G_i \times E_j) \tag{2.9}$$

which states that the value of trait i in environment j is equal to the genotype underlying the trait, the effect of environment on the trait, and the differential response of *different* genotypes with the environment. For the moment, let us ignore the genotype $\times$ environment ($G \times E$) interaction. Then Equation 2.9 can be rewritten in terms of variation in the trait,

$$V_T = V_G + V_E$$

where V = variance. We could then define the similarity in the value of the trait between offspring and their parents as a measure of heritability,

$$H^2 = V_G/V_T$$

where H^2 represents the so-called broad-sense heritability of the trait.[20] However, broad-sense heritability provides an unreliable measure of the change in a trait's value caused by adaptation. If the trait is influenced by interactions within genotypes, such as epistasis and dominance, then the value of the trait in offspring will not be a simple average of the trait's value in parents. We can overcome this problem by decomposing the genotypic variance into its additive and interactive components as

$$V_G = V_A + V_I$$

where I represents all possible interactions within a genotype and A corresponds only to those components caused by simple additive effects among alleles. The additive component will, in the absence of $G \times E$, 'breed true'. So we can calculate how similar the

---

[18] Modifier genes with large phenotypic effects can, in some instances, simplify the mechanics of otherwise complicated quantitative traits.

[19] Equations such as Equation 2.9 ignore the additional component of stochastic variation. We direct readers interested in its possible effects to the perspective by Kilfoil *et al.* (2009).

[20] What we refer to as var(T) is frequently denoted as phenotypic variance in the quantitative genetics literature.

expected value of the trait in offspring will be to that of their parents, *in a single population and environment*, by

$$h^2 = V_A/V_T$$

where h^2 is the so-called 'narrow-sense' heritability. Any factor (such as dominance and epistasis) that increases V_T will reduce heritability.

' In completely controlled populations, the change in a trait's mean value from one generation to the next can be predicted by the breeder's equation'

Narrow-sense heritability is a vital concept in plant and animal breeding, where it is used to measure the ratio of the response to selection (R)[21] divided by the selection differential (S, Fig. 2.1),

$$h^2 = \frac{R}{S} \qquad (2.10)$$

Equation 2.10 is one version of the so-called 'breeder's equation', which is often rearranged as $R = h^2 S$ to predict the expected response to selection by a pre-determined breeding programme. The response to selection is thus the change in the trait

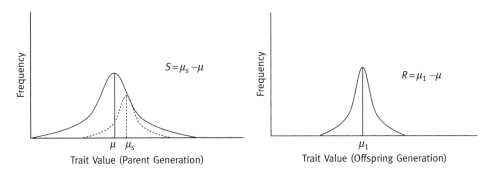

Figure 2.1. An illustration of the relationship between the selection differential (S) and the response to selection (R). Panel A illustrates the distribution of trait values in the parent generation (solid line), as well as the values of those individuals that successfully reproduce (dotted line). The difference in the mean trait value of the entire population of potential breeders (μ) and the mean of the successful breeders (μ_s) is the selection differential ($S = \mu_s - \mu$). Panel B illustrates the distribution of trait values in the succeeding offspring (F_1) generation. The difference in the mean trait value of the offspring distribution (μ_1) and that of the parent generation is the response to selection ($R = \mu_1 - \mu$).

---

[21] Selection is the proper term here because breeders typically choose only a subset of available individuals for reproduction. Be careful not to confuse the response to selection with a population's net reproductive rate, which is also typically denoted as *R*.

distribution between generations caused by the differential reproduction of individuals in the previous generation.

It is often very difficult to measure the selection differential in natural populations,[22] yet we would like to have some general measure of evolutionary change from one generation to the next. Since all offspring are produced by parents, evolutionary change must necessarily reflect the difference in the trait value in the offspring relative to that observed in the parents. Imagining for the moment that we are interested only in the mean value of the trait, the difference between generations can be written as

$$\Delta \bar{z} = (cov[w, z]) + E[w\bar{\delta}] \tag{2.11}$$

Equation 2.11 is one version of the Price (1970, 1972) equation,[23] where $\Delta \bar{z}$ represents the change in mean trait value between generations, $cov[w, z]$ is the covariance between relative fitness and the trait's value in the parent generation (a measure of how much change occurs in fitness when the trait's value changes), and $E[w\,\bar{\delta}]$ is the expected change in the trait's value *in the absence of differential reproduction and survival*. The covariance term corresponds to the selection differential. The selection differential in natural populations, in contrast to the controlled populations used by plant and animal breeders, includes both adaptation and random effects (drift; Rice 2004). The remaining term specifies several different biases in the 'transmission' of the trait's value in parents to offspring (such as underlying mechanisms of inheritance, changes in environment, and mutation rates that depend on fitness). Clearly, Price's equation for the change in trait values between generations includes more effects than are included in the classical breeder's equation. Heywood (2005) derived an alternative form of Equation 2.11 that clarifies what these differences represent. Heywood's version is

$$\Delta \bar{z} = B_{z'z}S + \sigma_{wz'.z} + E(\Delta z) \tag{2.12}$$

Here, z' is the mean value of the trait in the offspring undergoing adaptation and $B = h^2$ is the linear regression coefficient of the mean value of the trait in offspring on the mid-parent value. $\sigma_{wz'.z}$ is the partial covariance—the covariance controlled by the mid-parent value—between fitness and the mean offspring value—the component of Δz associated with the parent's fitness, but which is not determined by the trait value in the parent;[24] in other words, that component of the difference in the mean trait value between generations that is caused by factors influencing differential reproduction and survival among parental units, but that is not related to their value of the trait. $E(\Delta z)$ is

---

[22] There are a few outstanding exceptions where investigators have successfully identified and followed the success of virtually every individual.

[23] Rice (2004) provides a clear derivation of this important theorem.

[24] We provide an example dealing with the evolution of clutch size in Chapter 3.

the expected value for the change in the trait's value in the absence of fitness differences among parental units.[25]

'The breeder's equation will yield a biased measure of the change in trait values between generations in most natural populations'

Our purpose here is simply to demonstrate that the classical breeder's equation omits a variety of factors that can influence the distribution of trait values from one generation to the next.[26] To make this point explicit, we can rewrite Equation 2.12 as

$$R = h^2 S + \sigma_{wz'.z} + E(\Delta z)$$

It should not therefore be all that surprising to find, in natural populations, that the change in a trait's value cannot be predicted from the breeder's equation.

Interactions among genes and traits: trade-offs and constraints shackle adaptive evolution

'Inheritance of polygenic traits is complicated by non-additive genetic variation associated with dominance, epistasis, linkage disequilibrium, and environmental interactions'

The expected change in the value of a trait between generations, $E(\Delta z)$, includes a variety of complicating factors. Dominance, for example, does not transmit the value of traits additively from parents to offspring (Fig. 2.2). But allelic dominance can influence the change in the mean value of the trait between generations because the frequency of homozygous and heterozygous genotypes will vary with changes in allelic frequencies.

Epistasis (interactions between different genes) and linkage disequilibrium (linked genes that do not segregate independently) also violate the simple assumption of additive inheritance (though it is possible for epistatic effects to be converted into additive components, Table 2.1). And, as we shall see in Chapters 3 and 7, environmental effects can produce positive selection differentials on heritable traits, with no evolutionary change in the trait's mean value between generations. One explanation for this apparent paradox is that only a biased subset of parents reproduce (creating a selection differential). If the selection differential is actually caused by a different trait than the one we are observing (e.g. only individuals holding territories reproduce, but we are observing mean clutch size), then adaptive evolution of that second trait will have only

---

[25] Equation 2.12 applies only to situations where the mean trait value of offspring is the same before and after 'selection'. Heywood (2005) provides somewhat more complicated partitions for situations where this assumption is invalid. Equation 2.12 documents, nevertheless, our main point that the breeder's equation is an insufficient model of natural adaptation.

[26] We refer readers who wish to achieve a deeper understanding of the underlying mathematics to the original works by Rice (2004) and Heywood (2005).

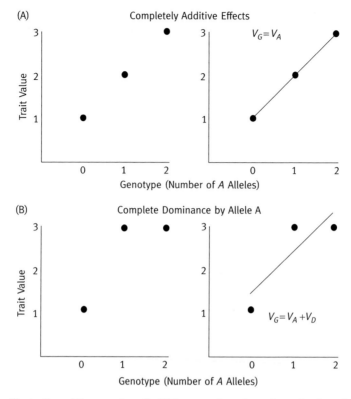

Figure 2.2. An illustration of the meaning of additive genetic variance for a simple trait controlled by two alleles (*A* and *a*) at a single locus. Graphs on the left illustrate the actual values of the trait for the three possible genotypes. Graphs on the right include the best-fit regression line to those trait values. Panel A illustrates a situation corresponding to purely additive genetic effects. Genotype *aa* codes for a trait value of 1. Each copy of allele *A* adds an additional value of 1 (*Aa* = 2; *AA* = 3). The variance in the trait is 'explained' perfectly by the regression (completely additive genetic variance). Panel B illustrates dominance. Allele *A* is dominant to allele *a*, so the heterozygote and *AA* homozygote yield the same trait value. The variance in the trait is only partially explained by the regression. The residual variation is caused by dominance. After Freeman and Herron (2004).

an indirect influence on the trait we are actually observing. In our example, adaptations to help secure and hold territories would continue to evolve, and those individuals would represent a non-random subset of the population. But if mean clutch size depends on the mean quality of territories, it could nevertheless remain constant even though it is an otherwise heritable trait.

'Adaptation of single traits depends on their genetic correlations with other traits'

The clutch-size example demonstrates a crucially important limitation of trait evolution. Adaptation of any single trait depends on its genetic correlation (covariance) with

Table 2.1 An example of epistatic interactions between two loci in a sexually reproducing population. The value of the trait for different genotypes at locus 1 depends on the genotype at locus 2. Note that if allele b was to be lost at locus 2 (e.g. through drift associated with a population bottleneck), then the epistatic variance would be converted into additive genetic variance (the values of the trait for locus 1 are completely additive for genotype BB at locus 2). After Mazer and Damuth (2001).

Locus 2	Genotypes	Locus 1		
		AA	*Aa*	*aa*
	BB	4	3	2
	Bb	4	6	2
	bb	2	2	2

other traits. Genetic correlations, in turn, emerge from two primary effects: pleiotropy and linkage disequilibrium.

Pleiotropy (one gene or gene complex influencing two or more traits) can produce either positive (an increase in the value of a single trait will necessarily increase the value in another) or negative genetic covariance (an increase in the value of a single trait is associated with a decrease in the value of another). Adaptation can be either reinforcing (the genetic covariance with the trait's values reflects the fitness covariance with trait's values) or antagonistic (there is a fitness trade-off; the genetic covariance has a different sign than does the fitness covariance).

'Adaptation of antagonistic traits can produce an illusion of maladaptive evolution'

Antagonistic adaptation is particularly interesting because adaptation of some traits carries with it the apparent maladaptation of others. In this sense, maladaptation of a single trait occurs when a change in the trait's value is associated with a decline in fitness.[27] Antagonistic traits are only apparently maladaptive because the increase in fitness caused by a change in the distribution of values of some traits is greater than the loss in fitness associated with changed distributions in others.

An interesting example of apparently maladaptive evolution can be found in a classic experiment performed by Oregon State University's Stevan Arnold (1981). Arnold was interested in investigating the geographical structure of genetic and phenotypic correlations among traits. He collected gravid female garter snakes (*Thamnophis elegans*) from coastal and inland races in northern California. Coastal snakes forage primarily on terrestrial slugs. Inland snakes are semi-aquatic and forage mainly on fish and salamanders. After the adult snakes gave birth, he tested the chemoreception (an indicator of diet preference) of more than 300 naive youngsters on odours extracted from 12

---

[27] Our use of maladaptation here differs somewhat from our treatment in Chapter 7 where we define it to represent *adaptive* trait values with negative fitness.

different potential prey items. Each offspring was scored on its relative chemoreceptive preference for, or aversion to, each type of prey.

Arnold's study had many interesting results, but one was particularly intriguing. There was a strong genetic correlation between the preferences for slugs and leeches. Snakes with a genetic preference for slugs also preferred leeches, and snakes with a genetic aversion to leeches also had an aversion to slugs. The relative preferences differed between populations. There are no leeches in the habitats where coastal snakes have a preference for slugs. And there are no slugs where the inland snakes have an aversion for leeches.

Snakes consume their prey whole. When a snake eats a leech, the leech remains alive, so it has the potential to wreak havoc on the snake's digestive tract. Thus, if an inland snake was released in the coastal population, then its innate aversion to slugs would be maladaptive. Such a snake would not consume the most common and valuable prey in its new environment, where 90–99% of the diet of native snakes is composed of slugs. A coastal snake released inland would also possess a maladaptive diet because it would possess a preference for harmful leeches. But the diet preference in each instance is only apparently maladaptive because the two races of snakes are geographically isolated. Somewhat different evolutionary outcomes are likely when apparently mal-adaptive evolution occurs within a single population.

Adaptation of single traits can also be compromised if the genetic bases for the traits are not randomly associated with one another (linkage disequilibrium). Linkage disequilibrium causes traits to be inherited together (again, their correlation with fitness could be either positive or negative). When traits are linked, adaptation will depend on whether the alleles at the linked loci reinforce one another in their 'separate' contributions to fitness or whether they are antagonistic in their fitness effects. If the linked loci reinforce one another, then directional adaptation that changes the mean value of both traits in the same direction is possible. But if the linked loci are antagonistic, adaptation is more likely to be 'normalizing', and any directional effect that increases the value of a single trait must come at the expense of reducing the value of the linked trait.

Plasticity: malleable responses are adaptive solutions to varying environments

Understanding adaptive evolution through the approaches of quantitative genetics is especially challenging for plastic traits whose value for a particular genotype changes with circumstance (Pigliucci 2001, 2005).[28] One of the best ways to understand trait plasticity, and its role in evolution, is through norms of reaction that summarize how a trait changes value from one environment to another. Figure 2.3 illustrates the reaction

---

[28] There are numerous other excellent reviews of phenotypic plasticity. Debat and David (2001) provide a concise overview of many key concepts. Readers interested in an in-depth perspective on developmental plasticity should consult West-Eberhard (2003).

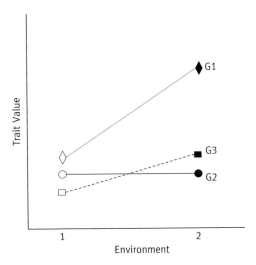

Figure 2.3. An illustration of reaction norms for three different genotypes that can occupy either environment 1 or environment 2. Open and closed symbols correspond to the expected value of the trait if the genotype occupies a given environment. Lines joining symbols are included only for clarity because we do not know the actual trait value in intermediate environments. The difference in trait value between environments corresponds to the genotype's plasticity (in those two environments).

norms for three different genotypes living in two environments. The difference in trait value between environments measures the genotype's plasticity. So, in this instance, we observe that genotype 2 yields exactly the same trait value in both environments. For this trait, and pair of environments, the genotype is 'canalized'[29] to produce the same value. Genotypes 1 and 3, on the other hand, produce different values of the trait in each environment. The difference in trait value is greatest for genotype 1. It is, in this pair of environments, a more plastic genotype than is genotype 3. Which of the three genotypes will be most adaptive? And if we know the answer, can we predict the response to adaptation?

The answers to both questions depend on the fitness of trait values in each environment. If higher values of the trait yield highest fitness, then genotype 1 will produce the most descendants in each environment. If the population occupies only these two environments, then adaptive evolution will yield a highly plastic genotype. If moderate values have the highest fitness in each environment, then genotype 2 would produce more descendants. Adaptation would yield reduced plasticity. But if genotype 1 has highest fitness in environment 1 and genotype 2 has highest fitness in environment 2, the adaptive outcome of evolution could be far less predictable. If the two environments are associated with separate habitats and thus different sub-populations of individuals, we might expect each population to diverge. Divergence would be opposed by gene flow.

---

[29] Canalized traits have the same value in all environments. There is no plasticity.

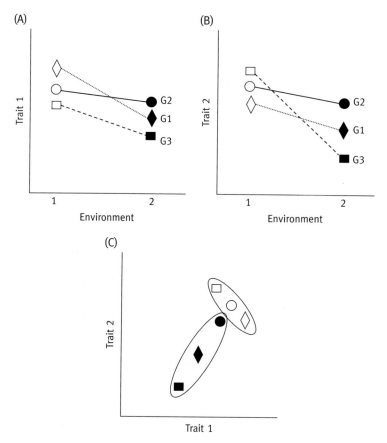

Figure 2.4. An illustration demonstrating how plastic traits can yield either positive (environment 2) or negative (environment 1) genetic correlations. Panels A and B plot the reaction norms of three different genotypes for two distinct traits in two environments (open and closed symbols). Panel C illustrates the resulting genetic correlations between the traits at low and high ends of the environmental gradient. After Stearns and Hoekstra (2000).

If the two environments exist at a much smaller scale such that all individuals are exposed to each one, then exposure and gene flow will restrict our ability to use the models of quantitative genetics to predict the response to adaptation.

The adaptive evolution of plastic traits will also depend on other correlated traits. In Fig. 2.4 we illustrate a simplified version of some of the complications that can arise.[30] We imagine two traits exposed to two environments whose non-parallel $G \times E$ reaction norms cross one another (panels A and B). If we then plot the correlations between the

---

[30] A simple one-locus model to 'explain' the genetic covariance between pairs of plastic traits can be found in Stearns *et al.* (1991).

two traits (panel C), the correlation is positive at the low end of the environmental gradient and negative at the other.

Recall, in this case, we also know that the trait values reflect different genotypes. So panel C also represents the genetic covariance between the traits. At the low end of the gradient, adaptation resulting in an increase in trait 1 will also yield an increase in the value of trait 2. At the high end of the gradient, the opposite occurs. An increase in the value of trait 1 can occur only if there is reduction in the value of trait 2. Please beware: it is incorrect to assume that either scenario will actually occur. We have, at this point, insufficient knowledge to predict the outcome of adaptation because we do not know how fitness maps onto the values of the traits (Chapters 3 and 4).

'A change in trait frequencies does not necessarily reveal genetic evolution'

At the University of California (Santa Barbara), Susan Mazer and Charles Schick (1991) explored $G \times E$ interactions in the wild radish. Norms of reaction for six life-history and floral traits were not linear with changes in population density (we illustrate two of these traits in Fig. 2.5). The distribution of values for each trait differed dramatically between low and high planting densities. The direction of reaction norms was often different, and the ranking of genotypes varied with density.[31] While the values for some

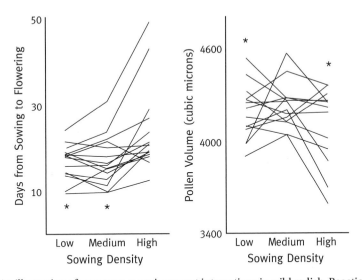

Figure 2.5. An illustration of genotype × environment interactions in wild radish. Reaction norms are drawn for flowering time and pollen volume for 15 different paternal (half-sib) families. Reaction norms for several other traits also demonstrated genotype × environment interactions. Asterisks correspond to planting densities where heritability was greater than zero. After Mazer and Damuth (2001).

---

[31] We address the effects of density, and ecological dynamics in general, in Chapter 6.

genotypes declined between density treatments, the values of others increased. Potential adaptation will depend not only on the $G \times E$ interaction, but also on geographical scale. Adaptation for different genotypes existing across a density gradient among widely separated populations could promote evolutionary divergence, but adaptation could be constrained if similar density variation exists within single populations. Regardless of which scale applies, we cannot evaluate the adaptive response unless we also know how fitness maps onto the trait value in each environment. It is nevertheless clear that a change in trait values between environments can occur without a change in allelic frequencies.

Mazer and Schick's research on wild-radish reaction norms reinforces several key principles in our understanding about evolution of quantitative traits:

1. *The degree of plasticity depends on which environments are being contrasted.* A genotype that appears to have little plasticity in two different environments may exhibit extraordinary plasticity if exposed to additional environments.
2. *The genetic correlation operating on different traits depends critically on which genotypes and environments are being compared.*
3. *Population density is a key component of environmental influence on quantitative traits.* A corollary of this final extremely important point is that we cannot possibly understand trait evolution without first understanding the interactions between population and evolutionary dynamics (Chapter 6).

Until now we have assumed quite simple reaction norms which take on but a single value in each environment. Some traits are so plastic, and some environmental interactions so complex, that traits may take on multiple values for each 'environment'.[32] Many organisms, for example, possess developmentally, or temporally, polyphenic traits that can take on multiple values at the same point along a single environmental gradient. Examples of such developmental flexibility include life stages of numerous species, seasonal changes in pelage colouration by northern vertebrates, and induced changes in antipredator adaptations such as cyclomorphosis[33] in aquatic invertebrates or secondary defences in plants.

> *'Extremely plastic traits, such as adaptive behaviours, allow individual genotypes to express many different values of the trait in a single environment'*

---

[32] We assume, implicitly, that environment corresponds to a single (but not necessarily continuous) gradient along which the response by several different genotypes can be assessed. If 'environment' is defined idiosyncratically for each different individual at a specific time and place then, by definition, only a single trait value is possible.

[33] Cyclomorphosis refers to a (usually seasonal) polymorphism in size and shape often interpreted as a tactic to reduce predation from size-limited predators. Perhaps the best-known examples are 'helmets' and 'spines' in water fleas (*Daphnia*) induced by the chemical cues of their predators.

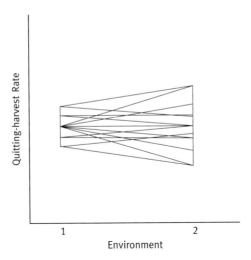

Figure 2.6. An example of how highly plastic (often behavioural) traits can create 'bands' of reaction norms that make any combination of genetic correlations possible. In this example, the trait of 'quitting-harvest rate' for a single genotype varies with such things as the cost of foraging, the developmental, physiological, and behavioural state of the forager, the risks of predation, and opportunities for other fitness enhancing activities. Only a few of the infinitely possible reaction norms are displayed (if all were included, the tetragon would be completely filled with overlapping and crossing reaction norms). Similar complexities arise with developmental polyphenism (because genetic correlations depend on when the investigator measures the covariances among traits) and through environmental interactions (the expression of the trait in one environment depends on its expression in others, see Chapter 4).

Multiple values are especially common for behavioural traits, or traits related to behaviour (Fig. 2.6). We illustrate this point with the clever enhancement of optimal foraging theory by Joel Brown of the University of Illinois at Chicago (Brown 1988). Brown's starting point was Charnov's (1976) marginal value theorem. The theorem states that individuals should forage in a patch only when they can make a profit. So, at equilibrium, each resource patch should be exploited just until the harvest rate in the patch is equal to that of the habitat at large. All patches yield the same return. Charnov's model did not include potential costs associated with predation risk while foraging in the patch, or costs associated with not engaging in alternative activities (that could also enhance fitness) during the time that the organism is foraging. So Brown included these effects to derive a series of related models. Each model maximized a slightly different formulation for fitness of organisms foraging in patches with depletable resources.[34] If individuals maximize the product of their survival and the fitness value procured from

[34] Houston and McNamara (1999) derived the same general model from principles of dynamic optimization. They also provide a 'theoretical summary' on the importance of an individual's state in determining its adaptive behaviour.

food (e.g. reproductive value), for example, then the optimum quitting-harvest rate (QHR) of the final forager to visit a patch is given by

$$QHR = C + \frac{\mu F}{\partial F/\partial e} + \frac{\phi t}{p(\partial F/\partial e)} \tag{2.13}$$

where C summarizes the metabolic cost of foraging and is constant for each type of patch, μ is the instantaneous rate of being killed by a predator while foraging in the patch, ϕt is the marginal fitness value of time that could be allocated to activities other than foraging, p is the probability of surviving the foraging period, F is the fitness obtained from foraging in the patch (F is assumed to increase with the net energy gain from the patch), and $\partial F/\partial e$ is the marginal value of energy in terms of fitness. The second right-hand term thus represents the marginal cost of predation (P), while the third is the marginal cost of missed opportunities (MOC) to enhance fitness through activities other than foraging in the patch.

Equation 2.13 demonstrates that the same quitting-harvest rate can emerge from several different effects in a single 'environment', which vary with such things as metabolic costs, predation risk, missed opportunities, and the marginal value of energy. It also illustrates that the encapsulation of several interacting behaviours (apprehension, vigilance, hunger) can fit together in different ways to yield the same harvest rate. But several different optimum values of QHR can also emerge for a single genotype depending on when it is active (can alter C, P, and MOC), and its current energetic state (modifies the individual's marginal valuation of energy). And numerous experiments, on a wide range of species, document that each factor does indeed modify QHR (Brown et al. 1992, Brown and Kotler 2004).

Others, most notably the University of California's Andrew Sih (Sih et al. 2004), have championed the view that suites of behaviours fit together as syndromes that can either constrain adaptive plastic responses or reflect underlying adaptive variation. Both views lead to what should now be familiar predictions. A single behavioural trait may often appear non-adaptive, or even maladaptive, because it is linked to others. The trait's evolution cannot be understood independent of its correlations with other traits, or independent of the context in which those correlations are expressed.

A challenge to the genetical theory of adaptive evolution: can developmental and behavioural plasticity force genes to follow traits?

Behavioural syndromes are but one class of exciting new discoveries that question whether our models of population and quantitative genetics truly represent the adaptive evolution of traits. The body plans of all but the simplest organisms are developmentally flexible (West-Eberhard 2003, 2005). During ontogeny, interactions between genetics and environment are modulated by an amazing variety of interconnected mechanisms. Subtle changes in otherwise highly conserved regulatory genes involved in morphogenesis can create vastly different types of organisms. Mutations and duplications of hierarchical Hox genes (which control the transcription of downstream genes in metazoans) yield major differences in body design. Hormones interact with developmental pathways to control the timing and duration of morphogenesis, and subsequent differences in morphology, physiology, and behaviour.

'Each individual organism has a genetic and environmental pedigree'

Although much of the variation in developmentally flexible traits is undoubtedly polygenic, classical models of quantitative inheritance are unlikely to guide our understanding of developmentally plastic trait evolution. Plastic traits, by definition, involve an interaction between an individual's genetics and its environment (but not necessarily a $G \times E$ interaction). Classical population and quantitative genetic approaches to adaptive evolution recognize that each individual shares its genetics with ancestors. Each individual has a genetic pedigree that we can use to map adaptation. But individuals also share aspects of their environment with their ancestors, and a true understanding of adaptation will require linking both genetic and environmental pedigrees (Fig. 2.7). The environmental pedigree represents an individual's 'inheritance' of its ancestors' selection gradients.

If environments change slowly relative to the lifetimes of individuals, then developmental plasticity is likely to yield somewhat similar trait values through time (different genetic pedigrees but a similar environmental pedigree). Different values should appear, however, in different environmental settings (the reaction norm comprises identical genetic pedigrees but different environmental pedigrees). And, if single organisms are exposed to multiple environments (and thus selection gradients) over their lifetimes, then we might expect an increasingly important role for flexible behavioural strategies over fixed and developmentally plastic ones. So we must expand our models of adaptive evolution to allow for the contingencies of past environments and the stochastic history of interactions between genetics and the environment.

'Developmental plasticity demonstrates that there are two different routes to adaptation—traits can follow genes, but genes can also follow traits'

Mary Jane West-Eberhard at the Smithsonian Tropical Research Institute has given us a glimpse of how our perspective of adaptive evolution needs to change in the face of developmental plasticity. West-Eberhard's (2005) starting point is a variable population whose individuals differ in their developmental responses to both genetic and environmental signals. The variability allows the different individuals to express different values of traits (so-called developmental recombination). Differences in trait values will often yield differences in how organisms perform crucial functions related to reproduction and survival. Subsequent genetic mutations that favourably adjust the

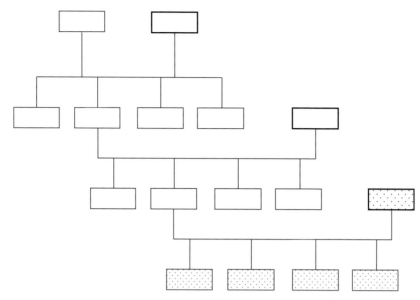

Figure 2.7. A simplified example of a combined genetic and environmental pedigree. The pedigree follows a single matriline of a sexually reproducing species through three generations. Each mother produced four offspring. Sires are denoted by bold boxes. Dense stippling indicates a sire from a different environment. Sparse stippling indicates that his offspring share ancestry with both environments. A complete pedigree would also include the genetic and environmental ancestry of the sires. The mechanisms and significance of environmental inheritance are poorly understood.

developmental expression of the traits (for example by adjusting the thresholds of responsiveness that control development) allow individuals with those mutations to produce more descendants than individuals lacking the mutation (genetic accommodation). Development, depending as it does on the interaction between genetics and environment, dictates that changes in the distribution of trait values have both a genetic and environmental cause. So adaptation can proceed simultaneously along two parallel paths. The distribution of trait values can follow slowly accumulating random mutations that alter function and ultimately fitness. Alternatively, gradual changes in the frequency of alleles can follow the development of newly arising and novel trait values.

We illustrate an example of West-Eberhard's point in Fig. 2.8. The classical gene-centred view recognizes that genotypes can create multiple phenotypes (illustrated by shading in the band of trait values; darker shading indicates a higher probability of occurrence), but most of the variation in mean trait values is caused by genetics. This means that both trait values and genotypes are closely linked with fitness (right-hand side of the figure; in Chapter 3 we will learn that this type of relationship is called a fitness-mapping function). Positive fitness means that individuals with those trait values have the potential, at low density, to increase when rare (feasible trait values).

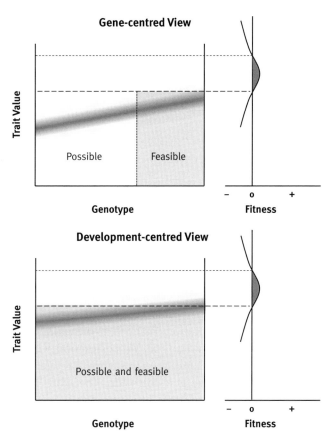

Figure 2.8. An illustration of two worldviews on what is possible and feasible for adaptation. Shaded bands on the left-hand figures represent variation in trait values produced by a single genotype (darker shading represents a higher probability of occurrence). Genetics accounts for most trait variation in the gene-centred view, development accounts for the majority of trait values in the development-centred view. Although all trait values are possible for the range of genotypes illustrated, only those capable of yielding positive growth rates at low density (right-hand figures) are feasible alternatives for subsequent adaptive evolution.

Negative fitness means that individuals with those trait values will decline in frequency toward extinction. Even though all trait values are possible, only a subset of genotypes produce feasible trait values. So although a genotype producing a barely feasible trait value can increase through its positive fitness, further improvements in trait values depend on the arrival of new genotypes (through mutation or migration).

The alternative development-centred view recognizes a significant role for genetic control of trait values but suggests that most of the variation is developmental. Whether the range of trait values for any given genotype is different from that of the genetic view depends on developmental programs and their interactions with the environment. In the Fig. 2.8 example, all genotypes produce feasible phenotypes. The trait can evolve to high values even if more favourable genotypes are not initially available. Those genotypes will nevertheless yield even higher mean fitness when they do appear in the population (genetic accommodation).

If environments change very rapidly, then we might expect even more developmental options. Two of these alternatives are particularly interesting.

'Differences in environmental variability and predictability yield a variety of developmental options'

Let us first consider a situation where environmental cues during development, such as maternal nutrient deficiency, correspond to expected future environments faced by the same individual later in life. An undernourished mammalian foetus, for example, is likely to mature into a 'thrifty' adult of relatively small body size. If the small adult's environment is nutritionally poor, then it may have an advantage over co-occurring larger and more profligate individuals. Gluckman and colleagues (2005) have argued that development under these scenarios can serve as a predictive adaptive response (PAR), where cues early in life modify development in a way that confers adaptive trait values later in life. PARs are thus adaptations that can, in principle, evolve whenever the environmental cues for development early in life correspond with the environment faced by the same individual later in life (the environmental pedigree is more or less constant during the life cycle). There is a downside. The adult may be maladapted whenever the cue and future environment fail to correspond.

In humans, the size and shape of the birth canal limits the size and development of the foetus, even in well-nourished mothers. So PARs could produce individuals with the ability to accumulate and store fat. The human foetus would thus be pre-adapted for the rather capricious and nutrient-limited environment faced by our recent hunter-gatherer ancestors. But in today's energy-rich human societies, the ability to store fat (e.g. insulin resistance) is a developmental trap causing epidemics of obesity, type 2 diabetes mellitus, and cardiovascular disease (Gluckman *et al.* 2005).

'Developmentally flexible traits allow organisms to track short-term environmental variability'

Now let us consider the case where organisms face a conflict of interest between the optimum fit of form and function in current as opposed to future environments. There are numerous examples. Energy expenditure and nutrient availability will often vary with environmental conditions and so too will optimum trait values. Are organisms that live in such variable environments capable of reversing development in order to hone trait values to current conditions? Piersma and Drent (2003) reviewed several examples of such developmentally flexible organisms. Gizard mass in Japanese quail and red knots is reversible. When quail diets include a high fraction of non-digestible fibre, the gizard (the organ that birds use to crush their food) enlarges. When fibre is reduced in the diet, the gizard follows suit (Starck 1999). Dekinga *et al.* (2001) measured the gizzard size of red knots with ultrasonography.[35] When red knots were switched from their preferred diet of small molluscs to softer trout pellets, their gizards contracted. And when the treatment was reversed, the gizards of the same birds increased in size (Dekinga *et al.* 2001).

Examples of developmental flexibility surround us. Pelage changes in mammals and birds reflect seasonal differences in climate and breeding opportunities. And, as we illustrated with our foraging example (Fig. 2.6), behaviour for many organisms is continuously flexible. Yet it is rather peculiar that we lack formal evolutionary models to deal with such prominent examples of the incomplete mapping between genetics and traits. Following Piersma and Drent (2003), we can partition the variance in trait values into a series of additive components

$$var(z) = var(G) + var(EP) + var(EF) + var(G \times EP)$$
$$+ var(G \times EF) + var(EP \times EF) + e \qquad (2.14)$$

where z is the trait value, $var(G)$ is the genetic contribution (which can be decomposed into additive, dominant, and epistatic components), e is the error in the trait not accounted for by the additive effects, and all other terms represent partitions of the environmental influence on the trait value (Box 2.1). In particular, $var(EP)$ corresponds to the irreversible component of plasticity (reaction norm), $var(EF)$ is the reversible component associated with developmental flexibility, and the remaining terms represent appropriate interactions. Clearly this treatment is far richer (and more challenging) than the corresponding model from quantitative genetics (Equation 2.9).

'Adaptive evolution occurs through both genetic and non-genetic inheritance'

Environmental pedigrees can be thought of as representing non-genetic inheritance from ancestors. Examples include various epigenetic effects (such as methylation of DNA), sex-dependent inheritance of alleles (so-called genomic imprinting), transfer of hormones and other substances from parent to offspring, and a wide range of cultural transmissions via learning and experience. How might we model the joint contributions of genetic and non-genetic inheritance? Russell Bonduriansky at Australia's University of New South Wales and Queen's University's Troy Day (Bonduriansky and Day 2009) suggest decomposing the mean phenotype into its expected genetic (g) and non-genetic (δ) components such that

---

[35] Starck also followed gizzard size in individuals with ultrasound, but on only a subset of the experimental birds. Ultrasonography systematically underestimated gizzard lengths measured after dissection of sacrificed birds. Once this bias was corrected, the patterns with diet in both samples were indistinguishable.

Box 2.1. What is a phenotype and how is it inherited?

How would you describe yourself? Would you include only physical features such as your height, weight, and complexion? Or would you also list your occupation, your interests and hobbies, your likes and dislikes? You can answer this question objectively. Simply look through the personal ads in your local newspaper, computer dating services, or the 'biographies' and blogs of movie stars, professional athletes, and models. Chances are that the descriptions will include information on such things as birthdate, education, hobbies, and mentors, as well as the usual dribble on fashion, fetishes, and pet peeves. No matter how mundane or jaded, each of these characteristics helps describe the individual person. They represent different components of that person's phenotype.[36]

Yet if you ask a typical biology student to define phenotype, chances are that the student will respond with something such as 'the expression of the genotype'. And if you press the student to elaborate, he or she should tell you that genotype expression is influenced by environment and development. Implicitly, then, this definition assumes that adaptation occurs only through genetics. The genotype leads the phenotype. But we have learned that adaptation applies to any system that possesses heritable variation, a struggle for existence, and heritable variation that influences the struggle. How might these two forms of adaptation interact? How might we map one onto the other?

Equation 2.14 provides a hint of how we might proceed with this difficult challenge. In this formulation, if reaction norms (EP) are perfectly parallel, then the interactions with genotypes ($var(G \times EP)$) and reversible developmental flexibility ($var(EP \times EF)$) disappear. Recall, however, that individuals have both genetic and environmental pedigrees. The two pedigrees emphasize that organisms inherit both their genes and their environment. Environmental inheritance, in concert with development, represents a form of 'acquired characters' that can nevertheless 'breed true' depending on the fidelity of the environment and the linearity and parallelism of the reaction norm.

In human society, for example, cultural evolution reinforces the inheritance of acquired characteristics. Many human societies were (and many still are) composed of caste or pseudo-caste systems where children inherit both their parents' genes and position. The English surname 'Smith'[37] became widely used as a descriptor of the family's skill set. Blacksmiths, in particular, developed similar musculature (and one supposes deafness) through the arduous tasks of forging metal objects from wrought iron; like father like son. As long as the cultural system remained intact, sons inherited their father's environment, and received an additive acquired component to their phenotype.

---

[36] Birthdate provides information on age and environment. It does not describe the phenotype directly, but gives context to the time at which different phenotypes can be compared with one another.

[37] The etymology of 'smith' is associated with the archaic 'smite' originally used to describe the verb 'to strike' as in striking metal with a hammer (hence smith was a common short-form for blacksmith). Etymology is, perhaps, the best example of non-genetic evolution.

University of California's (Irvine) Steven Frank (1997) points out that any form of evolution can be modelled via the Price equation. To see this, we write Price's equation as

$$\overline{w} \, \Delta \overline{z} = cov(w, z) + E(w \, \Delta z)$$

where $\overline{w}$ is the mean fitness associated with trait z, $\Delta \overline{z}$ is mean change in the character value from one generation to the next, $cov(w, z)$ is the covariance between the character and fitness in the parental generation, and $E(w \Delta z)$ represents the expected value of 'Y' given the change in the value of z between the two generations.[38] For our purposes we re-write the equation (see Equation 2.10) as

$$\Delta \overline{z} = \frac{cov(w, z)}{\overline{w}} + \frac{E(w \, \Delta z)}{\overline{w}}$$

which illustrates that we can partition the mean change in the character into a component (right-hand term) representing the 'transmission' of the character state from parent to offspring plus an additional component that corresponds to the change in the number of individuals in the population possessing different character values. If we use our blacksmith analogy with, say, arm circumference (a measure of musculature) as the character, we can think of the right-hand term as the similarity in musculature handed down from parent to son and the left-hand term as the change in the proportion of the population composed of blacksmiths relative to other 'professions'. Both terms include an 'acquired' component through cultural evolution. If, for example, society provided more opportunities for blacksmiths in the second generation than, say, thespians, then the 'fitness' of blacksmiths would be improved and a greater proportion would find employment. And, if blacksmiths and thespians tended to learn their trades from their relatives, then transmission of arm circumference would include both a genetic and acquired component. Similar processes operate in all populations. Individuals will, to differing degrees, inhabit the same environments as their parents. But environments vary on all spatial and temporal scales. So the proportion of individuals exposed to different environments will also change through time. How do these effects relate to the individual's environmental and genetic pedigrees? Imagine, for the moment, that there is no $G \times E$ interaction (parallel reaction norms). Then, although changes in the character value between generations will reflect both types of pedigree and will vary with changes in environment, the relative fitnesses of all genotypes will be independent of the environmental pedigree. If, on the other hand, the reaction norms are not parallel, then the transmission of environment from parent to offspring will influence the relative fitnesses of different genotypes, as will changes in the proportional representation of different environments in the population. The acquired character state will influence subsequent evolution.

[38] The Price equation can be written in many different ways to solve a variety of evolutionary problems. We refer readers interested in the theoretical underpinnings of Price's equation to the accounts by Steven Frank (1995, 1997).

One of the many advantages of the Price formulation is that it can be decomposed into even more components. We might imagine, for example, that there are a variety of factors, in addition to the additive genetic variance, that influence the expression of the character value. These terms can often be estimated by regression and included in the prediction of evolutionary change. We refer readers interested in exploring these many features of the Price equation to Frank (1995, 1997). We caution that even though one can use the Price equation to predict change from one generation to the next, it does not allow one to predict changes that may occur in underlying factors influencing trait values and fitness. Deconstructing adaptation into its components is not the same as predicting its future course. In this respect, then, the pace and direction of evolution is unpredictable.

$$\overline{g}(t+1) = \overline{g}(t) + M(p_{gz\delta}, \tilde{W}) \tag{2.15}$$

and

$$\overline{\delta}(t+1) = \overline{\delta}(t) + N(p_{gz\delta}, \tilde{W}) \tag{2.16}$$

In these equations, M is the change in the average genetic composition of the population from t to $t+1$, N is the corresponding change in the non-genetic component, $p_{gz\delta}$ is the joint distribution of the genotype (g), phenotype (z), and non-genetic inheritance (δ), and $\tilde{W}$ is a complex fitness function representing selection for or against the trait(s) under consideration (equivalent to the selection gradient in simpler genetic models). This approach is clearly much more complicated than those based on genetic correlations only, and it is unclear whether unpacking it into its numerous components will have empirical value (Bonduriansky and Day 2009). Fortunately, alternative frameworks exist that link the dynamics of populations with the evolution of traits independent of their mechanism of inheritance (Chapter 6).

Mechanics of population growth and decline

It is undeniably true, as demonstrated repeatedly and poignantly by Oxford University's Richard Dawkins, that the bodies of organisms function primarily as vehicles carrying genes through time and space.[39] But in order to do so, the genes must leave one body for the next. And in order for genes to go forth and multiply, their carriers must do the same. The mechanics of populations are therefore as important for evolution as are the mechanics of genetics and development.

The number of individual organisms alive in a given area at any particular time can be uniquely determined from only three key processes: births, deaths, and dispersal

---

[39] Dawkins' *The Selfish Gene* (1976) belongs on every literate person's bookshelf.

(both into and out of the population of interest).[40] A population's abundance is thus given by the so-called BIDE equation, the acronym standing for (births plus immigrants) minus (deaths plus emigrants):

$$N_{t+1} = N_t + B - D + (I - E) \tag{2.17}$$

where N is population size, B and D are the numbers of individuals that were born and died over the interval from time t to $t + 1$, and I and E are the numbers of immigrants and emigrants, respectively.

Ecologists have developed numerous other forms of the BIDE equation depending on such things as whether or not the life history can be categorized by discrete periods of reproduction, age, and stage structure, the form and intensity of density dependence, and interactions with other populations and species. We visit many of those formulations in Chapter 6, so here we simply note that the dynamics of gene pools emerge through the births, deaths, and movements of their carriers. Although it is often instructive to imagine that evolution occurs through the differential success of different alleles, loci, characters, and strategies, it is crucial to always bear in mind that those dynamics are tied directly to the success of the whole organism. It is equally as important to recognize that the dynamics of populations and communities are most important, from an adaptive evolution perspective, because they represent the mechanism by which changes in the gene pool take place.

The dynamics of populations include both stochastic and systematic effects. Each parameter in the BIDE model responds to stochastic environmental influences. Within populations, stochastic changes in demography also influence population persistence, stability, and growth, but so too do the functions of traits. Each parameter of the BIDE equation is thus available for adaptive evolution.

The limits of mechanics: mechanics, though essential, is an insufficient explanation for evolution

Phenotypic flexibility, as revealed by Equation 2.14, Brown's equation, and Sih's behavioural syndromes, yields poignant messages to evolutionary biologists. It will be virtually impossible to obtain meaningful measures of genetic heritability (and predict the adaptive response) of such crucially important and fitness-related summary traits as QHR. The optimum quitting-harvest rate has an obvious impact on fitness. But it is not a trait in the classic sense, and it is not under direct genetic control. Rather, QHR can best be thought of as an adaptive solution to strategies of foraging in environments with variable costs. Many other adaptive behavioural syndromes fall into the same category.

---

[40] The distinctions amongst individuals, and even among births, deaths, and dispersal, become blurred in some colonial organisms and in those with complex life-cycles alternating between aggregated colonies and individual free-living life stages.

Though there is obviously some underlying genetic control on behavioural flexibility, behaviours can represent sets of adaptations that allow single genotypes the plasticity they need to respond appropriately to rapid changes in environment. But syndromes of behaviour can also be adaptive and limit plastic responses. Quantitative genetics is unlikely to represent the best approach to understanding such behavioural complexity. We see similar constraints imposed on the classic mechanistic approaches of Mendelian and quantitative inheritance in the complex developmental options of polyphenic organisms. Expression of these traits also depends on genetics, environment, $G \times E$ interaction, and on the context (state) associated with any given individual.

'Though classic mechanistic approaches to evolution have limited application, they work wonderfully when their assumptions hold, and they can provide major insights into evolutionary processes'

This is not to say that we should avoid models of evolution based on population or quantitative genetics, quite the contrary. Those models have a deep legacy. They have yielded profound insights into evolution. And when their assumptions hold, they work. The evidence lies in our understanding of evolution, agreement of predictions with definitive experiments, and in the successes of plant and animal breeding. Problems arise only when the models' simplifying assumptions fail. Modes of inheritance complicate our ability to measure heritabilities and to predict adaptive responses, but they do not necessarily eliminate our ability to do so. Environmental interactions, and most especially those related to state dependence, would seem to require a different approach. Before we can develop that approach, we will need to understand how traits of individuals in different states living in different and changing environments are translated into fitness.

Reflection

We have seen how a variety of mechanisms can effect evolution. Mutations provide opportunities for novel solutions, but most are likely to have either neutral or negative influence on fitness. Sexual reproduction and recombination likewise yield potential for new, more effective combinations of alleles and genes, but also break apart existing and time-tested favourable combinations. Mate choice can change the distribution of trait values in a population, but does not alter underlying allelic frequencies.

Yet offspring resemble their parents. For simple traits, and in simple, closed, and controlled environments, we can combine knowledge of inheritance and relative rates of reproductive success to predict evolutionary change. Evolution becomes more complex as we relax those assumptions. Genetic trade-offs among traits force compromises. Individual traits do not evolve independently to maximize their separate contributions to fitness. Instead, groups of traits co-evolve toward moving targets of adaptation, reflecting optimum solutions in particular places and at specific times.

Gene flow among populations and environments erodes the ability of adaptation to fine-tune fixed trait values to local conditions. But gene flow also provides grist for adaptation's mill, and provides an opportunity for favourable genes and gene complexes to flex their muscles in other environments. Environmental variation, in both space and time, interacts with genetics and development to produce plastic responses to environmental variability. Plasticity culminates in adaptive behaviours that provide individuals with the ability to respond to changing conditions almost instantaneously. Behaviour, despite its flexibility, must also be optimized among numerous conflicting demands.

Our classic interpretation of adaptation driven by genes is brought into question by the role that environmental pedigrees might play in adaptive evolution. One is immediately drawn towards two of the main criticisms of Darwin: evolution through the use and disuse of characters and blending inheritance. Identical genotypes with plastic traits will look different if they have developed in different environments. Some of the plasticity will have arisen by use and disuse (across generations), and the values of those traits can be reinforced by subsequent mutations. So we may have judged Darwin too harshly. It is now evident that adaptive evolution is indeed possible via acquired characteristics (Box 2.1).[41] The book is still out on blending inheritance. We do not yet know completely how inheritance through environmental pedigrees might proceed.

We attempt, in subsequent chapters, to detail how we can make sense out of this bewildering and near-infinite array of possibilities. We need to understand the connections between traits and their function, as well as the underlying structure that details how genotypes, traits, and environments interact. And we need to understand how fitness and structure interact. After that we can begin to explore how adaptation influences evolution. We will find that the challenge is not to test for adaptation or its constraints. Rather we must learn how we can use adaptation to test other aspects of evolutionary theory. But we are getting ahead of ourselves. Before we can do any of those things, we must first learn how traits are converted to function, and how function effects fitness.

---

[41] Bonduriansky and Day (2009) review the importance of acquired phenotypes and other forms of non-genetic inheritance.

3

Function

HOW TRAITS INTERACT WITH THE ENVIRONMENT
TO INFLUENCE REPRODUCTION AND SURVIVAL

Overview

In evolutionary genetics, we ask how the genetic architecture, the units of inheritance, and their underlying mechanics influence trait values and vary in supposedly predictable manners. But what is a trait? This seemingly absurd question is crucial to ask when we want to understand adaptation. As we shall see, traits can only be evaluated through their influence on function. The function of the traits, and their influence on fitness and therefore on adaptation, can only be understood in the context of the environment.

In this chapter, we will illustrate that the mechanics of evolution is insufficient for understanding adaptation. We will show that traits can be understood only in an environmental context, and since the environment is ever changing, so are the functions of traits. We will also attack the elusive concept of fitness and attempt to give it a useful meaning in the theory of evolution. We will remind you that fitness cannot be viewed as a trait itself. Instead, we show how traits map onto fitness through the fitness-mapping function (FMF). The evaluation of the FMF is made possible by the adaptive function—the function that maps the distribution of fitness values originating from trait values to adaptation. This is an exercise in mappings from one realm to another, so we illustrate how alternative views of that mapping influence our interpretations of adaptation and evolutionary change. In doing so, we will (re)introduce Levins' elegant idea of fitness sets.[1] They serve as a versatile tool for illustrating the very notion of 'mappings'.

Traits are not independent of each other. The change in one trait may influence change in another. Thus, traits that are correlated with each other can strongly influence the course of adaptation. We illustrate this with a simple model, reaching back to mechanics (Chapter 2) and looking ahead toward the dynamics of evolution (Chapter 6).

---

[1] Introduced in the 1960s, they still have vast intellectual power and should not be forgotten.

Introduction: where traits meet the environment

During each rainstorm, the stark Cretaceous sandstones and mudstones of Canada's badlands bleed dinosaurs. The fossils are so numerous in some places that it is impossible to walk through the badlands without stepping, figuratively and literally, on dinosaurs. Vertebrate palaeontologists from around the planet gather each year to search for the newest treasures. The most spectacular location is a World Heritage Site in the rugged and picturesque Red-deer River valley. Here, among other gems, lie at least eight sprawling bone beds holding the remains of many hundreds, or even thousands, of Ceratopsians that perished together in massive floods 65 million years ago (Ryan *et al.* 2001).

The skulls of Ceratopsian dinosaurs are distinguished by two major features (Fig. 3.1).

1. Extensions of the squamosal and parietal bones supported large neck frills that extended backward from the base of the skull. The caudal surface of the frill in several species was ringed by triangular spikes called epocipitals.
2. Many species also possessed brow and nasal horns derived from the postorbital and nasal bones.

What function could these elaborate, and presumably expensive, structures have served? One early explanation was that the frills anchored the long, powerful jaw muscles used to close the 'beak' of these distinctive herbivores (Ostrom 1964). While the muscular role has been largely discounted, other proposed functions include defence, species recognition, mate attraction, intraspecific aggression, thermoregulation, and even a receptor/amplifier function for the receipt and broadcast of low-frequency sounds (Anton 2000).

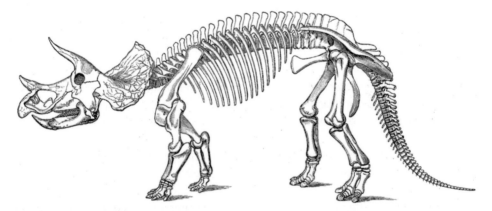

Figure 3.1. A reconstruction of a *Triceratops prorsus* skeleton from Wyoming by Zittel (Eastman 1902). Triceratops was one of the last remaining Ceratopsian dinosaurs. Other species had frills lined with horny projections. From Wikipedia commons, public domain (http://upload.wikimedia.org/wikipedia/commons/f/f5/Triceratops_prorsus_old.jpg, accessed 17 October 2010).

If defence was the primary function, then the horns should point forward to face the enemy, and the bony frills and epocipitals should protect the vulnerable neck region. But the bony frills in many species (including all members of the genus *Chasmosaurus*) had large openings where even thick skin would provide little protection from ferocious carnivores. Some species lacked the pointed epocipitals along the margin of the frill. Others, such as *Chasmosaurus irvinensis*, lacked a brow horn and possessed distinctive epocipitals that were flattened or curled away from approaching enemies (Holmes *et al.* 2001). And if defence was the primary function, then why do the nasal horns of animals found in a single bone bed vary from those pointing forward, to those that point backward? The weight of evidence does not present a convincing case for adaptive armaments.

Insights for alternative functions come from one of the first Ceratopsians discovered by the famous American bone collector Charles Sternberg. The specimen, described and named *Chasmosaurus belli* by Canadian palaeontologist Laurance Lambe, had rather small horns. Another, *Chasmosaurus kaiseni*, possessed quite long brow horns. But we also know that the horns of young Ceratopsians were smaller than those of older animals collected from the same bone bed. Some palaeontologists now believe that the horns were sexually dimorphic and that the two 'congeners' simply represent females and males of the same species. If so, the horns may have served a sexual function where males competed with one another for mating opportunities.

The sexual function of horns and frills is bolstered by incontrovertible evidence that Ceratopsians were herding animals. Not only have palaeontologists found huge con- centrations of animals killed by single catastrophes, they have also uncovered dinosaur trackways where small, presumably young, animals were flanked by large adults. The patterns bear a striking resemblance to contemporary mammalian herbivores. Herding mammals often possess sexually dimorphic 'armaments' in the form of antlers, horns, or tusks that are used in display and combat to establish dominance hierarchies amongst males. Anyone who has watched nature movies knows that weapons effective against other males can also help to protect individuals from predators. Protection is enhanced in species, such as musk oxen and elephants, where groups of individuals cooperate to face a common enemy. The point is that, while we can infer possible roles for some traits from their anatomy, we must know the environmental context if we are to relate those traits to their survival and reproductive functions.

'The function of a trait can be determined only in the context of the environment in which the trait is expressed'

Using contemporary ungulates coexisting with their predators as our model, it is thus likely that Ceratopsians also lived in a dangerous environment where their complex horns and frills served multiple functions. We can imagine males displaying massive and brightly coloured frills to ward off weak opponents. We can imagine similarly- matched males locking horns in Herculean contests of strength that determined access to females. And we can visualize how groups of individuals may have formed lines of defence around younger, smaller, and more susceptible animals. As vivid as our imagination may be, we can never be certain of the function unless we also know the context of how the traits interacted with the environment in which the animals lived. Knowing the context is also insufficient to determine function. We must be able to measure how the trait interacted with the environment to influence survival and reproduction. If we can do that, we also need to know how alternative functions interacted with one another. Can we predict why some species possessed larger frills and longer horns than did others? More generally, can we develop a theory that helps us understand the functional significance of variable traits?

We begin by revisiting the evolutionary map of polygenic traits. Each trait has a genetic (G), and environmental (E) component, as well as a $G \times E$ interaction. The genetic component includes the effects of interacting (epistasis) as well as pleiotropic genes that produce multiple phenotypes. Some biologists mistakenly think that evolution can be understood through this quantitative gene→trait map. To do so, they implicitly ascribe a fitness value to different expressions of the trait, evaluate its heritability, and 'predict' the response to selection with the breeder's equation (Chapter 2). The theory has some beautiful properties. Using the breeder's equation, you can measure a trait's heritability, monitor changes in the trait's distribution through time (the response to selection), and infer the selection differential. Or, if you know the selection differential and the response to selection, you can infer the trait's heritability. And the theory is confirmed by the unparalleled successes of plant and animal breeders.

But evolutionary ecologists know that the theory cannot easily be applied to natural populations that lack the breeder's foresight of designed selection. One of the best examples of this problem can be found in studies of clutch- and litter-size evolution.

'The breeder's equation fails to capture the dynamics of adaptive evolution in natural populations'

Beginning with insights from Oxford University's David Lack (1947, 1948), most models of clutch-size evolution assume a trade-off between the number of eggs that parents can produce and the subsequent survival of offspring to fledging. Large clutches may exceed the parent's ability to adequately care for, nurture, and protect individual offspring. Small clutches represent an inefficient use of parental resources that could be allocated successfully to rear a larger brood producing more descendants. An optimum clutch size lies between these extremes.

How should that optimum evolve? Can we model the evolution of the optimum number of offspring with the breeder's equation? We know that clutch and litter size are heritable. We know that parents produce clutches of different sizes. And, by monitoring populations of marked individuals through time, we can determine the sizes of successful and unsuccessful clutches (the selection differential), as well as changes in mean clutch size (the response to selection).

The white-footed mouse (*Peromyscus leucopus*) is a particularly attractive species for this type of monitoring. In the northern part of its geographical range this abundant North American rodent lives primarily in wooded habitats, where mice build nests in hollow trees and logs. White-footed mice are semi-arboreal and readily accept wooden nest boxes as alternative nest sites. Since the average lifespan of a mouse is measured in months rather than years it is possible, by monitoring mothers and their offspring living in the boxes, to calculate selection differentials from one generation to the next and to search for directional change in mean litter size.

The most common litter size produced by female white-footed mice in 'northern' populations is four offspring. But litters with five pups contribute more recruits to the population of mice than does any other litter size. Morris (1992) estimated the mean annual selection differential over 6 years to be approximately 0.3. Despite the consistent success of females producing litters larger than the population mean, there was no directional change in mean litter size (Fig. 3.2).

Similar patterns of positive selection differentials with no directional increase in clutch size have often been reported in long-term studies of both cavity-nesting and ground-nesting birds (e.g. great tits, *Parus major*, van Noordwijk *et al.* 1981, Boyce and Perrins 1987; lesser snow geese, *Anser caerulescens caerulescens*, Rockwell *et al.* 1987).

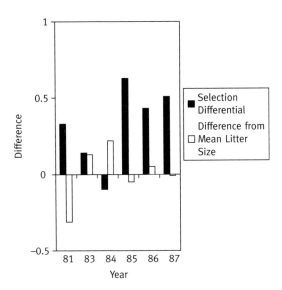

Figure 3.2. An example where the breeder's equation fails to predict evolutionary change in a natural population. Despite mostly positive selection differentials for litter sizes produced by white-footed mice in five of six different years in the 1980s, the mean litter size did not increase through time. Data from Morris (1992).

Two classical studies are especially revealing. van Noordwijk and colleagues (1981) analysed clutch-size evolution in great tits living in Dutch woodlands. Almost all adult birds nested in wooden boxes where each nestling was given a unique leg band that allowed the research team to follow its survival and breeding success. The research, begun by the famous ornithologist H. N. Kluyver in the 1950s, included data on selection differentials, heritability of clutch size, and the response to selection on several hundred clutches over a 16-year period. The number of clutches observed in any given year varied from a low of 10 clutches to 145. Parents from large first clutches were more likely to produce recruits into the population than were parents from clutches of average size (a positive selection differential) and clutch size was highly heritable. Despite this potential for rapid evolutionary change, there was no increase in mean clutch size.

Mark Boyce and Christopher Perrins (Boyce and Perrins 1987) amassed an even longer time series on nearly 4500 great-tit clutches in Oxford's Wytham Wood. Selection differentials calculated across 23 consecutive years averaged around 0.5, again indicating high potential for a rapid evolutionary increase in mean clutch size. There was none.

Evolutionary ecologists have many explanations for the 'failure' of an evolutionary increase in clutch size in populations with positive selection differentials (though it is debatable whether they also see it as a failure of the breeder's equation). In the case of white-footed mice, litters of size six and greater yield very few recruits to the population. So, even though females producing litters with five offspring have the highest fitness, females whose mean litter size is five offspring will often produce even larger litters with very low fitness (Mountford 1968). The optimum litter size will thus be less than the most productive one.

Beginning with seminal studies in the 1970s by Smith and Fretwell (1974) and Brockelman (1975), several evolutionary ecologists have also argued that adaptive evolution will yield females who invest the optimal amount of resources in reproduction. Recruitment from females that invest too little, or too much, will be lower than the optimum. So female white-footed mice that can afford to produce only four offspring will do so, and females that can afford larger investments will tend to produce litters with five youngsters. And the asymmetry of very low recruitment from the largest mouse litters constrains directional selection that would otherwise be adaptive.

Directional evolution towards increased brood size in great tits is also constrained by a similar process labelled, euphemistically, as the 'bad-years effect'. Recruitment from large broods exceeds that from smaller clutches during benign periods. But during years when birds are stressed by few resources or extreme weather, only those females laying small clutches produce descendants. The result is a life-history strategy that hedges its bets against environmental uncertainty. Mean clutch size is less than that predicted by the selection differentials because genes that code for the largest clutch sizes are eliminated during the bad recruitment years.

Two other possibilities deserve careful consideration. One view, promoted originally by Price and Liou (1989), is that adaptation is constrained because covarying traits are also being optimized. Price and Liou's model can be treated as a special case of a more general model described by Cooke and colleagues (1990). The 'Cooke model' modifies the breeder's equation to include an environmental component, $\Delta \bar{E}$,

$$R = h^2 S + \Delta \bar{E} \tag{3.1}$$

which reflects the change in environment from one generation to the next. Clearly, then, the response to selection cannot be predicted uniquely unless one knows how the environment is also changing. A positive selection differential is cancelled whenever the environmental change is negative. The environmental component includes the effects of other individuals in the population. The genes of all individuals compete with one another. Thus, as the population evolves, individuals might be expected to become better competitors for territories, resources, or mates. Increased mean competitive ability dictates that $\Delta \bar{E}$ will be negative and there need not be any response to a positive selection differential.

Some readers might suspect, then, that other traits related to competitive ability will change through directional selection. While such an outcome is possible, it is also possible that the best competitors are those individuals whose trait values correspond most closely with each trait's respective optimum. Since numerous traits are likely to influence competitive ability, it may not be possible for directional selection to operate effectively on any single trait. A change in one trait's mean value that increases fitness might be associated with a loss of fitness through another trait. Thus, similar to arguments we will make later regarding Red Queen evolution (van Valen 1973),[2] populations continue to evolve toward multiple optima even though there is no obvious change in trait distributions. It is as if the different traits are racing against one another on a treadmill. No single trait can win the race because, no matter how fast it evolves, all of the other traits maintain the same pace.

These various examples demonstrate vividly two crucially important and related principles:

1. We cannot predict the response to selection unless we also know how the environment is changing.
2. We cannot predict evolutionary change unless we know how a trait's value maps onto fitness.

'The response to selection depends on the environment in which the trait is evolving'

---

[2] The Red Queen analogy was taken from Lewis Carroll's *Through the Looking Glass*, and we can paraphrase it as 'evolve as fast as you can just to keep up with all the others running at least as fast as you'. We expand on this important analogy in Chapter 6.

Before we proceed, we need to evaluate whether or not fitness is a trait. A review of evolutionary texts reveals considerable confusion on this point. Thus, Stearns and Hoekstra (2000) state that 'fitness is under continuous selection in natural populations' (p. 86). Rice (2004, p. 6) also notes confusion in the literature, where fitness has been defined variously as a property of an individual, genotype, or allele. The distinctions are far from subtle. If fitness is viewed as a trait for adaptive evolution, then adaptation is tautological. Which individuals survive and reproduce? Those with high fitness. Which individuals have high fitness? Those who survive and reproduce. Thus, fitness cannot be a trait. Rather, *fitness is a necessary mathematical abstraction that we use to model adaptation.*

Evaluated in this light, fitness is not something that we measure on individuals. Rather, it is expressed as a consequence of evolution. Adaptive evolution occurs because the trait values of some individuals allow them to produce more descendants than other individuals with different trait values. To study evolution, we measure the traits (or infer strategies; Chapter 6). To estimate fitness, we evaluate changes in the moments of trait values (or the frequencies of strategies) through time.

Consider our previous examples dealing with the evolution of clutch size. To study its evolution in a population we might measure the distribution of clutch sizes by estimating the mean, variance, and skewness in clutch size at different times. We would conclude that the trait of clutch size evolved to some new value only if the distribution of clutch sizes changed. Do we need to know anything about fitness to study its evolution? Look again at Equation 3.1. Is fitness part of that equation? No.

So if we don't need fitness to study evolution in progress, why do we need the concept? There is only one reason. To understand evolution we need to do more than view nature and measure its dynamics. Understanding evolution implies that we can predict how evolution will proceed under different sets of assumptions. We need the abstraction of fitness to model evolution.

The fitness-mapping function

Our evolutionary models are constrained by the ways in which genes map onto traits and by the ways in which traits are mapped onto fitness. Often, we are misled into thinking that an understanding of evolution requires that we can infer the complete loop from genetics through development, expression of traits, their function and fitness in whole organisms, density and frequency-dependent adaptation, subsequent survival and reproduction, and back again to genetics (Fig. 3.3A). But the processes of evolution do not easily loop back onto one another. Evolutionary change progresses from one link to the next (Fig. 3.3B). Evolution proceeds in lock-step sequence with its mechanics and dynamics. Thus, to understand evolution, we need to understand the various mapping functions that translate genes into traits, as well as those that translate traits onto their adaptive value.

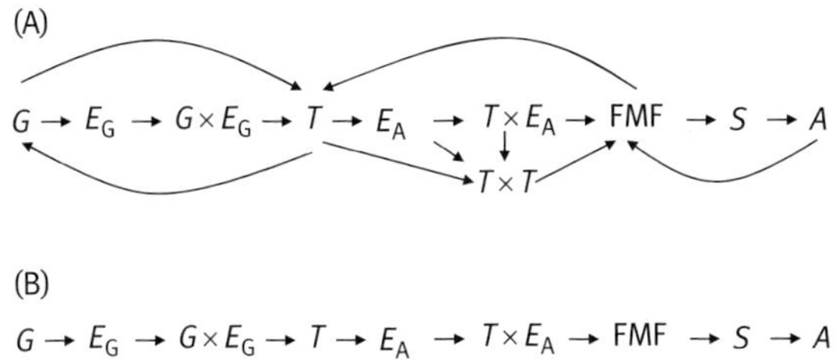

(A)

$$G \rightarrow E_G \rightarrow G \times E_G \rightarrow T \rightarrow E_A \rightarrow T \times E_A \rightarrow FMF \rightarrow S \rightarrow A$$
$$T \times T$$

(B)

$$G \rightarrow E_G \rightarrow G \times E_G \rightarrow T \rightarrow E_A \rightarrow T \times E_A \rightarrow FMF \rightarrow S \rightarrow A$$

Figure 3.3. An illustration of two world views of evolution. In panel A, genotypes, environment, and the genotype × environment interaction produce traits that interact with one another and whose functions are influenced by density and frequency dependence. The value of the different functions is reflected in differences in survival and reproduction that feed back onto the values of traits, allelic frequencies, and subsequent evolution. The loops imply that an evolutionary biologist should be able, in principle, to follow evolution not only from genes to fitness, but also should be able to work backwards from fitness to the gene. In panel B, most of the interactions are the same, but one cannot easily follow evolution backwards. Trait × trait interactions are subsumed in the fitness-mapping function. Changes in allelic frequencies occur as a consequence of differences in survival and reproduction caused, at least in part, by the way that trait values map onto fitness. The values of the traits depend on the way that genes map onto traits. The mapping, in each case, is unidirectional. An effective study of evolution can begin anywhere along the gene→adaptation sequence and trace evolution foreward through time. We revisit these mappings in Fig. 3.13 and in Chapter 6. G, underlying genetics; E_G, genetic/developmental environment; T, trait value; E_A, adaptive environment; FMF, fitness-mapping function; S, fitness set; A, adaptive function. Interactions are denoted as products.

'Adaptive evolutionary change can be predicted only through the fitness-mapping function'

Occasionally, the mapping is direct. A single gene produces an enzyme that modifies survival and reproduction. In these rare cases the mapping functions are so simple that we can trace differences in fitness back to their genetic causes. Frequently, however, traits with large effects on survival and reproduction represent complexes of genes and developmental pathways. Our challenge is to develop a single theory that will let us predict the adaptive evolution of both complex and simple traits.

Adaptive evolution implies a two-step process linking the values of traits with their adaptive value (Fig. 3.3B). The first step, where traits are translated into fitness, defines the fitness function (we prefer the term fitness-mapping function, FMF). The FMF assumes that each value of a trait can be represented by its expected contribution to fitness. In reality, of course, the expected fitness depends on the inter-relationships among all traits that define each different individual. Fitness emerges only because individuals possessing a particular trait value tend to leave either more or fewer descendants than do other individuals with different values for the same trait. Thus, even though many traits are not independent of one another, we can pretend that their contributions to fitness are independent because any measure of fitness is based on the whole organism and necessarily includes interactions among traits.

Note that our use of fitness in this case corresponds to our interest in forecasting the expected adaptive response for a specific trait. We are not interested, here, in actually measuring the fitness of a particular trait value in an individual or group of individuals where it may often be necessary to understand interactions among traits (see Endler 1986, which remains a highly readable and appropriate reference for readers interested in measuring fitness in natural populations). Nor are we interested, at this point, in predicting how different traits 'coevolve'to produce the whole organism.

Fitness sets and the fitness-generating function

Nevertheless, fitness of a particular trait value, even if defined as the expectation of fitness across many individuals, also depends on environment. Returning to our clutch-size example, a large clutch may yield high fitness in an environment lacking nest predators, but low fitness in an environment where predators encounter nests in proportion to the number of feeding visits made by parents. Richard Levins (1962) solved the environmental-dependence problem with his inventions of fitness sets and the adaptive function. Levins reasoned that the mean fitness of a particular trait value depends on the relative weights given to FMFs in different mixtures of environments. So far so good. But how do we translate the fitness of single trait values that we estimate in one environment or habitat into a state space that represents their expected fitness in all environments used by an individual?

'Adaptation is determined by two functions that describe, firstly, the ways in which traits map onto fitness and, secondly, their environmentally derived adaptive value'

Let us make the problem tractable by considering only two habitats. First we imagine that we can plot the FMFs of trait values in each habitat separately. Then we plot the fitness of each trait value in Habitat 2 against the fitness of the same trait value in Habitat 1. The resulting fitness set thus specifies the joint fitness of all possible trait values.

We can use our clutch-size example to make the fitness-set concept clear. Imagine a semelparous species the members of which are genetically predisposed to produce clutches of different sizes (we invoke semelparity to simplify the analysis, the approach can be readily generalized to iteroparous species[3]). Offspring mortality differs between two habitats. The FMFs reveal that the fitness achieved from producing different numbers of eggs also varies between the two habitats (Fig. 3.4). The most descendants are produced from small clutches in Habitat 1, and from somewhat larger clutches in Habitat 2. To create the fitness set we graph, for each clutch size (the sequence of trait

---

[3] Semelparity and iteroparity represent fundamental differences in life history. Semelparous species reproduce only once in their lifetime and often die shortly thereafter. Iteroparous species are capable of two or more reproductive episodes.

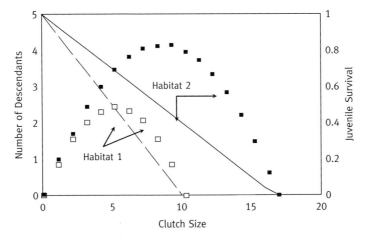

Figure 3.4. An illustration of how fitness can be mapped onto a heritable quantitative trait (clutch size) in two different habitats. Juvenile survival (lines) declines linearly with increased clutch size, but at a different rate in each habitat. The resulting trade-off between number and survival of offspring yields a different fitness-mapping function (the products of clutch size multiplied by juvenile survival in this case) for each habitat. The optimum clutch size (eight in this example) is greater in Habitat 2 than is the optimum (five) in Habitat 1. After Charnov and Krebs (1974) and Morris (1998).

values), the fitness expected in Habitat 2 against that in Habitat 1. The shape of the resulting fitness set depends on the shapes of the FMFs, and on how similar one habitat is to another.

Thus, if fitness is more-or-less normally distributed among clutch sizes, and if the mean and variance of clutch sizes produced in the two habitats are similar, then the fitness set will be concave (Fig. 3.5). If the means are quite different from one another, the fitness set will be convex (Fig. 3.6).

Let us review what we have done thus far. First, we imagined that we were able to measure the probabilities of offspring survival for different clutch sizes produced by semelparous parents living in a stationary population occupying two habitats.[4] The product of juvenile survival multiplied by clutch size estimated the number of descendants produced for each clutch size in each habitat. But because individuals exploit both habitats, the optimum clutch size will represent a compromise between the fitness achieved in each one. So we expressed that compromise by drawing the fitness set.

Our analysis to this point has ignored a variety of potential complications. Clutch sizes are unlikely to be genetically or developmentally fixed. (There are some notable

---

[4] A stationary population is one where both the number of individuals and their age-distribution are constant through time (which implies a constant environment). If the environment varies temporally, then the optimal life history will evolve to minimize losses during periods of low fitness. We provide a worked example illustrating this principle in Chapter 6.

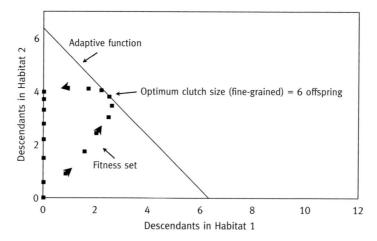

Figure 3.5. An illustration of how we can determine the optimum clutch size in a mixture of habitats using fitness-set analysis. Begin by plotting the fitness value of each clutch size simultaneously for Habitats 2 and 1 (from Fig. 3.4) to produce a series of points travelling in a counter-clockwise rotation (the fitness set). Then overlay the family of curves that represent the adaptive function for a given mixture of the two habitats. The optimum clutch size corresponds to the point on the fitness set that is tangential to the adaptive function. No other clutch size yields higher fitness.

exceptions to this rule, for example many seabirds produce clutches with only one egg and pigeons and humming birds lay two eggs.) Instead, different genotypes will produce a spectrum of clutch sizes around some modal value. The mode will vary with the total environment and with the developmental map. The habitats will also vary and so too will their FMFs. Clutch sizes and juvenile survival are likely to depend on population density and on the relative abundances of individuals occupying the two habitats. All of these effects may interact with one another.

There are at least two possible solutions to the added complexity. Imagine, for example, that we can count the number of descendants produced under each different scenario, and that we then plot the FMF for every case. Each FMF would allow us to predict the optimum clutch size for that particular case. We could then combine different scenarios for each habitat and plot the respective fitness sets. However, there would be so many alternatives that we would be unable to make any general predictions on the evolution of clutch size. We need a different and more general solution.

Imagine instead that we can count the number of descendants produced from different clutch sizes under the best circumstances in each habitat. We let these distributions represent the FMFs. We then combine these functions in a fitness set to create the composite FMF in both habitats. But we still do not know how to generate the expected fitness when individuals possess different modes of inheritance and development, or when they are exposed to different mixes of habitats, habitat heterogeneity,

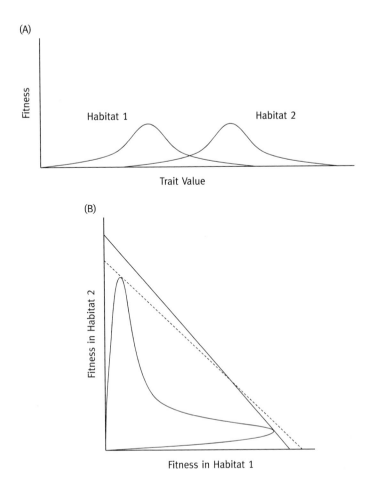

Figure 3.6. An illustration of adaptive evolution in a fine-grained environment where large differences between habitats cause the fitness-mapping functions of each separate habitat to lie far apart from one another (panel A). The fitness set is convex (panel B). A small change in the slope of the linear adaptive function can switch the optimum trait value from one that has high fitness in Habitat 1 (specialist in Habitat 1, solid adaptive function) to one with high fitness in Habitat 2 (dashed line). The scales differ between panels. After Levins (1968).

population density, and frequency. We need a new function that generates the expected fitness of each clutch size produced under the influence of all of these additional complexities.

Many evolutionary biologists subsume this new function in the fitness map. By doing so, they imagine that this fitness-generating function and the FMF can be merged statistically along a 'fitness surface' (e.g. Fairbairn and Reeve 2001). Adaptation will favour the trait value(s) corresponding to the maximum 'height' of the fitness surface. While such an approach has proven valuable, it assumes that the investigator is aware of, and has incorporated, all features of the environment that alter the fitness of a particular trait value.[5] To quote Levins (1968, p. 17): 'The fitness set alone does not define an optimum strategy. Over-all fitness in a heterogeneous environment depends on the fitnesses in the separate environments, but in a way which is determined by the pattern of the environments.'

Our aim, therefore, is to build a fitness-generating function (G)[6] that allows us to predict the evolution of trait values from their FMFs. The simplest G-function will allow us to calculate the weighted mean fitness in the two different habitats.

The adaptive function

In our example, each individual uses the two habitats in proportion to their availability (a so-called fine-grained environment). Thus, with fine-grained exposure to habitat, the expected fitness of different clutch sizes is given by their fitness in each habitat weighted by the habitat's frequency in the environment. Levins called this weighting the 'adaptive function'.

To build the adaptive function in our example we note that the total environment consists of only the two habitats, 1 and 2, in proportions p and q respectively ($p + q = 1$), The adaptive function (A) is given by a set of curves obeying

$$A = pw_1 + qw_2 \qquad (3.2)$$

where the actual value of A depends on the fitnesses (w_i) of the different trait values in the two habitats. Rearranging equation 3.2 we obtain

$$w_2 = \frac{1}{q}(A - pw_1) \qquad (3.3)$$

which can be plotted on the same graph as the fitness set. The optimum clutch size in the mixture of the two habitats is the one lying tangential to the adaptive function (Equation 3.3, Fig. 3.5). The optimum clutch size, given our example's restrictive assumptions, corresponds to an evolutionarily stable strategy (ESS). No other clutch size yields higher fitness.[7]

'Adaptation will create a frequency distribution around the optimum trait value'

---

[5] Vincent and Brown (2005) avoid this problem with their concept of 'evolutionary feasible strategies'.

[6] The fitness-generating functions similar to those we use here were invented by Tom Vincent and Joel Brown in the 1980s (e.g. Vincent and Brown 1984). The Vincent and Brown G-function incorporates the fitness-mapping function as well as density and frequency dependence.

[7] Our example, and Levins' original fitness-set approach, ignore the effects of density and frequency-dependence, which are crucial for determining evolutionarily stable strategies. We develop these details explicitly in Chapter 6.

In order for the optimum clutch size to become fixed, three assumptions must be met:

1. The mixture of the two habitats must remain constant.
2. Each clutch size must yield a single value of fitness.
3. Each genotype must be associated with a unique clutch size (narrow-sense heritability = 1).

None of these assumptions is likely to apply. The slope of the adaptive function will vary through time (and in different environments) as the proportion of the two habitats changes. Natural variation and stochastic events will produce fuzzy fitness sets. Incomplete heritability will generate additional variation around the optimum trait value. Thus, when we consider evolutionarily stable strategies, we should not expect a single trait value to emerge, but rather a frequency distribution of values. The ESS corresponds to the mean of that distribution.

Our prediction of evolution toward an intermediate trait value applies only to similar habitats that yield a concave fitness set. If the fitness set is convex, then evolution in a fine-grained environment will again lead to a compromise, but one that is biased towards the habitat with the greatest frequency in the environment (Fig. 3.6).

Levins also considered evolution in coarse-grained environments where individuals are capable of moving between habitats, but can exploit only one of the habitats at any given time. Under these conditions fitness will vary through time. The total number of descendants at some future time will depend on the number produced at earlier times. The same principle applies to the value of savings accounts and pension funds that accrue compound interest through time. Our estimate of fitness must account for the temporal variation. Instead of using a fitness estimate based on the additive characteristics of the arithmetic mean, we need to base it on an average that explicitly incorporates the multiplicative effect of variation through time. The geometric mean is such a function.[8] The adaptive function, expressed in terms of geometric mean fitness, is given by

$$A = w_1^p w_2^q \qquad (3.4)$$

which can be rearranged as

$$\log w_2 = \frac{1}{q}(\log A - p \log w_1) \qquad (3.5)$$

where p and q represent the proportion of time that individuals with different trait values spend in each habitat.

---

[8] An example using the geometric mean to understand the evolution of clutch-sizes can be found in Boyce and Perrins (1987).

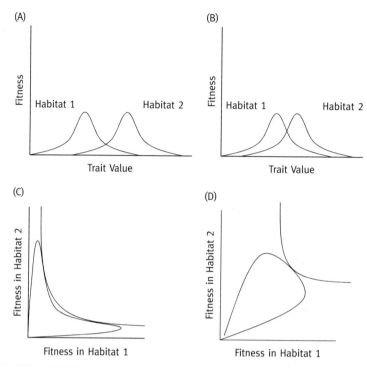

Figure 3.7. An illustration of adaptive evolution in a coarse-grained environment consisting of two habitats. The concave adaptive function yields a single intermediate trait value with concave fitness sets (panels B and D), but a polymorphism is possible if the fitness set is convex (panels A and C). After Levins (1968).

Equation 3.5 defines a convex adaptive function (Fig. 3.7). Predictions of adaptive evolution now depend on the shape of the fitness set. If the fitness set is concave, adaptation will again yield a single intermediate optimum. But if the fitness set is convex, a single adaptive function may lie tangential to the fitness set at two different values (Fig. 3.7). The adaptive solution, in this instance, would create a balanced polymorphism in the trait.

'Adaptation in fine-grained environments is most likely to yield a single optimum, whereas adaptation in coarse-grained environments can produce a polymorphic trait'

The polymorphism could represent a mixed strategy, where trait values emerge from randomly mating individuals sharing an optimum frequency of competing alleles in the population. The polymorphism could also emerge as the optimum solution between two competing pure strategies, where assortative mating occurs among individuals sharing the same optimum trait value. Regardless as to cause, stable polymorphic traits are particularly interesting because they may provide a heightened opportunity for disruptive selection and diversification. If individuals select the habitat that best corresponds with their trait value, assortative mating within that habitat could quickly lead to population divergence.

Our discussion of polymorphic traits has re-introduced us to the concept of adaptive strategies, which we discuss formally in Chapter 6. The strategy may be mixed such that the polymorphic population is produced through variable expression of the trait in different individuals. Each individual has the potential to express different values of the trait. The trait's value in any one individual depends on genetics, development, and exposure to the environment. Alternatively, the strategy may be pure. The polymorphic population represents a composite of pure-breeding individuals whose genetics and development always yield a single trait value.

But what, exactly, do we mean by strategy? The answer emerges from our understanding of FMFs and fitness sets. We note that the FMFs in Fig. 3.4 assume, implicitly, a constant environment. In our representation, we plotted only those points that define the outer bounds of fitness in the two habitats. There is a unique fitness associated with each different trait value. In reality, the fitness of a trait value will vary with the total environment (including genetics and development) in which the trait is expressed. A different value of fitness will emerge with different combinations of environments, and with environmental variability. Fitness will also depend on the density and frequency of individuals with other trait values. Thus FMFs, as well as their emergent fitness sets, are best thought of as more-or-less continuous clouds of points that represent all possible fitness outcomes for each trait value in the population.

The combined pairs of points in the fitness set represent the trait's bauplan;[9] the total range of adaptive possibilities for that trait. But the set of points on the outer negatively-sloped margin of the clouded fitness set yield higher combinations of fitness in the two habitats than do any others. This set of exterior points represents the set of possible adaptive strategies for the trait in the two habitats. Our analysis of adaptive functions demonstrated that the value of the 'best' strategy varies with the mix and scale of habitats. A completely different set of adaptive strategies could emerge from the bauplan in a different set of environmental circumstances (we discuss these important issues more fully in Chapter 7). Similarly, in our simple two-habitat caricature, both the bauplan and the strategies could be quite different in an alternative pair of habitats. More generally, we can imagine that the composite of all traits represents a taxon's bauplan, but that only certain combinations of traits and trait values correspond to adaptive strategies.

' The outer negatively-sloped portion of a trait's fitness set represents the set of possible adaptive strategies for that trait'

---

[9] We use the Anglicized version 'bauplan' (plural = 'bauplans'). The term originates from the German 'Bauplan' (plural = 'Baupläne').

We can clarify the distinction between bauplan and adaptive strategy with one of Darwin's favourite foils for adaptation, the evolution of domestic breeds of plants and animals. Darwin noted, for example, that pigeon fanciers created numerous distinctive breeds ranging from the expressive pouters and fantails to the aerobatic rollers and tumblers. Each breed represents a strategy along which assortative mating by fanciers favours some combinations of traits and trait values over others. But when released into the competitive and dangerous world of the common pigeon, the specialized strategies yield low fitness. Though part of the pigeon bauplan, birds with programmed rolls and tumbles are easy targets for peregrine falcons and other aerial predators. The proud struts and head bobs of the pouters are likely to compromise their foraging efficiency, and colourful, expansive tails may simultaneously fail to attract mates while catching the attention of enemies. In the wild, the specialised breeds are quickly replaced by the tried-and-true rock-dove strategy.

Similarly, when we look closely at a clade of species, we see groups of similar species arranged along the same strategy set (e.g. variation in body size caused by allometric growth of the same general morphology), as well as somewhat more distantly related clusters of species following alternative strategies (e.g. different morphological plans). All of the species would belong to the same bauplan as long as their strategies are, with time and opportunity, reversible and interchangeable. The species would belong to different bauplans when their strategies are so fundamentally different that they can no longer converge on one another.

In its original form, Levins' fitness-set analysis was most useful as a model of phenotypic evolution. In the case of fine-grained environments, adaptation produced a single optimum adaptive strategy. But in addition to differences in fitness for single trait values, we also know that $G \times E$ interactions associated with developmental and behavioural plasticity allow single genotypes to express different trait values in different environments. Can we modify fitness sets to incorporate the evolution of these reaction norms?

We return to the evolution of clutch size as our hypothetical model. First, we plot the reaction norms for clutch size in the two habitats (Fig. 3.8). Each set of parallel lines represents a different reaction norm. Positively sloped lines, for example, represent reaction norms that yield higher clutch sizes in Habitat 2 than in Habitat 1. Negatively sloped reaction norms yield lower clutch sizes in Habitat 2 than in Habitat 1.

In order to conduct a fitness-set analysis, we need to redraw the same reaction norms as fitness sets by plotting the fitness of each clutch size produced by each different reaction norm (e.g. Fig. 3.9). Unlike our previous graphs, here each fitness set represents the range of fitness values produced by different reaction norms. The adaptive function is unchanged. The optimal reaction norm corresponds with the fitness set tangential to the adaptive function with the highest fitness value. Thus, we are simultaneously able to predict not only the adaptive reaction norm, but also the best combination of trait values.

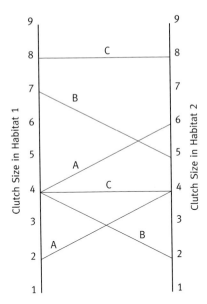

Figure 3.8. An illustration of different potential reaction norms for clutch size in two different habitats. Each reaction norm (A, B, C) is represented by a different set of parallel lines demonstrating that differences and similarities between habitats, for a given reaction norm, do not depend on clutch size. After Futuyma (1998).

'Fitness sets can also model adaptive phenotypic plasticity'

We can use our clutch-size example to explore three additional issues that are crucial to our understanding of adaptive evolution:

1. The optimum trait value may change with differences in density.
2. Changes in density may also alter the frequency of exposure to different habitats.
3. The resulting density and frequency-dependent evolution of the trait may depend on other traits.

We can explore each issue by imagining that one habitat yields higher fitness than does the other, that fitness declines with increasing density, and that individuals preferentially occupy the habitat that maximizes fitness. Stephen Fretwell and Henry Lucas (1969) demonstrated, in one of the most cited papers in evolutionary ecology, that populations existing under these conditions will achieve an ideal distribution such that the expected fitness is the same in each habitat (Fig. 3.10). In a coarse-grained environment, each habitat will equilibrate with a different number of individuals. In a fine-grained environment, the frequency of use of will reflect the density-dependent fitness value of the habitat.

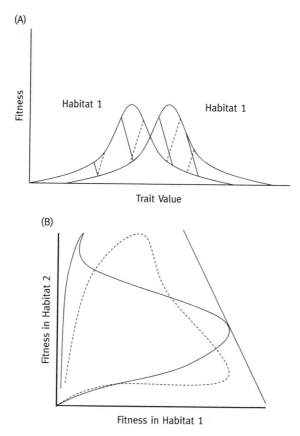

(A)

Fitness

Habitat 1   Habitat 1

Trait Value

(B)

Fitness in Habitat 2

Fitness in Habitat 1

Figure 3.9. An illustration that demonstrates adaptive evolution of reaction norms. In panel A, different sets of parallel lines connect two reaction norms with their expected fitness in two habitats. The approximate values are plotted as different fitness sets in panel B. The optimum reaction norm for a given mixture of habitats is the one that yields the highest combined fitness (tangential to the maximum achievable adaptive function).

For simplicity, imagine that fitness declines linearly in each habitat with increasing population size (this simplification allows us to model either fine-grained or coarse-grained habitat use). In our example, therefore, any increase in population size will reduce mean fitness in each habitat and alter the frequency of exposure to the two habitats. To make our graphical model tractable, let us further imagine that the relationships between juvenile survival and clutch size in each habitat become steeper as population size increases.

We examine the consequences for three different population sizes in Fig. 3.11. Panel A evaluates the FMFs for Habitat 1, panel B does the same for Habitat 2. The reduction in juvenile survival alters the FMFs for clutch size, as well as the corresponding fitness sets (Fig. 3.12). The adaptive function is also altered because it must now reflect not only the

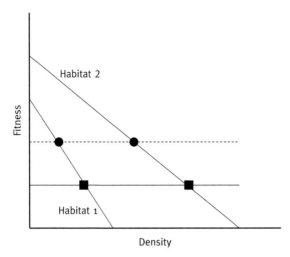

Figure 3.10. An illustration of ideal habitat selection. Fitness declines at different rates in two different habitats (1 and 2). If individuals select the habitat yielding maximum fitness, the density (or frequency of use) in each habitat will be adjusted such that the expected fitness is the same in each (solid circles and squares). Thus when both habitats are occupied, the frequency of individuals exploiting each habitat will change with population size (the frequency would be constant for linear fitness functions sharing the same intercept).

frequency of occurrence of the habitat in the landscape, but also changes in the frequency of exposure to each habitat with increasing density. For a fine-grained environment the adaptive function becomes

$$A = f_1(N)pw_1 + f_2(N)qw_2 \tag{3.6}$$

where the functions $f_i(N)$ represent the frequency of use of habitat i with changes in population size (N).

'Density and the frequencies of alternative strategies alter the fitness-mapping function, whereas exposure to different environments alters the adaptive function'

Our more complex adaptive analysis (Fig. 3.12) illustrates how the optimum trait value (clutch size in our example) changes with density and also with the frequency of exposure to different habitats. Moreover, in this example, the pattern of frequency dependence emerges through the evolution of an additional trait, the ability to select habitat. Thus, the adaptive value of clutch size in our hypothetical organism depends on its strategy of habitat selection. Offspring inherit not only the genes for clutch size and the ability to choose habitat, they actually 'inherit' the habitat itself. This exciting and revolutionary form of evolution (called 'niche construction' by its main proponent,

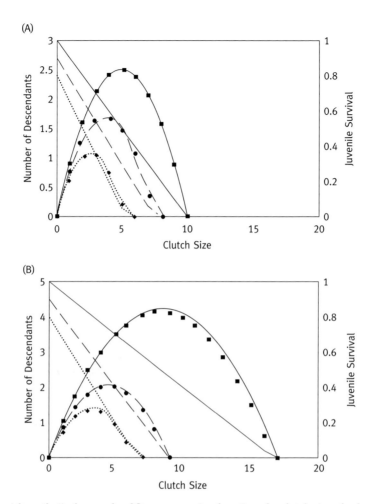

Figure 3.11. A hypothetical example of fitness-mapping functions for clutch size of a density-dependent habitat selector occupying two habitats. Panel A illustrates how density-dependent differences in juvenile survival with clutch size in Habitat 1 alter the number of descendants produced at three different population sizes. Panel B illustrates the same in Habitat 2. Solid line, small population; dashed line, intermediate population; dotted line, large population. Curves characterize the fitness-mapping functions given by the solid symbols.

Oxford's John Odling-Smee; Odling-Smee *et al.* 2003) thus creates evolutionary feedback where trait values depend not only on genetics and $G \times E$ interactions, but also on the ways in which organisms modify the environment.

Our analysis of frequency dependence was based on the idea that the proportion of individuals using one or the other habitat will change with population size. But population size will vary through time. To predict the optimum clutch size we should now extend our analysis to incorporate changes in population size (and associated density

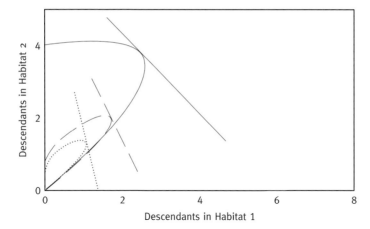

Figure 3.12. Fitness sets and examples of adaptive functions corresponding to the fitness-mapping functions illustrated in Fig. 3.11. The evolutionarily optimum clutch size depends on the decline in fitness in each habitat, on the relative densities in each habitat, on the frequency of each habitat in the environment, and also on the frequency, through time, of each population size.

and frequency-dependent evolution) through time. The simultaneous analysis of density and frequency-dependent evolution in space and time cannot be explored easily with simple graphs. Even so, our simplified graphical analyses of fitness sets and adaptive functions have illustrated several principles of adaptation. Armed with these principles, we can soon embark on a more formal analysis of density and frequency-dependent adaptation. First, however, we need to formalize our understanding of mapping.

Mappings

The corollas of many flowers are brightly coloured. The colouration helps attract insects to the flower because they expect the reward of nectar and, in return, the plant is pollinated and has its own pollen carried to others. The function of brightly coloured petals and sepals is pollination enhancement. The plant can use many different strategies in order to maximize pollination efficiency, bright colours being one of them. Red colours can be one strategy to solve the pollination game, yellow another. The *trait* corolla colour has the *function* to enhance pollination. Having brightly coloured petals is a strategy to solve the pollination game. The reproductive strategy may involve many other traits as well, such as odours, shape and size of the petals, and the timing of flowering. Traits are components of the phenotype and they map onto function. Function in turn maps onto fitness.

What do we mean by 'mapping'? A map is a projection or translation from one realm to another. For example, clutch or litter size maps onto fitness, but typically not in a simple and linear manner. Having four young surviving to weaning does not necessarily mean that fitness is twice as high compared to an individual producing only two, and eight young does not inevitably give the parent four times the fitness (e.g. Fig. 3.11). Sometimes mappings are simple. Lacking the ability to produce a critical enzyme for proper metabolism might mean death, whereas having it means survival (everything else being equal). If the enzyme is coded for by a single simple gene, then there is a very straightforward mapping from gene to trait (the enzyme) to function (metabolism) to survival and to fitness. For most traits of most multicellular organisms, things are not this easy. We will explore the ubiquitous complications of these mappings in Chapter 4. Here, we look in more detail at the function-to-fitness mapping.

Earlier, we asked 'what is a trait'? Is a trait unambiguously defined through its function? Function is only evolutionarily meaningful if it affects demographic rates, i.e. ultimately fitness. We can illustrate this by inspecting the conceptual formulation of a mapping $w = f(D(T(G)))$, where G is a genotype distribution, T is a trait distribution, D the demographic rates (survival and reproduction), and w is fitness. This is a nested mapping from genes to fitness and we may ask how changes in the genotype distribution contribute to changes in (mean absolute) fitness by writing

$$\frac{\partial w}{\partial G} = \frac{\partial w}{\partial D}\frac{\partial D}{\partial T}\frac{\partial T}{\partial G} \tag{3.7}$$

This is the approach that Tim Coulson at Imperial College and coworkers took when trying to develop a demographic framework for mapping genes to communities (Coulson *et al.* 2006). The three components of Equation 3.7 operate at different levels of biological organization (e.g. as in Fig. 3.3). Figure 3.13 provides more detail of that

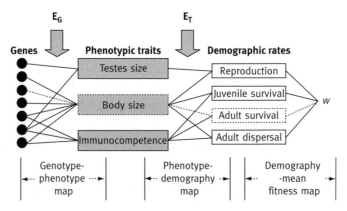

Figure 3.13. A schematic of the demographic framework showing how alleles (or the proteins they code for) can interact to produce traits, which in turn influence demographic rates and w. E_G is the influence of the environment on gene expression and E_T is environmental effect on trait expression that influences demographic rates. The dotted lines represent a path between an allele, a trait (body size), a demographic rate (adult survival), and w. After Coulson *et al.* (2006).

mapping with specific examples. Changes in the genotype distribution affect the trait distribution (responses to selection), changes in trait distribution change the demographic rates (the traits are exposed to selection), and the opportunities for adaptation arise from variation among individuals in their demographic success (survival and reproduction). The different terms in Equation 3.7 are very simplified maps that translate changes at one level to changes in another.

'Fitness emerges from the nested mapping of the influence of genotypes and environment on trait distributions, the effect of traits and environment on demography, and the opportunities for survival and successful reproduction'

In this mapping, unlike Fig. 3.3, there is no environment. If we include environmental terms in the equation, assuming that they affect both the expression of traits (through $G \times E$ interactions) and the demographic rates (through, for example, density and frequency dependence), then we can write an expanded version as

$$\frac{\partial w}{\partial G} = \frac{\partial w}{\partial D}\frac{\partial D}{\partial T}\left[\left(\frac{\partial T}{\partial G} + \frac{\partial T}{\partial E}\right) + \frac{\partial D}{\partial E}\right] \tag{3.8}$$

where E is the environmental influence. This map has some obvious interpretations. The last term ($\partial D/\partial E$) represents how the environment influences demographic rates, i.e. the density- and frequency-dependent effects. The term $\partial T/\partial E$ is the environmental influence on trait distributions, which can be thought of as phenotypic plasticity, and $\partial T/\partial G$ is, as before, the effect of the genotype distribution on the distribution of traits. If this latter term is zero, then the trait can be thought of as canalized (we briefly introduced this term in our discussion of how genes and genotypes effect traits in Chapter 2). The concept of canalization is usually credited to Waddington's 1942 research on the robustness of developmental programmes (Figure 3.14).[10] Small changes in the environment have no effects on the resulting phenotype. Also, small changes in the genotype, as above, should result in small or no changes in the values of canalized traits. Bergman and Siegal (2003; see also Siegal and Bergman 2002) have also shown that gene networks[11] can be rather strongly canalized, thereby also accumulating large genetic variation outside the functional parts of the genome. In a similar vein, the University of Florida's Robert Holt and Tristan Kimbrell demonstrated the joint roles of canalization and genetic variability in adaptation to novel environments (Kimbrell and Holt 2007, Kimbrell 2010). Using individual-based models, they showed that

---

[10] Waddington (1942, 1957) used the word 'canalization' rather than 'robustness' to indicate that developmental programmes are strongly shaped by evolution, reducing random fluctuations around the rather narrow 'channel' leading to the fully grown organism.

[11] Many genes function in concert with other genes and any given gene may be up- or downregulated depending on the activities of other genes. Their mutual influences are thus organized in sometimes complicated networks.

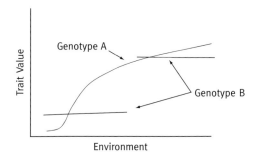

Figure 3.14. A simplified illustration of canalization. Genotype A (the curve) responds to changes in the environment by changing trait values. Genotype B, on the other hand, is canalized within two regions of the environmental variation. Small changes in the value of the environment have no or little effect on the resulting trait values, but large changes do.

reasonably complex gene networks tend to become canalized when adapting to a source habitat producing emigrants, but it is necessary for this canalization to break down when a novel (sink) habitat is colonized. Unless canalization that was beneficial in the source habitat is broken down, genetic variation necessary for successful adaptation to the novel habitat will remain 'hidden' and inaccessible to further adaptation. Here, we use canalization to eliminate the $\partial T/\partial G$ term and thus simplify Equation 3.8. Since our focus in this chapter is on the function of traits, we will now turn to the trait–demography mapping.

A trait's function can be entirely neutral, that is, have no appreciable effect on survival or reproduction. The question is, however, whether such traits would ever be considered as traits at all. For example, consider the two European birch species *Betula verrucosa* and *B. pubescens*. On the surface they are quite similar in appearance, but differ in some morphological respects, and to a degree in habitat requirements. *Betula verrucosa* has somewhat more triangular leaves than *B. pubescens*'s more rounded ones. The trait 'leaf shape' differs between the two species (and botanists use that difference, among other things, to tell them apart). What function would the more triangular leaves of *verrucosa* have as opposed to the more rounded ones in *pubescens*? How would the change, for whatever reason, in leaf shape of *pubescens* towards a more triangular, elongated, or even more rounded shape affect the reproduction and survival of the tree? Probably very marginally. The length:width ratio of birch leaves is demographically neutral. But leaves must be there and the leaves must have some length:width ratio, otherwise the birch tree would not be functional at all. So leaf shape does have a function, but the mapping is flat.[12]

---

[12] An appreciation of function often requires very careful assessment. A kiwi's wings, for example, are incapable of flight. The inability of kiwis to fly does not mean that their wings lack function, nor does it mean that they are 'neutral' characters. Development of wings is expensive, so ancestral kiwis developing frugal vestigial wings would have achieved higher fitness *ceteris paribus* than those with more profligate and elaborate wings.

Figure 3.15. The neutral mapping of trait values onto demographic rates (survival and reproduction). For both traits A and B the mapping is neutral such that the demographic rate does not change with changes in trait values. In the case of B the trait is truly neutral in that it has no influence on demographic rates (it has no function). Trait A does have function, but a constant one across trait values.

Without the trait, fitness is zero, but with it some basic level of survival and reproduction is guaranteed. We may also think of traits that have no bearing on demographic rates, whether they are present or not. Such traits have no function at all and are truly neutral (Fig. 3.15). It is questionable whether such phenotypic characters should be called 'traits' at all. Recall our definition of a trait as heritable phenotypic variations the functions of which modify survival and reproduction. Perhaps more interesting are traits that do have a function but where function is determined by trait value. Now, the value of the (quantitative) trait, given its function, will potentially have strong influence on demographic rates. Suppose the mapping of trait values onto juvenile survival rate (an important demographic rate and therefore important fitness component) looks like the relationship depicted in Fig. 3.16. High trait values yield high juvenile survival. Individuals with higher trait values would supposedly be better adapted, eventually leaving behind more descendants. We would hence conclude that there would be a selection gradient towards higher trait values. There are two principal caveats to this scenario. First, the mapping shown in Fig. 3.16A may only be true *in a given environment* (recall the last term in Equation 3.8). Instead, we could have a family of curves, each representing a different environment (Fig. 3.16B). Of course, different environmental conditions are not necessarily discrete; population density, a continuous variable, can also be an important part of the environment (Chapter 6). High dispersal propensity, if we identified that as a trait, could have the function of bringing the young individual into new and perhaps more profitable or safe habitats, hence rendering higher survival. But this may be true only under certain density conditions. Should the density in the patch in which the young animal lives be considerably lower, perhaps a more sedentary behaviour would enhance survival.

Second, we have to remind ourselves that juvenile survival, our function in this example, is not the same thing as fitness. Juvenile survival might be greatly enhanced

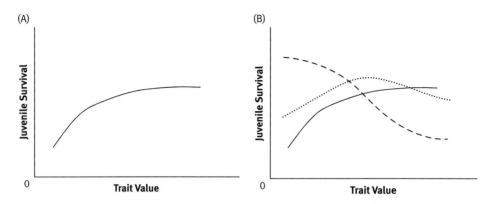

Figure 3.16. Panel A shows an example of a trait that maps onto a demographic rate (here juvenile survival) in some nonlinear fashion. Panel B shows that the relationship may only be true in a given environment. In other environments (dashed and dotted lines), the mapping may be slightly or even totally different.

by having a larger trait value, but if juvenile survival does not map onto fitness anywhere near proportionately, then the trait could possibly be neutral! Inspecting Equation 3.8 further we can also rather intuitively understand what 'neutral' means. If either of the two first terms on the right-hand side ($\partial w / \partial D$ [how demographic rates map onto fitness] or $\partial D / \partial T$ [how changes in trait values map onto demographic rates]) are zero, then there would be no effects on fitness by varying any of the other terms.

Note also that the mappings are not always linear (Fig. 3.16). If they are not linear, then the original trait distribution may be translated into something quite different in terms of means and variances. Given that we know something about the mapping function (how trait values translate into demographic rates, which is to say that we know something about the function of the trait) and possibly something about the properties of the trait distribution, then the moments of the resulting distribution can be (approximately) determined. The trick is to use what is called the Delta method of moment approximations (Box 3.1 fleshes out the mathematics of this translation). It is thus possible, at least in theory, to forecast changes in trait distributions (evolutionary change). Traits are typically not isolated parts of an organism's phenotype but are often correlated or otherwise contingent on each other. We will now briefly address this complication.

Multiple traits

If the functions of two traits are totally uncorrelated, and the genetic control of the two traits likewise is uncorrelated, then the traits evolve independently of each other. The assumption of independence is the cornerstone of Mendelian inheritance, which we reviewed in Chapter 2. But this is not always the case: traits often covary such that the

Box 3.1. The Delta method

Suppose we have a quantitative trait x. If we measure the value of that trait in a population, we could calculate the mean, $\bar{x}$, and the variance, σ^2. The exact nature of the distribution of trait values in the population is not important, but many quantitative traits are often approximately normally distributed. The function of the trait may now depend on the value of the trait. The relationship between trait value (x) and function (y) is, however, not always linear but determined by some function $y = f(x)$ mapping the distribution of trait values to a distribution of functions. The Delta method[13] is an approximation method so that you can calculate the mean and variance (and other moments) of the distribution of y.

The expectation of y is given by

$$E[y] \approx f(\bar{x}) + \tfrac{1}{2}\sigma_x^2 \frac{\partial^2 f(\bar{x})}{\partial x^2} \tag{B3.1.1}$$

where the last part of the last term is the second derivative of the function $f(x)$ evaluated at $\bar{x}$.

The variance of the new distribution is

$$\sigma_f^2 \approx \sigma_x^2 \left[\frac{\partial f(\bar{x})}{\partial x}\right] + 2\bar{x}_{3x}\frac{1}{2}\frac{\partial f(\bar{x})}{\partial x}\frac{\partial^2 f(\bar{x})}{\partial x^2} + (\bar{x}_{4x} - \sigma_x^4)\frac{1}{2}\frac{\partial^2 f(\bar{x})}{\partial x^2} \tag{B3.1.2}$$

where $\bar{x}_{3x}$ and $\bar{x}_{4x}$ are the third and fourth moments of the original distribution of x, respectively. The middle term is zero if the x-distribution is normal. Also, the third moment of the x-distribution is zero and the fourth moment is $3\sigma_x^4$ if the x-distribution is normal, significantly simplifying the calculations.

change in one trait value is constrained or facilitated by changes in another. This is a classic problem in quantitative genetics (e.g. Lande and Arnold 1983). Despite strong directional selection gradients, the character in question may not respond as expected (given also that sufficient genetic variance for the trait is present; see Chapter 2) because it may be locked to traits that are not changing, consequently hindering the expected result. This can be illustrated by considering two traits and their respective quantitative values z_1 and z_2 (Agrawal and Stinchcombe 2009). The change in the mean of those trait values from one generation to another is given by

$$\Delta \bar{z}_1 = \sigma_1^2 \beta_1 + Cov(z_1, z_2)\beta_2$$
$$\Delta \bar{z}_2 = \sigma_2^2 \beta_2 + Cov(z_1, z_2)\beta_1 \tag{3.9}$$

[13] More details, as well as extensions to multivariate cases, can be found in e.g. Otto and Day (2007) or Lynch and Walsh (1998).

Box 3.2 Correlated traits and the G-matrix

The problem with change in correlated traits is a classic one in quantitative genetics (e.g. Lande 1979, 1980 and Lande and Arnold 1983). The problem amounts to understanding the breeders equation (see Chapter 2) when more than one trait is involved. The additive genetic variance of the single trait is now replaced by the G-matrix, the matrix of the traits' variances and the pair-wise covariances. Mathematically, we have

$$\Delta \bar{z} = \frac{1}{\overline{W}} G \nabla \overline{W} \tag{B3.2.1}$$

where $\Delta \bar{z}$ is a vector with the relevant trait values, $\overline{W}$ is mean fitness, and $\nabla \overline{W}$ is the selection gradient (a vector with elements $\partial \overline{W} / \partial z_i$). G is the additive genetic variance–covariance matrix. The diagonal elements of G are the trait variances and the off-diagonal elements the covariances between trait i and j. Understanding long-term evolution (beyond from one generation to another) requires that the G-matrix is constant, which is far from certain.

---

where $\Delta \bar{z}_i$ is the change in trait value, σ_i^2 is the genetic variance for the respective trait, β_i is the selection gradient,[14] and Cov indicates the covariance (see Box 3.2 for a more general treatment of covariances).

'The evolution of correlated traits depends on the strength and sign of their correlation'

For illustrative purposes, we can now make some simplifications. First, let us assume that the genetic variance of the two traits is equal: $\sigma_1^2 = \sigma_2^2 = \sigma^2$. Second, let the selection gradients also be equal: $\beta_1 = \beta_2 = \beta$. Then recall that the definition of the correlation coefficient ($\rho_{i,j}$) for two variables is $\rho_{1,2} = Cov(1,2)/\sqrt{\sigma_1^2 \sigma_2^2}$. Remembering that the variances and selection gradients are equal, and after some rearrangements, we then have

$$\Delta \bar{z}_1 = \Delta \bar{z}_2 = \sigma^2 \beta (1 + \rho_{1,2}) \tag{3.10}$$

If the two traits are uncorrelated ($\rho_{1,2} = 0$), then the two traits will change independently and just follow the univariate breeder's equation that we introduced in Chapter 2. Should the two traits be perfectly negatively correlated ($\rho_{1,2} = -1$), then neither of the traits could change at all ($\Delta \bar{z}_i = 0$). Should they be positively correlated ($\rho_{1,2} > 0$), then

---

[14] The 'selection gradient' in this model, and other models of this kind stemming from quantitative genetics, actually accounts for both function and its mapping onto fitness. This assumption is sometimes, but not always, an accurate short-cut.

the change in one trait value would enhance the change in the other. Conclusion: genetic correlation (or lack thereof) between two traits can have a great influence on the rate of adaptation.[15] These are not just theoretical possibilities emerging from the mathematics of quantitative genetics. It is well-known among plant and animal breeders that attempting to change the value of certain desired traits can be difficult or even impossible because they are correlated with other traits.

Are correlated traits also widespread in natural populations? An innovative approach to this problem was taken by Aneil Agrawal and John Stinchcombe at the University of Toronto (Agrawal and Stinchcombe 2009). Their starting point was the Lande and Arnold variance-covariance models described above. They then devised an index that measures the rate of adaptation with covariances relative to the expected change without such correlations. A careful search of the published literature found a sufficient number of studies to test whether correlated traits influenced the rate of adaptation. Agrawal and Stinchcombe conclude that negative correlations can indeed make adaptive changes less likely, but also the reverse. There was no apparent bias towards covariance constraint, and facilitation seems to be equally common. In many other cases there was no effect of one trait on another. So, we learn that genetic correlations do or do not influence the rate of change of trait values.

This conclusion is, strictly speaking, only about the genotype–phenotype mapping. The trait to fitness mapping is assumed to be straightforward, but it is not. It is true that one typically cannot consider traits in isolation. It is ensembles of traits (the phenotype) that are exposed to the environment and it is ensembles of traits that are adapted. The environment is key. The mapping from trait value to fitness cannot be established unless the environment that influences the selection gradient is characterized. For example, the amount and types of food available would constitute an environmental dimension typically worth considering. This would in turn be influenced by the density of conspecifics and the frequencies of foraging modes and preferences, as well as the densities of, for example, predators that alter the time individuals spend foraging (or in another habitat) and the time they allocate to vigilance. In the following, we are going to see how the environment affects the trait–fitness mapping.

Optimal trait values

We will return to the scenario of a fine-grained environment consisting of two habitat types. The adaptive function in this situation is

$$A = pF_1 + (1 - p)F_2 \qquad (3.11)$$

---

[15] It is rather straightforward to extend the analysis to any number of traits, see, for example, Lande and Arnold (1983) and Box 3.2.

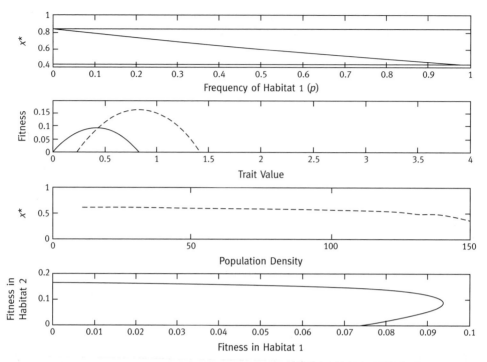

Figure 3.17. The frequency and density dependence of an optimal trait value. The top panel illustrates how the optimal trait value, x^*, varies with the proportion of Habitat 1 in the environment. As the proportion of Habitat 1 increases (for a given population density, here $N = 50$), the optimal trait value decreases because the optimal trait value in Habitat 1 only is lower than for Habitat 2. The horizontal lines indicate the optimal trait values in respective habitats. The second panel shows how trait value, x, translates into fitness in Habitat 1 (solid curve) and Habitat 2 (dashed curve). As population density increases (third panel, proportion of Habitat 1 is constant at 0.5), the optimal trait value also decreases. The bottom panel shows the fitness set (fitness in Habitat 2 against fitness in Habitat 1). The second and bottom panels apply to $N = 50$.

where p is the proportion of Habitat 1 in the environment. F_i is the density-dependent, and here also trait-value-dependent fitness-related reward in the respective habitats, the FMF. The habitats are different and the efficiency by which an individual can survive and reproduce will depend on a single trait value, x. The trait–fitness map is different in the two habitats (we will here assume a quadratic function). Density dependence enters, as before, in a linear fashion, and if we put it all together we have

$$F_i = (\alpha_i - \beta_i N)(a_i x - b_i x^2) \tag{3.12}$$

where the first bracketed term represents the linear density dependence and the second one, trait dependence (a quadratic, dome-shaped function). The parameters α_i and β_i determine the strength of the density dependence and the parameters a_i and b_i dictate the shape of the function over the trait axis. So, we have an environment (fine-grained) with two habitat types, each associated with an FMF, F_i, that maps trait value x onto fitness. Having a given trait value may yield a high fitness reward in one habitat, but much less so in the other habitat. Which trait value would be optimal, i.e. which would yield the highest fitness under the assumption of a fine-grained environment? It depends. If Habitat 1 is the dominating (most frequent) habitat, then a trait value close to the one that maximizes fitness in that habitat would be optimal (and the reverse). Note also that the FMF is density dependent, so the solution depends on population density. In order to find the solution, we need to identify which trait value maximizes the adaptive function, the function that translates the FMFs to realized fitness. The trait value that maximizes the adaptive function is found by calculating the derivative of the adaptive function with respect to x, dA/dx, putting that expression equal to zero and solving for x.[16] This exercise is reasonably straightforward and we will arrive at

$$x* = \frac{a_1 \Lambda + b_1 B}{2(b_1 \Lambda + b_2 B)} \tag{3.13}$$

where $\Lambda = p(\alpha_1 - \beta_1 N)$ and $B = (1 - p)(\alpha_2 - \beta_2 N)$. Obviously, the optimal trait value (the one maximizing the adaptive function A), x^*, depends on frequency (p) and density (N). It is not easy to visualize Equation 3.13 directly, so we illustrate the optimal trait value solution in Fig. 3.17. The upper panel shows that, for a given constant population density, the optimal trait value decreases as the frequency of Habitat 1 increases in the environment. When the frequency of Habitat 1 increases, more and more time is spent in that habitat (remember that in a fine-grained environment, the habitat types are used in proportion to their frequencies) and smaller and smaller trait values will be favoured. This is seen in the second panel where trait values are mapped onto fitness depending on which habitat the organism uses. The third panel illustrates how population density changes the optimal trait value. The bottom panel illustrates the fitness set (Levins 1968).

This exercise in solving for the optimal trait value in a fine-grained environment illustrates the many roles that function plays. First, we have to identify relevant traits, which can only be done when mapping them onto function. In the above example this was easy because we made up a trait with one fitness function for each habitat. For the theorist this is easy, but when faced with a real problem, finding the (relevant) trait FMF may not be a simple task. The next step is to determine the adaptive function in order to be able to evaluate the probable (and not only the possible or feasible) outcomes of

---

[16] Recall the usual optimization procedure of finding the maximum of a function. The value on the abscissa corresponding to the maximum value of the function is the 'optimal' one.

adaptation.[17] Habitat selection in a fine-grained environment is again a rather straight-forward problem in this respect, at least from a theoretical point of view. Calculating the adaptive function in the field can be difficult, but it is nevertheless a necessary step if we want to understand how populations of organisms change in the course of evolution. Our example also taught us that the solution may be sensitive to both population density and frequency. There is also an issue of scale—it was decided from the outset that the environment should be considered fine-grained. How do we know that the organism is operating at a (spatial) scale that corresponds to our idea about the environment? There is much to learn before we can arrive at a complete picture. The following chapters will lead us toward that goal.

Reflection

Function is the crucial link between what organisms 'are' and what they will become over generations. This is because function links the values of traits to differential reproduction and survival. We can measure infinitely many genetic, physiological, morphological, and behavioural properties of organisms and call them 'traits', but many, if not most, would be evolutionarily uninformative because they have no function and therefore no adaptive value is associated with them. This can, however, only be judged given the environment in which the organism lives. Should the environment change, new functions may appear. The mapping of, say, juvenile survival to fitness may be weak or absent in one environment, but much stronger in another. Any evaluation of function must, therefore, be associated with a clear specification of the environment.[18] The specification of the environment goes beyond the physical proper-ties of it, e.g. whether it is fine- or coarse-grained from the point of view of the organism. The biotic environment is equally important, for example the density of conspecifics, or of resources and predators.

Fitness is not a trait. Fitness is the outcome of function. Whether a trait renders high fitness (is adaptive) or low fitness (is potentially ephemeral or even maladaptive) is evaluated by the adaptive function. Here, we have used the approach that Levins invented when paving the way for an elegant and comprehensive understanding of adaptation. His tools have since been refined, as we shall see in Chapter 6, but they serve us well when clarifying how we can understand the relationship between traits and adaptation. This is done through the FMF. The 'fitness function' has many appear-ances and disguises. One can think of it as the function describing the adaptive landscape *sensu* Sewall Wright with alleles, not traits, as the independent variable(s).[19]

---

[17] The difficulties associated with the 'probable', 'feasible', and 'possible' will be further developed in Chapter 7.

[18] This is formally called the 'evolutionary feedback environment' and is discussed in Chapter 6.

[19] Wright's idea was to map genotypes (alleles) onto fitness. Some allelic combinations would render high fitness, others low. By plotting the fitness values over the genotype values (allele frequencies) one could thus create a landscape with troughs (fitness minima) and peaks (fitness peaks).

Often, the fitness function is the name for the relationship between trait values and some measure of 'success' (e.g. winter survival or clutch size). This definition runs the risk of confusing fitness components (such as survival) or contributions to fitness with fitness itself. Those pitfalls are more easily avoided if we carry with us an appreciation of the different mapping steps, and how we ultimately translate the FMF into realized fitness through the adaptive function. The *G*-function (an FMF with explicit frequency and density dependence) approach developed by Tom Vincent, Joel Brown, Yosef Cohen, and others helps us understand how to do that.

To fully understand how the seemingly hopelessly complex mappings are integrated,[20] we will now introduce the pillar called structure, the synthesis of mappings from genes to adaptation.

[20] See Fig. 3.3.

4

Structure

HOW GENOTYPES, TRAITS, STRATEGIES, AND ENVIRONMENT INTERACT

Overview

A thorough understanding of evolution requires much more than mechanics and function. We need to know the transformation rules that convert genotypes living in different environments into the traits we study as evolutionary biologists.[1] We also need to know how those traits influence the frequencies of future genotypes through their effects on fitness. But traits effect fitness only indirectly through their function in whole, working organisms. The expression, and function, of traits varies with development and depends on interactions among genes, interactions of genes with their environment, interactions with other traits and strategies, and interactions among individuals living in different places.

Our objective in this chapter is therefore to explore the often complex structure that describes how genotypes, traits, and the environment interact. We begin by describing the intriguing relationships between the anatomical structure of gill rakers in northern fishes and their function in foraging. We then review a furious debate on evolutionary structure that demonstrates why we must map the values of biological traits, such as gill rakers, onto their function.

Organisms perform numerous functions in order to live and reproduce. The maps we draw must recognize that traits are the adaptations enabling organisms to perform those essential functions. In order to map traits onto function, we first need to understand how an individual's state modifies not only its traits, but also the trait's function.

An individual's state is often influenced by density and the frequency of other types of individuals with which it interacts. We probe these crucial density and frequency-dependent interactions by asking what is optimal, and by assessing evolutionary strategies. Optimum trait values, and optimum strategies, are constrained by history, genetics, development, and the environment in which they are expressed. Some solutions are reinforced by synergistic interactions among traits performing similar or

---

[1] We can do no better than to quote Gomulkiewicz and colleagues (2010): 'There are countless ways to map genotypes to phenotypes' (p. 100).

co-dependent functions. Others are opposed by trade-offs that restrict possible evolutionary solutions. Convergence on single trait values and strategies depends on the underlying spatial and genetic structure in populations.

We attempt to make sense of this bewildering array of possibilities by summarizing the complexity with a structure matrix. The matrix helps us explore what is possible through evolution. Those explorations will reveal that an appreciation of structure is far more interesting and important than it might appear on first reading.

Introduction: mapping traits onto fitness

Only 20,000 years ago, less than a wink in geological time, Earth was a dramatically different place than it is today. Much of the northern hemisphere was layered in ice. Continental ice sheets flowed across Canada and the northern United States, most of northern Europe, and throughout large expanses of Asia. With much of the world's fresh water trapped in ice, sea levels dropped by as much as 150 metres. So it should hardly be surprising that the ice sheets had major effects on the distribution and diversification of northern fishes.

During the time of continental ice sheets, anadromous and estuarine fish species that could live in both salt and fresh water occupied different river systems than they do now. Many northern freshwater fishes barely hung on in glacial refuges. As the ice sheets melted, remnant populations spread across the continents in postglacial lakes and drainages. Meanwhile, rising sea levels provided salt-tolerant species with new but often ephemeral access to coastal waterways. Glacial melt waters allowed many of these fish species to also move among watersheds. Watersheds shifted as Earth's crust rebounded isostatically from the weight of the ice. The colonization of new emerging lakes and waterways was thus followed by physical isolation of the colonizing populations in separate basins. Many lakes and rivers contained few species, but with huge ecological opportunities for divergence into 'unoccupied' niches.

'Numerous species of northern freshwater fishes coexist as sympatric polymorphic ecotypes'

The fish did not squander their chances for diversification in this massive, replicated experiment. Today, both Nearctic and Palearctic lakes frequently contain two or more sympatric, diverging, polymorphic populations of fish. The pattern is exemplified most clearly in salmonids (salmon, trout, whitefish), but is also repeated in at least four other families of fishes including sticklebacks (Gasterosteidae), smelts (Osmeridae), sunfishes (Centrarchidae) and suckers (Catostomidae) (Saint-Laurent *et al.* 2003). A typical polymorphic pair in a northern lake consists of a small, pelagic, planktivorous form and a closely related but much larger benthic feeder or piscivore. In the case of three-spined sticklebacks, the polymorphism is expressed as a bottom-feeding 'benthic' type and a

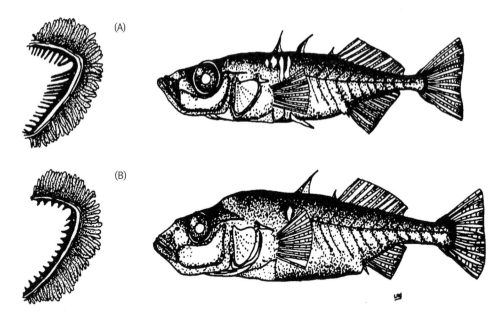

Figure 4.1. An example of polymorphic ecotypes of three-spined sticklebacks representative of fish populations that coexist in many northern lakes in North America, Europe, and Asia. Figures on the left illustrate the number and length of gill rakers (along the inside edge of the gill arch) found in limnetic (A) and benthic (B) forms of sticklebacks from Paxton Lake, British Columbia, Canada. From Schluter (1993), reproduced with permission from the Ecological Society of America.

distinct open-water 'limnetic' form (Fig. 4.1)[2]. In addition to differences in body size and shape, the pairs typically differ in a variety of other structural characters, including differences in the number and length of gill rakers, the location and size of pectoral and pelvic fins, the shape and length of the caudal peduncle, and the shape and position of the mouth.

Traits and function

Gill rakers, small cartilaginous structures arranged like the teeth of a comb along the gill arches (Fig. 4.1), are thought to aid in foraging by altering water currents and sieving prey. Many fine gill rakers should increase the rate at which dwarf, pelagic individuals consume small zooplankton. But benthic feeders easily disturb the substrate, so if the gill rakers are too numerous or too long they can clog with sediment and reduce foraging and respiratory efficiency. The tight connection between form and function

[2] It may be instructive to pause for a moment to contemplate whether this pattern is consistent with our understanding of fitness sets (Chapter 3). What does it suggest about the shapes of the fitness set, the adaptive function, and the course of evolution through time?

in these vital characters is reflected in their utility in taxonomy (the number of gill rakers is a key trait in the systematics and classification of *Coregonine* fishes). The number and length of gill rakers is one of the diagnostic differences between benthic and pelagic/limnetic ecotypes of numerous fish species, and the number of gill rakers is often, but not always, a reliable morphological indicator of genetic divergence (Næsje *et al.* 2004).

Genetically distinct coexisting fish ecotypes in northern lakes tend to eat different foods and live in different habitats. Morphologically, they split into large, benthic and small, pelagic, limnetic forms. Trophic traits, measured by the number and length of

---

Box 4.1. What roles do adaptation, geographic isolation, and plasticity play in the evolution of polymorphic traits in northern fishes?

Northern lakes in both the Old and New World frequently contain divergent poly-morphic populations of limnetic and benthic fishes. This very strong and repeated pattern should help us understand the mechanisms and dynamics of diversifying lineages. Evolutionists have concentrated on three questions:

1. Did the populations diverge through competition for resources?
2. Were populations isolated long enough to become reproductively isolated?
3. Or is the divergence explained by developmental plasticity?[3]

The University of British Columbia's Dolph Schluter is the leading proponent of the role of competition in the ecological speciation of these closely-related fish populations. Schluter (1996) identified several lines of evidence that support eco-logical speciation. One of the most important observations is that assortative mating (often associated with differences in spawning times or locations) and morphological differences are maintained in wild populations despite high poten-tial for gene flow. Assortative mating, or post-mating differences in offspring fitness, must occur in the wild because hybrid progeny created and raised in the laboratory survive and reproduce about as well as their 'purebred' parents. The morphology of hybrid sticklebacks is intermediate between that of purebred strains. When laboratory-reared hybrids and their purebred cousins are raised in natural habitats, the purebreds grow more rapidly in their preferred habitats than do the hybrids. Schluter's ecological interpretation is bolstered by studies docu-menting direct correspondence between the degree of morphological and genetic divergence of sympatric populations.

---

[3] David Pfennig and colleagues (2010) review the importance of phenotypic plasticity to diversifica-tion, speciation and adaptive radiations.

Much of our understanding of the genetics of northern polymorphic fish eco-types comes from teams led by Louis Bernatchez at Québec's Laval University. In one classical study Bernatchez's group examined ecological and genetic divergence of coexisting dwarf and normal whitefish (*Coregonus clupeaformis*) ecotypes sampled from two eastern North American lakes (Bernatchez *et al.* 1999). Diets of adult fish had little in common. Dwarf ecotypes consumed mostly zooplankton while normal whitefish ate mostly large zoobenthos, fish, or molluscs. Genetic analyses based on microsatellite loci documented clear genetic differences between the two ecotypes in each lake. Other than differences in body size, ecotypes in only one of the lakes were morphologically distinct. Dwarf fish in Maine's Cliff Lake had more gill rakers (27.6) on average than did normal fish (24.9). These patterns are not what we would typically expect if diverging ecotypes reflect genetically-determined adaptations to different niches. Indeed, Bernatchez's group had earlier documented patterns of genetic divergence suggesting that different ecotypes may have developed reproductive isolation while living in separate glacial refugia (Lu and Bernatchez 1998). But the degree of genetic difference among ecotypes is nevertheless low and adds indirect support to a third alternative: different morphotypes may often emerge through phenotypically plastic traits.

Robinson and Parsons (2002) evaluated the plasticity hypothesis with a meta-analysis of 36 different studies testing for phenotypic plasticity in 23 different taxa of northern freshwater fishes. Each study found some evidence for phenotypically plastic morphology. Ten of twelve studies examining gill rakers documented plasticity in the predicted direction (more or longer gill rakers in dwarf ecotypes than in normal fish). So at least three interacting evolutionary mechanisms are involved in creating and maintaining the dramatic morphological ecotypes of northern fishes:

1. Ecologically driven diversification into separate niches.
2. Reproductive isolation originating in refuge populations.
3. Phenotypic plasticity.

gill rakers, often correlate with the morphological, ecological, and genetic divergence. There are at least three interdependent routes by which the differences could have evolved (Box 4.1). What sense can we make out of these patterns? What do they tell us about evolutionary structure? To answer these questions, we first need to explain what, exactly, we mean by structure.

'Structure' is a loaded term. The online *Compact Oxford English Dictionary* (http://oxforddictionaries.com/view/entry/m_en_gb0821990#m_en_gb0821990; accessed 9 March 2011) provides three definitions:

1. 'the arrangement of and relations between the parts of something complex'
2. 'a building or other object constructed from several parts'
3. 'the quality of being well organized'.

All three apply to biology. When we speak of an anatomical structure, such as a single gill raker, we are probably thinking of it as an object (definition 2). But when we speak of gill rakers as trophic structures, we are probably thinking about the organized arrangement of, and relations among, the parts of something complex (definitions 1 and 3).

'Evolutionary structure is the core of a long debate on the role of intelligent design in evolution'

The organized, systematic relationships among several parts that form complex traits (such as eyes) have served as the foil in a long and tempestuous debate between theologians and evolutionists. The never-ending, sometimes rancorous, differences of opinion centre on a famous book, *Natural Theology*, written in the early 19th century by the Archdeacon of Carlisle, William Paley (Paley 1802).[4] Paley's treatise focussed on the so-called 'argument from design', a ploy often used by creationists to discredit evolution. Here is a nutshell encapsulation of the argument. Complex entities such as clocks and telescopes (and such 20th- and 21st-century inventions as aeroplanes, computers, video cameras, satellites, cellular telephones, BlackBerries, and iPads) are designed purposefully to fulfil a function. They are the product of intelligent designers. So when we assess complex traits in nature (human eyes, the necks of giraffes, aposematic colouration, and possibly gill rakers), we see that they also serve a function, and must similarly be the product of intelligent design (God). The debate rages on even though numerous evolutionary thinkers have demonstrated, time and again, that traits such as human eyes evolved through many, cumulative, small, adaptive modifications (e.g. Dawkins 1986, 1997, Ruse 2003).

Each side defines traits in the context of their function or purpose.[5] The human eye is an interesting and adaptive character (trait) because it provides vision. Components within the eye, such as cones and rods, are interesting traits because they fine-tune the eye's sensitivity to movement, light, and colour. The bright colours of unpalatable or poisonous animals such as coral snakes interest us because their colouration reduces mortality from predators that recognize the danger signal. And for humans, brightly decorated venomous snakes heighten the value of our colour vision. Clearly, then, traits fulfil one or more functions, they have purpose. But since traits evolve, we must be able to relate function to fitness. By defining traits through their connection to fitness from function, we force ourselves to treat evolution as a set of hypotheses that can be tested, and rejected, by careful experiments. A character that has no function, or a function that is unrelated to fitness is, by definition, immune to adaptation. By restricting 'trait'

---

[4] Michael Ruse (2003) provides a lucid history of natural theology.

[5] An instructive exercise is to ask your friends 'What is a clock?' Most will answer 'A device to measure time'. Clocks are defined by most people through their function, not through their elaborate and varying mechanics used to keep, display, or record time. Now repeat the question with reference to a biological trait (e.g. 'What is a gill raker?'). Is the emphasis still on function?

to represent only characters whose function either improves or reduces fitness, we can mimic evolution with adaptive thinking to quickly generate and weed out competing explanations. Would coral snakes with washed-out colours be more susceptible to injury or death? On average, would pale snakes produce fewer descendants than the normal brightly-coloured snakes? Would even more brightly-coloured snakes be less prone to attack and produce more descendants than normal snakes?

> *'The argument that traits must emerge from intelligent design can be resolved only by linking biological characters to both function and fitness'*

Our attention on both function and fitness forces us to evaluate what, exactly, we mean by characters versus traits, and whether a particular trait or group of traits is adaptive or not. The word 'character' is shorthand for 'inherited biological variable'. Characters can be either meristic (present versus absent, or occurring as discrete entities that can be counted, e.g. the number of gill rakers) or metric (continuous variables such as the length of gill rakers). The character could be as simple as a single anatomical entity (gill raker) or represent something more 'complex', such as a cognitive ability to solve novel problems. Regardless of whether it is simple or complex, a character that has no fitness consequences is not a candidate for adaptive evolution; it is not a trait. We learned in Chapter 3 that, in some cases, the expression of biological variables is genetically fixed, or developmentally canalized, with little or no variation. The character lacks the variability that we would normally use to assess its adaptive value (we address the evolutionary dynamics of traits in Chapter 6).

We also learned that different character values may have no fitness consequences whatsoever. So, in the case of the human eye, whether the iris is blue, brown, or some other colour is unlikely to modify directly the number of descendants we produce (though it could do so indirectly if human mating preferences are based on eye colour). But the inherited anatomy that defines our interest in the trait we call a human eye may nevertheless be adaptive because individuals with impaired vision living in dangerous, capricious, or otherwise heterogeneous environments may tend to produce fewer descendants than individuals with normal eyesight. We thus restrict our use of 'trait' to represent only those inherited variables (characters) for which different values (including presence/absence for meristic variables) yield differences in fitness.[6]

The complex layers that connect a character with fitness from function represent the evolutionary structure for that trait. Evolutionary structure includes the mechanics of genetics and development responsible for the trait's expression, as well as the associated genetic and developmental environments. A trait's evolutionary structure also includes the physical–biological environment in which the function is performed, and

---

[6] This definition of 'trait' makes no assumptions about the mode of inheritance.

the population–community context in which fitness is accrued through function, as well as the possibility for non-genetic inheritance.

'A trait's evolutionary structure includes its expression through genetics and development as well as its function and the fitness accrued from the physical-biological environment in which individuals possessing different trait values live'

So how do we relate our understanding of structure to characteristics such as gill rakers and their role in the morphological divergence of northern fishes? First, we must specify clearly which specific trait we are interested in (e.g. the length of gill rakers). Then we must identify which population of individuals we are considering. Once these decisions have been made, we need to know that gill-raker length in that population is an inherited and variable character.[7] Next, we need to identify the supposed function of the trait (in our example, foraging efficiency). Then we must map the function onto the trait's value, and finally, map the fitness value onto the trait's function (Chapter 3 deals with this problem in detail).

We illustrate a hypothetical example of this structural mapping as it could apply to northern fishes in Fig. 4.2. Our interest is focused on the role that habitat might play in the adaptive evolution of fishes. So we need to evaluate the foraging efficiency of the gill rakers separately in benthic (lowest layer of a water body adjacent to the sediment) and limnetic (the portion of open water where photosynthesis occurs) habitats. Each habitat supports different types of prey and requires different foraging behaviours. Longer gill rakers should be more efficient in the open, clear water of the limnetic zone, where fish feed on small zooplankton. If the gill rakers are too long, however, they will inhibit effective foraging. And there is also a much shorter optimum gill-raker length for benthic feeders, which probe the substrate in search of larger, less mobile prey. But knowing the relationship between a trait's value and its function is still not structure. We need to know how the function maps onto fitness. In our gill-raker example, we imagine a simple map (Fig. 4.2B) where changes in fitness are directly proportional to changes in foraging efficiency.

The two maps taken together represent key elements of the adaptive structure of gill rakers. Knowing this structure, we can associate traits with their function and fitness, and evaluate the possible outcomes of evolution. Of course we can short-circuit the process by mapping trait values directly onto fitness (we actually do this in Chapter 6), but an implicit assumption when we do so is that we already understand the structural connections of the trait to its function in real organisms. If our understanding is incomplete, we lose insight into the underlying structure that determines success and failure. We

---

[7] We ignore the genetical–developmental components of the evolutionary structure of gill rakers in this example only because they are not essential to answer our specific question of morphological divergence based on habitat.

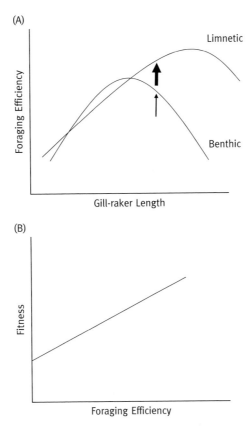

Figure 4.2. A hypothetical illustration of the ecological component of evolutionary structure that could apply to gill rakers in northern fishes. Panel A illustrates one of many possible functional relationships between the length of gill rakers and their role in foraging efficiency in limnetic versus benthic habitats. Panel B illustrates the possible relationship between foraging efficiency and fitness. Both figures taken together represent the adaptive structure of gill-raker length for fish living in limnetic versus benthic habitats. Note, in this case, that the length of the gill rakers has two optima, one in each separate habitat. The arrows point toward the efficiency of an imaginary fish with gill-rakers intermediate to the two optima. The broad arrow represents a fish living in the limnetic habitat, the narrow arrow corresponds to the efficiency of the same fish living in the benthic habitat.

would thus have an incomplete understanding of adaptation, and even less understanding of the processes and sequences of events influencing the evolution of traits.[8]

Now, with a general understanding of structure in hand, we can begin to explore the options that are available to adaptive evolution. We begin our quest by asking whether the adaptive structure of a trait is constant for all individuals or whether it varies amongst them.

---

[8] We do not expect, or for that matter recommend, that single research programmes probe all scales necessary for a full understanding of evolutionary structure.

Traits, states, and strategies

Actually, we have already answered this question. In Fig. 4.2, we mapped the adaptive structure of gill-raker length for fish living in two separate habitats. We imagined that the length of gill rakers maximizing foraging efficiency was shorter for benthic foragers than it was for individuals feeding in the limnetic zone. Our structural map tells us that maximum efficiency in each habitat occurs at a different trait value. In the jargon of evolutionary biology, fish living in one habitat are in a different state than individuals living in another.

We can define state as any variable that differentiates individuals (e.g. Houston and McNamara 1999). But as we have seen with our fish example, it is convenient to subdivide state variables into meristic (countable) or metric (continuous) traits that are fixed properties of the organism (e.g. the number of gill rakers or their length at maturity), and those that represent categorical states differentiating large groups of organisms from others (age class, sex, habitat). Fish living in the limnetic zone are in a different state than fish living in the benthic habitat. Similarly, young fish are in a different state (age, size, status) than are older ones. Fish living at low density are in a different state than fish living at high density. And fish living at low population size may be more likely to live in a particular habitat than are fish in a large population. The adaptive value of a trait thus depends on which of many states an individual is in. Put another way, the optimum value of a trait depends on its evolutionary structure. The structure changes with differences in an individual's state.

'The function and fitness of a trait depend on the current state of the individual'

Unfortunately it is not always clear in print, or in practice, which characteristics should be treated as traits, and which should be considered part of the organism's state. Where an organism currently lives is an expression of its ability to choose habitat, but is not itself a trait. If the organism can, in principle, choose which habitat to occupy (or whether to disperse its offspring), then the current habitat may not correspond with future or past habitats. So rather than being a property of the organism (trait), habitat in this example is a state that individuals (or their ancestors) choose. But the ability to disperse from one location or one habitat to another is a trait that deserves its own adaptive analysis.

The state of an organism has huge consequences on adaptive evolution. Perhaps the most intriguing of these is the concept that individuals inherit not only their parents' genes, but also components of their parents' state (Odling-Smee et al. 2003).[9] A classic example emerges from polygynous species, where one male may fertilize several females. Males with high social status (often correlated with large, or otherwise

---

[9] We also learned in Chapter 2 that individuals can inherit their ancestors' environments. Much of the environmental inheritance may, however, be captured by the state of the parents.

prominent, individuals in a high physiological state) are more successful at siring offspring than are males with lower status. The opportunity to rear a high-status male also varies among females. Females that are themselves in a high state often produce larger male offspring than do females of lower quality. And, in species with post-reproductive parental care, females in a high state are better able to provision their expensive male offspring. Males inherit their mother's state. Males with high-state dams (who will often also maintain high social status) will themselves achieve a high state and social status and sire more offspring. This means that females in a high state should be more likely to produce male offspring than females in lower states, whose best strategy is to concentrate their investment in daughters (Trivers and Willard 1973). The distinction between 'trait' and 'strategy' is somewhat arbitrary. We prefer to use the term 'trait' when evaluating the evolution of *measurable characteristics of individuals*, and 'strategy' when assessing *any collection of evolutionarily feasible options about which it is interesting to model fitness*.

Male red deer, called stags, compete with one another for access to large harems of females during the autumn mating period. The most dominant stags maintain larger harems and procure more matings than do less dominant animals (Clutton-Brock *et al.* 1982). And, as the theory predicts, female red deer of high social rank tend to produce more sons than do females of lower rank (Fig. 4.3, Clutton-Brock *et al.* 1984). Most importantly, the sons produced by dominant females have higher lifetime reproductive success than do sons produced by subordinate females.

Until now we have been interested in the adaptive evolution of traits, such as the length of gill rakers or the ability to select habitat. Often, however, we will be interested in the evolution not of specific traits, but of strategies. In the case of habitat choice, for example, an ecologist or conservation biologist might be more interested in what determines the relative densities of individuals living in different habitats (where each frequency represents a different emergent strategy of habitat selection) than in the underlying adaptive decisions (cognitive trait) that determine an individual's ability to choose one habitat over another.

But we could also argue that different combinations of the size and number of gill rakers represent different trophic strategies. The dichotomy between a trait and a strategy may appear mostly semantic, yet there is a crucial difference. Recall that we defined traits as inherited biological variables whose values yield differences in fitness. The distribution of trait values depends on such things as environment, development, and the states of individuals. A strategy, on the other hand, represents the adaptive 'plan' for maximizing fitness.[10] So while trait distributions reflect the panoply of inter-actions that create variation amongst individuals, the strategy emerges through the evolutionary architecture that we call 'structure'. This also means that different trait

---

[10] Our concept of 'strategy' differs from Vincent and Brown (2005), who define strategy as a 'heritable phenotype'.

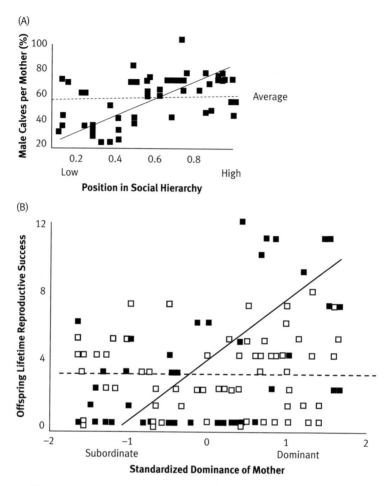

Figure 4.3. An illustration of the effect of a female's status on the adaptive evolution of sex ratio (trait). Panel A shows that high-ranking red-deer mothers tend to produce more sons than daughters. The opposite is true of mothers with low rank. Panel B shows that sons produced by dominant mothers have higher lifetime reproductive success than sons produced by subordinate mothers (closed symbols and solid line = sons, open symbols and dashed line = daughters). After Clutton-Brock *et al.* (1984, 1986) and Ridley (1993).

values represent different possible strategies to be chosen or rejected by adaptive evolution. We expand on this theme in Chapters 6 and 7.

> *'According to the classic view from population and quantitative genetics, adaptation increases mean fitness and changes the frequency distribution of the trait'*

Emphasis on traits echoes the historical tone of a classic paper by Mitchell and Valone (1990). Mitchell and Valone noted that adaptive analyses of trait evolution have most often been couched in population and quantitative genetics. From the quantitative genetics perspective, adaptation is modelled as a change in a trait's value. Traits are imagined to climb slopes in the adaptive landscape and, as they do so, mean fitness rises. Fitness will continue to increase as long as there is additive heritable variation in the trait. As this process of adaptation proceeds, the distribution of trait values will change through time, and the rate of evolution will be directly proportional to the fitness gradient multiplied by the additive heritable variation (Fisher's fundamental theorem of natural selection). As we have seen earlier (Chapter 2), however, the ability to predict the evolution of single traits depends on their often complex genetic interactions with other traits. It will also depend on density and frequency dependence. The ultimate adaptive outcome will also be determined further by the traits and strategies of other individuals (and taxa). Thus for the theorem of natural selection to become 'fundamental', it must be elevated to an adaptive landscape based on strategies.

> *'An alternative worldview demonstrates that adaptation changes the relative frequency of competing strategies, but does not necessarily increase mean fitness'*

Mitchell and Valone championed an approach free of genetics. They imagined an 'optimization research program' based not on the genetic structure of traits, but based instead on strategies. The analysis has five main assumptions:

1. New strategies are formed by mutation.
2. Strategies are heritable (but we do not need to know the mechanism).
3. Strategies serving the same function differ from one another in their per capita growth rates (fitness).
4. A strategy's growth rate depends on the environment.
5. Strategies are constantly under evolution and thus exist near an equilibrium.

The structural analysis of evolutionary strategies proceeds in the same way as our analysis of traits. We need to define the strategy's function, we need to understand how the function maps onto the strategy, then we need to define the relationship between the strategy's function and fitness. The best strategy is the one that yields the highest per capita growth rate (this may be zero) in competition against all other available strategies. The composition of those strategies also becomes an important component of evolutionary structure. Viewed in this light, the process of adaptation does not necessarily change the mean trait value, but rather changes the relative frequency of strategies as they approach the optimum solution (Mitchell and Valone 1990).

> *'The distinction between "trait" and "strategy" depends on the scale of measurement and the degree to which fitness varies with density and the frequency of alternative character values'*

Imagine that we wish to evaluate the adaptive evolution of gill-raker length. An appropriate experiment would contrast the fitness of individuals with long versus short gill rakers foraging on pelagic versus benthic prey. If we observed higher foraging efficiency and fitness of individuals with long gill rakers fed only pelagic prey, and similarly for individuals with short gill rakers fed only benthic prey, then we could conclude that the mean length of gill rakers is indeed an adaptation that improves their function in foraging. The experiment would not reveal anything about the expected frequency of short and long gill rakers in the population. It would not reveal the evolutionary strategy emerging from the prey-dependent adaptive value of gill rakers, and it could not reveal anything about the roles of density or of other individuals on the equilibrium distribution of gill-raker lengths.

The distinction between a trait and a strategy depends on what we hope to understand about the roles of density and frequency dependence in the evolutionary game. We refer to traits as those characters with fitness consequences that we can measure on individuals. The fitness of static, as opposed to dynamic, traits is invariant with density and the frequency of different trait values amongst competing individuals or groups of individuals. Since the fitness of any single genotype is relative to all others in the population, we expect static traits to often represent characters the expression of which has major consequences (such as survival versus death) on fitness. Strategies[11] are characters or characteristics for which fitness depends either directly or indirectly on the density and the frequency of individuals (or groups of individuals[12]) expressing different characters or characteristics. Dynamic traits thus represent a subset of strategies where the character of interest is measured on individuals.

Evolutionary games, such as those involving the evolution of gill-raker length, are often hierarchical. In the absence of fish with short gill rakers, individuals with long gill rakers feeding on benthic prey are likely to live and reproduce successfully. But those same individuals, faced with competition from far more efficient benthic foragers, are unlikely to match the benthic specialists' fitness. Analysis of the game, including individuals with different gill-raker lengths, and using a single habitat and prey distribution, should reveal the expected gill-raker length for a population of fish exploiting only that habitat. Now consider evaluating a similar game played in the mixture of benthic and pelagic habitats that we might find in a series of typical northern lakes. It would be reasonable to expect higher proportions of short gill-raker benthic specialists in those lakes with a higher proportion of benthic habitat. The expected value of the trait that we measure on a randomly chosen individual varies between habitats and among lakes; it depends on the strategy emerging from the larger game,[13]

---

[11] We provide a more inclusive definition at the end of the chapter.

[12] Evolutionary games, including all those related to interactions among species, are often played amongst groups of unrelated individuals. If a character's expression depends on the environment, the underlying reaction norm represents the evolving strategy, but usually it can only be measured on groups of individuals.

[13] Chapter 5 delves more deeply into such issues of 'scale'.

Evolutionary games are particularly useful in understanding the evolution of trait distributions when the traits are phenotypically plastic. In our gill-raker example, high gene flow between coarse-grained habitats[14] is likely to favour developmental pathways that modify the length of gill-rakers contingent on an individual's encounter with the different types and sizes of prey associated with each habitat. The distribution of trait values of otherwise identical genotypes would vary with habitat. Analysis of the evolutionary game should reveal the underlying phenotypic plasticity as a mixed strategy of short gill rakers in benthic habitat and long gill rakers in pelagic habitat that can be tested against nature. A quantitative genetic analysis of gill-raker length in the same system is unlikely to be as productive because its inferences would be limited by the trait's low heritability.

Optimization

While the concept of strategies simplifies our ability to understand adaptation in evolutionary games, it will often be difficult to predict the expected distribution of trait values. If, for example, the expression of a trait depends so intimately on its evolutionary structure, including the effects of other individuals, then how do we know which value is best? At one level this is a trivial question. Adaptation arises from the survival and reproduction of individuals capable of passing strategies and traits to their offspring. There is no choosing to be done. The best value of the trait simply emerges from the process of adaptive evolution. But at another level, the question is incredibly complex. The distribution of trait values emerging from adaptive evolution represents the 'best available fit' of traits with the recent environments and states of individuals.

' The distribution of trait values in a population will mirror the trait' s evolutionary structure'

The answer depends on structure. In Fig. 4.2, for example, we mapped the adaptive structure of gill-raker length for benthic and limnetic habitats. Our structural map illustrates that maximum efficiency in each habitat occurs at a different trait value, and that evolution rewards efficiency. We expect a bimodal distribution, with one peak representing many, long gill rakers for fish living in the limnetic zone, and another peak corresponding to the fewer, shorter gill rakers of fish in the benthic zone. Can our structural map can tell us more?

Let us imagine that the common ancestor for both fish morphotypes was intermediate between our two extreme optima (arrows in Fig. 4.2). The gill rakers were longer than in the benthic form, and shorter than in the limnetic one. How efficient would that ancestral fish be? Quick inspection of Fig. 4.2 reveals the answer: efficiency differs

---

[14] We learned in Chapter 3 that the grain of habitat is 'coarse' when individuals spend most of their reproductive lifetime within a single habitat. Grain is dealt with in detail in Chapter 5.

between habitats. Thus, if our imaginary fish lives in the benthic habitat, its foraging efficiency (and fitness) will be low. But if it occupies the limnetic habitat, its efficiency will be high. Efficiency and fitness depend not only on the value of the trait, but also on habitat. And so too does the expected distribution of trait values following adaptation.

'The adaptive structure of traits reflects trade-offs in their function'

So we must be certain that our structural maps are complete. If we return to the red-deer example for a moment, we can see why. Recall that large stags are dominant to smaller ones and that they procure higher mating success. Large stags assert their dominance by displaying and successfully jousting with smaller opponents. If this was the only function associated with male size we might expect continual increase in stag size through time. But large size exacts a heavy price. To achieve large size, male calves maximize growth rates by carrying low fat reserves into winter. And large males that were successful during the autumn rut also enter winter in poor condition (Clutton-Brock *et al.* 1982). Death, particularly during long, hard winters, weighs heavily on the calves that grew too quickly, and on the large dominant males that expended too much energy warding off opponents. And though the difference in body-size is undoubtedly sex-linked, a significant portion of size variation will be unrelated to sex. If males play to their strength of growing to larger size, females will follow suit. Even if large body size is adaptive for females, the adaptive ledger balances the benefits of increasing body size against the cost of reduced male survival. Thus the distribution of body size will represent a compromise or optimum reflecting the different functions that the trait fulfils. The optimum size for a red-deer stag depends on how much fitness is gained through the function of increased mating success versus how much fitness is lost through correlated size-dependent mortality.

The red-deer example highlights two of the most fundamental features of biological organization. No organism can simultaneously be good at everything. There is no such thing, to quote the University of York's Richard Law (1979, p. 399), as a 'Darwinian demon which can maximize all aspects of fitness simultaneously'. A jack-of-all-traits is master of none. Time and energy are limited, and time and resources allocated to one purpose can rarely be allocated to another. Life must obey fundamental laws of physics. So life is a compromise dictated by trade-offs and constraints. All successful organisms specialize in time and energy management. Energy devoted to reproduction can be recovered (if at all) only at huge cost by means such as resorbing zygotes or cannibalising young. Time spent as a juvenile can never be recouped as an adult. Early copious reproduction can be achieved only at the cost of reduced survival. Production of many offspring, for a fixed investment, can be accomplished only through a reduction in mean offspring size. Large body size reduces an organism's surface-to-volume ratio, but requires a disproportionate increase in support and transport structures.

> *'An understanding of structure emerges from the analysis of trade-offs*
> *and constraints, and the assumptions we make between traits and fitness'*

Adaptation, to a large extent, can be viewed as a problem of optimization (Vincent and Brown 2005). Thus, much of our understanding of structure will emerge from our comprehension of trade-offs and constraints. Some specific examples will help to illustrate our point.

> *'Many trade-offs emerge because resources cannot be allocated simultaneously*
> *to different functions'*

Smith and Fretwell (1974) developed a simple optimization model that can be used to evaluate the evolution of offspring size. The model makes three assumptions:

1. Offspring survival will increase with size (i.e. with increasing parental investment).
2. The gain in survival with offspring size fits a curve of diminishing returns.
3. There is a trade-off between number and size of offspring.

We illustrate the assumptions in panels A and B of Fig. 4.4. The figure represents the structure necessary to understand Smith and Fretwell's model for the evolution of offspring size. And if that model is a fair representation of nature, the figure summarizes the underlying structure for the evolution of offspring size.[15]

In this example, the optimum offspring number is given by the product of the two curves, corresponding to the assumptions of offspring survival and number (panel C). The mother's fitness increases quickly to a maximum at the optimum offspring size. Any female that produces more, but necessarily smaller, offspring than this optimum will have lower fitness. Any female that produces fewer, larger offspring will also have lower fitness. And we also see that, if offspring survival varies between environments, the optimum size of offspring can also differ.

Trade-offs are particularly striking in beetle species belonging to the genus *Onthophagus*. These exotic animals live on all continents except Antarctica. All dig tunnels beneath dung piles, in which males and females mate. The females make brood balls constructed from the dung above. The balls are packed into the ends of the subterranean tunnel chambers where a single larva develops from the egg that the female deposits in each ball. Males (and in some cases females) of many species possess elaborate 'horns' located at various sites on the head and thorax. The horns, in many species, are dimorphic between sexes, and between small and large beetles (Fig. 4.5). Females and small males of most species either lack horns or have much smaller horns than large males.

---

[15] It is curious that scientists frequently list the assumptions that models make, but often fail to describe them as caricatures of nature's structural maps.

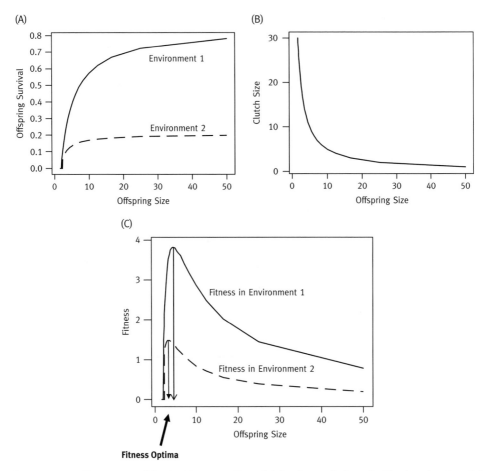

Figure 4.4. An illustration of the Smith–Fretwell model for the evolution of offspring size. Panel A illustrates the assumption that offspring survival varies with offspring size. Note that increased size has diminishing returns on offspring survival and that this relationship differs in two different environments. Panel B illustrates the assumption that the number of offspring produced must decline with mean offspring size (the 'principle of proportional investment', Morris 1985). Panel C illustrates the two single-peaked fitness-mapping functions (defined in Chapter 3) that summarize the 'structure' in panels A and B. After Messina and Fox (2001).

Two developmental models have been proposed to explain the pattern. According to the 'developmental reprogramming' viewpoint, horns represent a threshold polyphenic character. Horn development is regulated by hormone thresholds that modify subsequent cell proliferation to either create functional horns or rudimentary ones (Emlen *et al.* 2005a). Typically, levels of juvenile hormone are higher for 'undernourished' small male larvae than for well-fed large males. Concentrations of juvenile

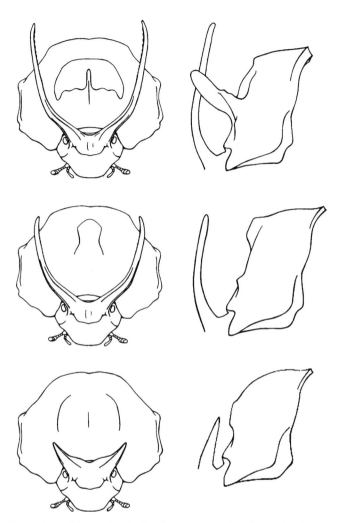

Figure 4.5. An illustration of horns in *Onthophagus watanabei*. Note that horns occur on different parts of the body and that the size and shape of the horns varies amongst large males (top), small males (middle) and females (bottom; all drawn to the same scale). Males of several *Onthophagus* species use the horns in combat with other males in order to maximize mating opportunities. From Moczek *et al.* (2004), reproduced with permission of Wiley-Blackwell on behalf of The Linnean Society of London.

hormone in small males lie above the threshold that signals an off–on switch for subsequent 'downstream' horn development. Small males and females also produce a pulse of ecdysone that reprograms gene expression to produce a shallower growth trajectory for (rudimentary) horn growth.

It is also possible that the apparent threshold simply reflects the power function of size-dependent allometric growth (Tomkins *et al.* 2005).[16] Horn growth is exponential, but nevertheless yields small horns in small individuals. As individuals grow, their horns grow disproportionately long until large individuals exhaust the resources that can be allocated to growth. Intermediate forms are relatively rare because they occur at body sizes where a small change in body size creates a large increase in horn length. So we have two explanations for the development of horns, but why are they dimorphic?

'Polymorphic traits can arise when extreme values of the trait serve different functions'

The relative advantages of functional versus rudimentary horns have been worked out in clever experiments on the common dung beetle, *Onthophagus taurus*, by Armin Moczek and the University of Montana's Douglas Emlen. Moczek and Emlen (2000) built a series of ant-farm-like nest chambers in a darkened laboratory in order to observe the nocturnal beetles under red-filtered light. Common dung beetle males use their horns as weapons to battle for access to, and in defence of, females in the tunnels. Males with the longest horns win most battles. Small hornless males are easily defeated. Yet these diminutive males are able to copulate with females by using a variety of sneaky behaviours. The sneakers' tactics include entering unguarded tunnels while large males and female mates are collecting dung, as well as digging secret accessory tunnels (Moczek and Emlen 2000). Large horns on dominant males appear to impede their agility inside the tunnels, and increase the amount of time that sneaky hornless males can court and mate with females before being challenged by larger, horned, suitors. Small males in many dung-beetle species allocate more resources to testis development and sperm production than do larger males. Each 'trait' maximizes function. Long horns on large males increase their chances of success in intra-sexual contests, and thereby increase mating opportunities. The 'absence' of horns allows small males to increase mating opportunities as they outmanoeuvre their horned competitors. Intermediate males are weak combatants and inept sneakers. So adaptation will yield bimodal patterns in body size and horn development between the two alternative strategies (Fig. 4.6), and will similarly reinforce their relative advantages (longer horns in large males, increased sperm development in small males).[17]

---

[16] It is not yet clear which hypothesis best explains horn 'polyphenism' in dung beetles. We direct readers interested in the debate to Moczek (2006a) and Tomkins *et al.* (2006). Interestingly, developmental reprogramming is accepted by both sides as an explanation for dimorphism in forceps length of European earwigs. In the case of dung beetles, major alterations in adult forms also take place during pupal development (Moczek 2006b), when regulation by Hox genes has a significant impact on future horn growth (Wasik *et al.* 2010).

[17] Recall that high-status female red deer produce a disproportionate number of sons. How might the Trivers and Willard hypothesis apply to dung beetles? Do female beetles change the size of the balls they create to alter the ratio of horned versus 'hornless' male offspring? Can we predict the expected size distribution of dung balls?

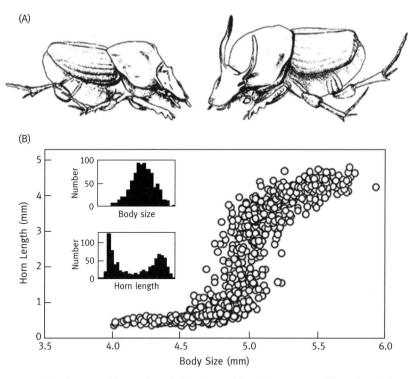

Figure 4.6. Panel A shows an illustration of size dimorphism between small hornless (left) and large horned (right) males of the common dung beetle *Onthophagus taurus*. Panel B illustrates the body-size and horn-length allometry of 810 male beetles collected from a pasture in Durham County, North Carolina. Note the pronounced bimodal pattern in horn length despite the unimodal distribution of body sizes. From Moczek and Emlen (2000), reproduced with permission of Elsevier on behalf of The Association for the Study of Animal Behaviour.

'Developmental trade-offs can have dramatic effects on trait evolution'

Beetle horns are extraordinarily expensive structures because they obey the 'principle of allocation' (Levins 1968) during development. Enlarged horns cause stunting in other nearby structures (Emlen *et al.* 2005b). Horns on the thorax reduce flying ability because the wings are stunted. Horns in the front or middle of the head cause stunting of antennae (and loss of olfaction). Horns at the back of the head stunt eye development (and vision).

Emlen's team (Emlen *et al.* 2005b) explored the consequences of these trade-offs. First, they used nucleotide sequences from both nuclear and mitochondrial genes to derive the phylogeny of the horned species. Then they used the reconstructed phylogeny to document lineages with numerous evolutionary losses and gains of horns at different sites on the head and thorax. Horns, or at least their locations on the body, have multiple independent evolutionary origins. We might expect, then, that the location of the horns would reflect the relative costs of flight, smell, and vision in different environments.

Emlen's team tested the environmental trade-off idea by associating the gains and losses of horns with environment. They reasoned as follows: beetles living at high density travel shorter distances to find dung than beetles living at low density. So in high-density environments, the cost of thoracic horns mediated by stunted wings would be less than in low-density environments. There would be no penalty for head horns (because they do not impede flight). But in open environments (grasslands) where beetles use their antennae to detect dung by olfaction, horns on the head would be more costly than thoracic horns. The penalty would not be nearly as severe in closed forest habitats, where olfaction plays a smaller role in detecting dung. And horns at the base of the head, which impede eye development, might be most costly for nocturnal species that have the largest eyes.

The Emlen team's phylogeny confirmed each trade-off prediction (Fig. 4.7). Gains in thoracic horns were associated with high population density, while gains in head horns were not. But gains in head horns were associated with forest environments while gains

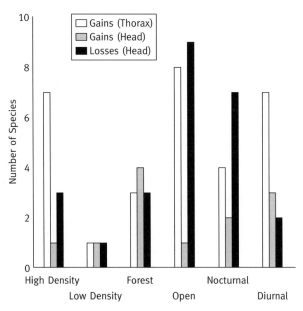

Figure 4.7. An illustration of trade-offs in the location of elaborate sexually-dimorphic horns in the dung-beetle genus *Onthophagus* revealed by phylogenetic analysis. Gains in thoracic horns that stunt wing development are associated mostly with species living at high density (less value for flight). Gains in head horns that stunt antennae are most prevalent in forest-dwelling species. Losses of the ancestral horn type located at the base of the skull (which impedes eye development and vision) are most common in nocturnal species. Data extracted from Table 2 in Emlen *et al.* (2005b).

in thoracic horns were not associated with habitat (presumably because they have no trade-off with the growth of antennae). Most lineages losing horns at the base of the head were also active at night.

> *'A thorough understanding of trade-offs requires an assessment of the relative magnitudes of traits on adaptation as well as the correlations among traits'*

Onthophagus beetles teach us that trade-offs can emerge from multiple mechanisms. Often, we imagine that a single gene influences two or more traits. A trade-off occurs when an increase in the function associated with one trait comes at the expense of reduced function associated with a genetically correlated trait (negative or antagonistic pleiotropy). We do not know what the underlying genetic structure of horns might be in the beetle genome. Perhaps a single gene complex (and its associated developmental machinery) determines how exoskeleton can be manipulated to create horns. Relatively simple developmental pathways may even determine where such protrusions occur. What we do know is more interesting. Horns, and their locations, have numerous independent phylogenetic origins. The shape and location of the horns varies. Yet all appear to fulfil a shared (but perhaps not exclusive) function of increasing mating opportunities. Horns on the head are traded off against a different trait than horns on the thorax, and those correlated traits perform different functions (e.g. vision versus flight). In a sense, the trade-offs among functions are translated through their adaptive disadvantages onto altered trade-offs in traits (we explored some of these sorts of complex interactions in Chapter 3).

Constraints and reinforcement

The distribution of traits can also be constrained. Look again at the shapes of the efficiency curves in Fig. 4.2. We assumed that there is an optimum gill-raker length for each habitat. Many long gill rakers catch more prey in the limnetic zone, provided that they are not too long, and few short gill rakers improve foraging efficiency in the benthic zone unless they are too short. The underlying structure determining the efficiency of short versus long gill rakers constrains their adaptive evolution.

> *'Adaptive evolution can be constrained by historical, physical, genetic, developmental, and environmental limits'*

Constraints come in a variety of forms. There is a limit to how large an organism can be without a sophisticated transport system for fluids, nutrients, and waste products. Transport systems are constrained by the need to produce pressure or concentration gradients to move material from one location to another. Hydrodynamics dictates the size and amount of 'tubing' required for transport, and those relationships dictate the total length of plumbing for organisms of different sizes. Biochemical kinetics and the laws of thermodynamics determine rates of metabolism. Stoichiometric rules place limits on permissible ratios of elements in living tissues, their abundance and procurement from the environment, their transformations through metabolism, and their eventual flux through abiotic and biotic systems (Brown *et al.* 2004).

In addition to physical realities, evolution and adaptation are further constrained by genetics and history. Epistasis among genes can constrain evolutionary options, and those options are limited by all organisms' evolutionary history. Development can often constrain traits (recall the hormonal control of horn development in dung beetles), as can environmental conditions.

*'Adaptive evolution of life histories and mating systems is often limited
by a wide variety of constraints'*

Many of our best examples of these phylogenetic, genetic, and physiological–developmental constraints come from studies of life-history evolution. Many traits that are diagnostic of particular taxa or clades are invariant within the taxon; they are phylogenetically constrained.[18] All individuals sharing a common line of descent 'inherited' the same fixed trait from a common ancestor (called a synapomorphy by systematists). Thus, for example, the evolution of large clutch sizes in pigeons is constrained because all members of the Columbidae produce only two eggs per clutch. Viviparity is not an option for birds. The fruits of nut-producing tree genera such as *Quercus* (oaks), *Juglans* (walnuts), and *Carya* (hickories) are not suitable for wind dispersal. And long adult life with iterated reproduction is absent in the insect order Ephemeroptera (mayflies), whose adult life stages do not feed. This does not mean that pigeons cannot evolve to produce larger clutches, or that mayflies could not live longer. What the constraint does mean is that if pigeons are to evolve larger clutches, then they must do so from their current clutch size of two. If mayflies are to live longer, they start with adult stages that do not feed, and if nut trees are to evolve wind dispersal, they begin to do so with nuts as fruit.

Genetics, most especially antagonistic pleiotropy, often constrains otherwise optimal life-history solutions. George Williams invented what is perhaps the best-known, but still controversial, model of senescence. Williams (1957) championed the view that senescence evolves indirectly when adaptive traits expressed early in life also reduce survival or reproduction late in life. This pleiotropic effect is enhanced whenever deleterious effects of mutations are expressed preferentially in old individuals. Selection against such traits is diminished because their carriers have previously reproduced and passed the trait on to the next generation,[19] so deleterious mutations are more

---

[18] Phylogenetic constraints have major implications for use of the 'comparative method' in evolutionary biology. See, for example, Felsenstein (1985) or Harvey and Pagel (1991).

[19] Tatar (2001) provides a cogent review of senescence and its evolution.

likely to accumulate in older age classes (Medawar 1952). If such mutations also benefit younger individuals, they will be even more likely to persist in the population.

Mating behaviour provides particularly illuminating examples of physiological, developmental, and behavioural constraints. Sexual cannibalism of males by their female mates occurs in several families of insects and arachnids. Cannibalism by mates might at first appear as an obvious constraint on male-mating behaviour. High mating costs (death in this case) should constrain males to seek the highest quality females available. And if cannibalized males produce more descendants than those who survive copulation, then the sexes should agree on male mortality. Such an extreme form of male suicide appears to exist in Australian redback spiders, studied by the University of Toronto's Maydianne Andrade (1996). Male redback spiders selectively choose virgin females with high reproductive value over non-virgin females with lower value (Andrade and Kasumovic 2005). The amorous males somersault while copulating so that their abdomen is maximally exposed to the female's voracious mouthparts. Over 60% of all copulations end in male suicide. But females possess paired sperm-storage organs that can only be inseminated by two separate copulations. Suicidal males, constrained in the grasps of their mate's fangs, possess a unique constriction in the abdomen that prolongs female feeding until the doomed but adaptively successful male completes both copulations (Andrade *et al.* 2005). Similar constrictions are absent in closely related non-suicidal species.

While cannibalism is, perhaps, the most extreme form of sexual conflict,[20] other forms of intersexual antagonistic coevolution may be common in promiscuous mating systems (Rice 2000). The seminal fluids of male fruit flies (*Drosophila melanogaster*), for example, are toxic to females and reduce female survival. The toxicity to females is likely a side-effect of accessory gland proteins targeted against competitors' sperm (Civetta and Clark 2000). The apparent optimal female strategy of increased longevity would thus appear constrained by mechanisms of sperm competition among males.

'Adaptive evolution often proceeds by bending constraints, rather than breaking them'

Despite constraints, evolution finds incredibly inventive ways to bend, if not break, the rules. The most energy-efficient photosynthetic and nutrient acquisition surfaces of terrestrial plants are small, so terrestrial plants have evolved as composite organisms that maximize photosynthesis with numerous repeated structures sharing the supply of nutrients and the harvest of sunlight. Adaptation caused by competition for light among terrestrial plants has produced a wide diversity of support structures and strategies in the race to the sky. Walk through a tropical rainforest. The massive buttressed trunks of the largest trees help disperse roots and spread the tree's weight on shallow soils. Yet the entire infrastructure is built and sustained by a thin layer of

---

[20] Readers interested in sexual conflict may wish to consult the review by Arnqvist and Rowe (2005).

canopy leaves. Trees function only because the common support tissues (wood) do not participate in metabolism (Li *et al.* 2004). Numerous other species avoid the compromise by cheating on their large cousins. Climbing plants snake their vines skyward along the trunks and branches of trees. Epiphytic lichens, mosses, ferns, orchids, and bromeliads rise above the dark forest floor by living on their hosts. Strangler figs start out as epiphytes. Using their host tree as a scaffold, they drape an encompassing root system into the soil below, ultimately choking off the nutrient supply to their surrogate trunk.

Earlier, we discussed the implications of trade-offs associated with negative (antagonistic) pleiotropy. However, single genes that modify multiple traits can also reinforce the functions performed by each one (positive pleiotropy). An increase in the value of one trait is often associated with increase in another. Fecundity in many organisms increases with body size. So an increase in body size that may allow individuals to secure additional resources by foraging over larger areas, or to secure more mates, also enhances the correlated function of increased recruitment through expanded clutch size.

'A trait's reaction norm can often be quantified by its allometric coefficient'

Correlations amongst traits have both genetic and developmental roots. Many morphological traits, for example, undergo differential rates of growth (allometry). Allometric relationships are typically expressed as a simple power function:

$$y = ax^b \tag{4.1}$$

where y and x represent different morphological traits or characters (such as the diameter of a tree's trunk and the tree's height). If the allometric scaling exponent (b) equals unity, Equation 4.1 becomes an equation for a straight line passing through the origin. The value of trait y will then be a constant proportion of the value of trait x. If b is less than one, the value of y increases more slowly than that for x, and if b is greater than one, then y increases more rapidly than does x. Allometric relationships represent one of the most effective mechanisms capable of modifying the expression of genotypes under different environmental circumstances. In these instances, the allometric exponent provides a convenient and precise measure of the trait's potential for phenotypic plasticity: its reaction norm.[21]

Any change in an allometric relationship can profoundly influence positive or negative reinforcement in traits and their function. An increase in b will yield a phenotype with a more exaggerated value of y for each value of x. The opposite occurs if b is reduced. And if the relative value of y is altered, its function will be altered as well.

---

[21] We return to this important point, and provide an example, later in the chapter.

The constancy of function, relative to some trait value (e.g. metabolic rate and body size) helps to explain why allometric coefficients tend to cluster around similar values.

'Heterochrony, a change in developmental rate, timing, or duration, can reinforce or reduce correlations (allometry) between traits'

Heterochrony often emerges when organisms (or organ systems) obey the same allometric growth relationship but have different rates or durations of development. If development occurs at a slow rate or is curtailed 'early', then the value of *y* will be reduced relative to *x*, producing a so-called paedomorphic or juvenile state. If development proceeds more rapidly, or for a longer period, then the trait is 'overdeveloped' or perimorphic. So, if 'more is better', then prolonged development will enhance the trait's function. Developmental periods can be 'pre-programmed' or responsive to the environment, as may occur when large-horned beetles exhaust resources for further growth (Tomkins *et al.* 2005).

The University of Manchester's Christian Peter Klingenberg invented a simple graph to illustrate the close relationship between heterochrony and development (Fig. 4.8; Klingenberg 1998). The figure assesses the growth of two traits through an individual organism's lifespan. Heterochrony occurs when the growth rates of the two traits differ

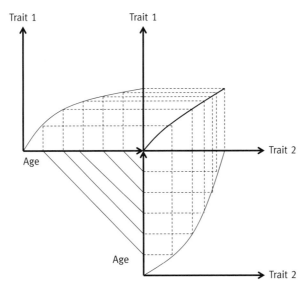

Figure 4.8. The correspondence between heterochrony (differences in growth rate of a trait with age) and allometry (differences between traits in growth rate). Growth rate decelerates with age for Trait 1 but accelerates with age in Trait 2 (heterochrony). The emergent allometric relationship is revealed when the values for each trait are plotted against one another for constant ages. After Klingenberg (1998).

from one another. The consequence of heterochrony in this example is that the covariation between the traits reveals their allometric relationship.

'Functionally correlated traits are often integrated into developmental modules'

Covarying traits often represent integrated modules that interact to perform function. When variation in performance of that function has large effects on fitness, adaptation will produce further integration of the traits by genetic, developmental, or epigenetic processes.[22] The modular traits will then tend to be inherited together. Some of the best evidence for the roles of form and function in the evolution of modular structure comes from studies of changes in skull anatomy of domestic dog breeds (Drake and Klingenberg 2010). The short flat (brachycephalic) faces of so-called companion dogs set them apart from other breeds and their wild cousins. These differences are in addition to those caused by allometric relationships with body size. Variation amongst dog breeds in their facial (nasomaxillary) characteristics and cranial shapes suggest that sets of traits represent modular features that evolve together. Correlated facial features producing brachycephalic faces in lap dogs likely originated as a functional module, the form of which was directly associated with performance, such as securing and subduing prey (e.g. bite force) in wild canids. Intense selection for facial shape by humans in an otherwise benign environment revealed the underlying modular structure even though the traits are associated with numerous respiratory disorders. We can expect similar modularization to emerge whenever correlated morphological, physiological, behavioural, developmental, or genetic traits interact to produce a common function.

Structure at different scales

We restricted evolutionary structure, in our treatment of Mendelian genetics and mutation (Chapter 2), to mappings associated with specific traits. We started by examining the influence of such traits on the ability of individuals to survive and reproduce. It was as though we assumed that we could dump all of the traits and their values into a boiling caldron, stir them around with an adaptive spoon, sequentially scoop each one with a statistical ladle, and use their 'structure' to model evolution. We imagined that each trait value 'replicates' according to its contribution to fitness. Then we tossed all the 'offspring' back to simmer before sipping from the ladle with another draw. If we repeat this process many times, then we would observe that the distributions of each trait's values converge on some stable set of frequencies. If we knew where to find them, we could even add a dash of epistasis and a pinch of pleiotropy to give extra zip (and unpredictability) to our witches' brew of evolution.

---

[22] We direct readers interested in the interaction between evolution and development of morphological traits to a review by Klingenberg (2010).

Next, we learned that epistasis and pleiotropy emerge when we consider the values of traits that we observe in a single individual, and that not all trait values are possible because they are constrained in different ways. We learned that some of the constraints can be bent, if not broken, by plastic developmental and environmental interactions with the genome, while others may be even further constrained through canalization. But we have mostly avoided discussion of structure above the level of the individual. In this case it is as though we dumped each of the traits for all individuals into the same pot and then let them bond together to form new, matched groups (individuals), which we then scooped up at random. We could model evolution by letting the individuals replicate, then extract their offsprings' trait values before tossing them all back for another draw. Epistatic effects would bias the way in which the traits bonded together, development and canalization would limit their expression, and pleitotropy would alter their joint effects on the whole phenotype. Through time, the trait values might, or might not, converge on a single set of frequencies.

But now we must ask what structure would appear if we separated only some of the values, or if we extracted the values from only some of the individuals. And what would happen if we tossed them into, and sampled from, different pots? Two kinds of population structure would emerge (Nunney 2001):

1. Each population might be expected to depart, uniquely, from a random distribution of genotypes (genetic structure).
2. Several additional levels of structure might exist among and within pots depending on which individuals ended up in close proximity to one another (proximity structure), and depending on how vigorously nature stirred the brew.

Numerous processes can create each kind of population structure. Any form of partial reproductive isolation, including non-random mating, will create a non-random distribution of genotypes. Local adaptation within the separate populations (often referred to as demes by geneticists) is also likely to create non-random distributions of genotypes, and especially so if different favourable combinations of alleles and trait values arise in the different populations.

Various proximity structures emerge depending on how many other individuals influence a target individual's fitness. Part of this structure will depend on the spatial and temporal scale of the environment. So a landscape with many different large pieces (coarse-grained) might be occupied by many different closely-interacting groups of individuals. But groups might coalesce if the same landscape was cut into many small pieces. Populations of organisms with limited mobility might be expected to possess greater spatial heterogeneity than would those of species with greater movement potential in the same landscape. Species with social systems centred on extended-family, age, or sex groups would be more heterogeneous amongst those clusters than species congregating in large herds, flocks, or shoals. One of the intriguing evolutionary implications of proximity structures is that they can apply to any organizational level where inheritance plays a role. Temporal, spatial, and social heterogeneity can thus create a multi-levelled hierarchical system. Interacting and coordinated components grade from congregations of genes into chromosomes, prokaryotes into eukaryotes, cellular organisms into multicellular creatures, individuals into groups, and groups into the massive social organizations of some insects and humans (Wilson, 2001, 2002). Such multi-level structures have rather pronounced implications for adaptation. We will revisit this theme in Chapter 5.

The structure matrix

It is easy to be overwhelmed by the complexity of structure. Trait values are determined by genetics, development, and interactions among genes, as well as interactions between genes and the environment. Traits can be constrained or reinforced through all of these numerous mechanisms. Ultimately, the functional relationship between any single trait and its 'fitness' is determined by interactions among traits and their interactions with the environment.[23] Variation in traits and the way that they map onto fitness can be enhanced or masked by various forms of plasticity and canalization. All are integrated into the genetic and proximity structures associated with time and space. How can we make sense of this incredibly complicated structure?

Imagine your favourite species. In most cases, the species will interact with several others, it will occupy a variety of environments varying in space and time, and individuals will differ both within and among populations in the values of ecologically important traits. Now imagine that you actually know such things as the number of individuals living in each environment, the number and identity of genotypes in each population, the range of trait values, how different traits influence one another's functions, and the relationships between those functions and fitness. Of course we do not expect that you can actually know all of these sorts of details, we ask only that you imagine you can. In order to make evolutionary sense out of this mass of facts, we organize the details into a structure matrix (Fig. 4.9). Each of the $I \times J \times K \times L$ elements of the matrix is filled with the value of 1 to L possible traits. But there is also a 'sub-matrix' composed of $I \times J \times K$ 'elements', each of which is filled with the value of 1 to K functions. The accumulation of all traits and their values within a single genotype describes what an individual organism might look like. The accumulation of functions and their values would describe how the organism 'works'. And if we summed the traits and values across all I to J different genotypes we would have a measure of variation among different individuals of the species in a single environment. We would need to repeat the process in all environments to measure individual variation for the entire

---

[23] Evolutionary biologists often use 'environment' as shorthand referencing mechanisms and patterns that we do not currently understand. These include the usual suspects of biochemistry, inheritance, development, behaviour, and ecology, as well as the numerous 'hidden players' that live within us (Holt 2007). For the purposes of trait evolution, however, we restrict our discussion to a scale that allows different individuals to experience different environments (habitats).

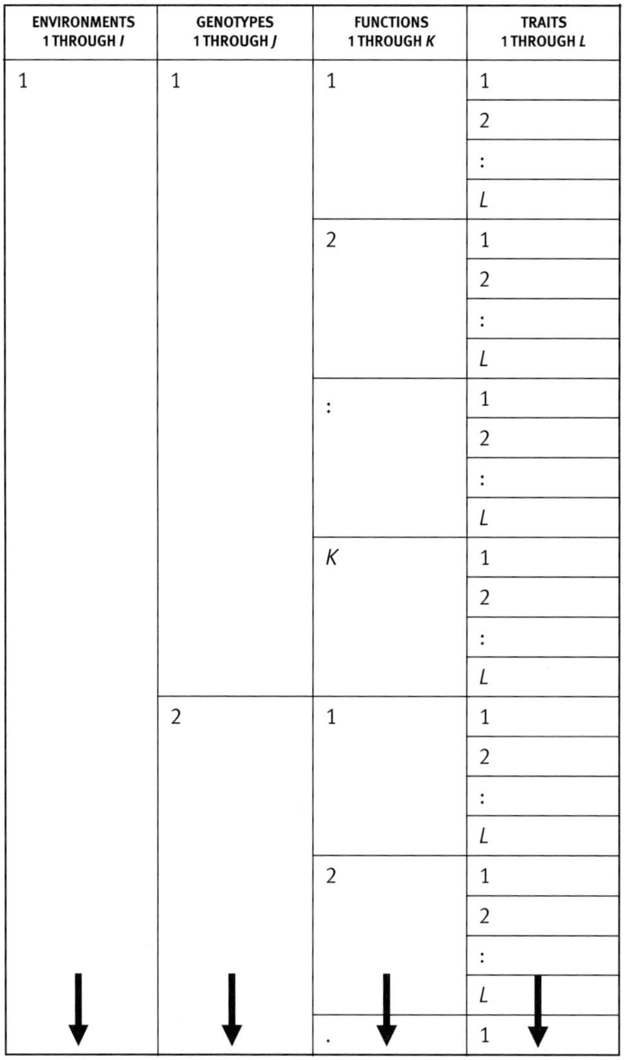

ENVIRONMENTS 1 THROUGH *I*	GENOTYPES 1 THROUGH *J*	FUNCTIONS 1 THROUGH *K*	TRAITS 1 THROUGH *L*
1	1	1	1
			2
			:
			L
		2	1
			2
			:
			L
		:	1
			2
			:
			L
		K	1
			2
			:
			L
	2	1	1
			2
			:
			L
		2	1
			2
			:
			L
↓	↓	↓	1 ↓
		.	1

Figure 4.9. An illustration of the structure matrix associated with evolution of a single species. Only a small portion of the matrix is shown. Arrows signify continuation deeper into the $I \times J \times K \times L$ cells of the matrix. Some rows and elements can be composed of null sets, but columns cannot. Structural rules (some of which reflect adaptation) determine which elements are 'empty', and which elements possess the same value. The structure matrix illustrated here subsumes genetic and developmental matrices underlying genotypes that connect them with traits. Our diagram of the structure matrix also assumes that population dynamics, other species, and ecological communities can be incorporated into 'environment'. A similar matrix could be developed to reveal the structure of evolutionary strategies.

species, and we would need to ensure that our definition of 'environment' includes such additional complexities as group formation[24] and population dynamics.

Consider, for example, horns on the thorax and in the middle of the head in an *Onthophagus* male. The traits share a central function in battle, when males compete for mating opportunities. If the beetles live in an open environment for many generations, we expect reduction or elimination of head horns because they impede the development of the antennae used to find dung. But we do not expect any pattern in the thoracic horns other than what might be associated with their trade-off with mobility. The values of the traits depend on environment. We can also expect that the absolute size of the two traits varies with environment. If dung is abundant, females may make larger brood balls, and their larvae should grow to a larger size and produce longer horns. There may also be feedback from the density of individuals in a given population as well as from the frequencies of different genotypes (we treat these formally in Chapter 6).

Examine Fig. 4.9. Note that every element (value of a particular trait) in the matrix is nested into functions, genotypes, and environments. We hope that this nestedness looks familiar. It is the same nested structure that we incorporated into the canonical equation for fitness ($W = f(D(T(G)))$, Chapter 3). Each trait can occur in all or only a few genotypes. One trait can serve one function or many. Each genotype can occur in only one or many environments. Traits emerge from genotypes through the mechanics of inheritance, development, and $G \times E$ interactions. Some traits are more closely related to survival and reproduction than are others. An important corollary of this complex organization is that it is virtually impossible for us to understand, completely, the path of mechanisms determining fitness for anything other than the simplest of traits. It is even more difficult to trace the fitness value of a trait through its function(s).

Fig. 4.10 illustrates some of the complexity that we are likely to encounter in any species' structure matrix. Different genotypes will produce different expected trait values than will others. The vagaries of development and life experience of each genotype will, except for the simplest of traits, yield a frequency distribution of different trait values. Epistatic and pleiotropic differences among genotypes will change the range and frequency of each genotype's expected trait value.

Environment, development, and the growing individual's state interact with genetics to determine the mean and frequency of trait values that each genotype expresses. The pattern of trait values among environments maps each genotype's reaction norm. If the rank of trait values remains constant among environments, then the mean reaction norm is an accurate representation of each genotype's separate reaction norm (they are parallel). But if the rank of expected values changes among environments, as in Fig. 4.10A, the expression of the trait depends on a $G \times E$ interaction, and the mean could mislead our attempts to predict future adaptation (the reaction norms cross).

---

[24] We deal with the problem of groups and multi-level adaptation in Chapter 5.

(A)

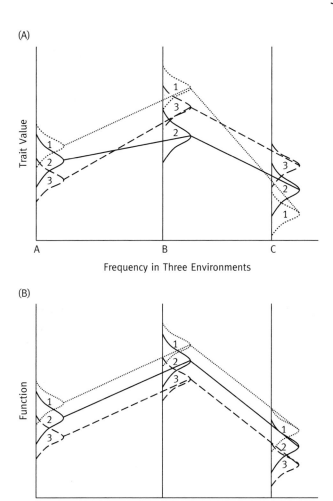

Frequency in Three Environments

(B)

Frequency in Three Environments

Figure 4.10. An illustration of some of the complexities associated with adaptive evolution of traits. The expected trait values, function, and fitness of three different genotypes (numbers) are represented by frequency distributions in three different environments (letters). Lines connect the expected (mean) value for each genotype. In panel A the trait values of the different genotypes vary across the three environments. Lines in this panel represent the trait's reaction norm and reveal a $G \times E$ interaction. Panel B shows the correspondence between the trait's value and its contribution to function. Lines in this panel reflect the 'norm of performance'. Panel C shows the correspondence between the trait's function and fitness. Lines correspond to the 'norm of fitness'. Panel D shows the emergent relationship between trait value and fitness for the three genotypes (inheritance). The rank of fitness (in parentheses) differs among environments because the $G \times E$ interaction in the reaction norm illustrated in A is unopposed by parallel performance and fitness norms.

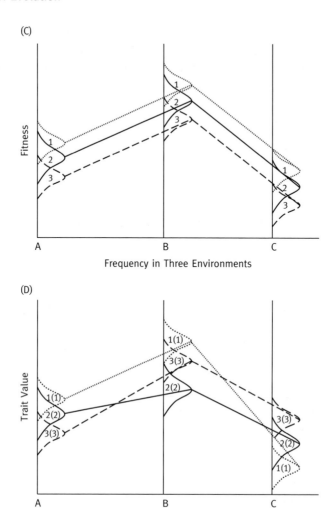

Figure 4.10. Continued.

The potential evolutionary contribution of any trait value depends on its relationship with function (performance). If the function is independent of the environment, as might occur for traits closely linked to survival, then the contribution of each trait value will be identical in all environments (Fig. 4.10B).

The adaptive value of the trait also depends crucially on the mapping of function onto fitness. Again, we might expect functions linked with survival to have similar fitness rankings in all habitats (Fig. 4.10C), but it is easy to think of alternatives (e.g. colouration that is cryptic in one environment may not be in another). The ultimate relationship between the trait's value and fitness (Fig. 4.10D) thus includes the mechanics of inheritance and development, the function that the trait performs, the relationship between the trait's value and its function, and the correspondence between performance and fitness. These relationships can be either constant or variable among environments, and they can also vary with the scale of the environment (Chapter 5),[25] the density and the frequency of alternative trait values and strategies (Chapter 6), and the state of the individual or group of individuals expressing the trait (strategy).

These complexities demonstrate why, in breeding programmes, some traits respond quickly to selection while others do not. Plant and animal breeders have a long history of 'improving' traits closely related to fitness, such as egg and milk production, seed size, and crop yields. Much of the success has been achieved by purposefully developing breeds and varieties for use in single environments. Similarly, the dramatic morphological differences that we associate with many pet and livestock breeds often emerge from selective breeding of single allometric and paedomorphic relationships. Each programme takes advantage of relatively simple structural maps that yield highly heritable traits and strategies. A thorough understanding of structure should shed light on the apparently low inheritance of many other traits and strategies that fail to respond quickly to selection.

Although no-one is ever likely to draw a complete structure matrix, such matrices are a necessary 'characteristic' of all species. Knowing this we can imagine moving through the matrix in search of patterns that may reveal some of its rules. What might we find?

'Although adaptation operates directly on a trait's function,
it is nevertheless possible to map the trait's value onto fitness'

It should be clear from the structure matrix, and our discussion of examples, that the fitness value of traits to organisms occurs through their function: their ability to influence survival and reproduction by how well the organism 'does its work'. Careful assessment and measurements of traits representing a cheetah's limb morphology, for example, can help us determine its biomechanics that are associated with locomotion. With enough careful measurements and knowledge of biomechanics we could calculate each cheetah's maximum speed. Acceleration and speed help to fulfil the additional function of catching prey. The frequency with which a cheetah successfully captures and consumes prey fulfils additional functions that determine how many resources can be diverted from survival to reproduction. And the value of those functions changes with the density and distribution of cheetahs and their prey.

'The definition of traits and their functions reflects the research objective'

---

[25] Environmental scale will also determine modifying factors such as a population's spatial and temporal genetic structure.

Two important principles emerge from this somewhat contrived example:

1. Traits are arbitrary characteristics that interest us.
2. Definition and assessment of function depends on the research focus.

A scientist interested in functional morphology might measure limb traits to help understand the detailed biomechanics of animal movement. Another scientist, interested in foraging behaviour, might measure the same characteristics to evaluate their role in prey capture. Yet a third scientist, also interested in foraging, might use a composite trait arising from the morphological study of biomechanics as an indicator for prey capture success.

'Adaptation operates only indirectly on all but the simplest and most essential traits'

We seek a broader research programme that links our understanding of structure to the fitness of whole organisms. It would be tempting to imagine that we could construct such a model of adaptation simply by incorporating the covariation that exists among different traits. In a sense we can, but only by also including differences in the relative contributions of traits to fitness. How might we construct this map (Fig. 4.11)?

First, we need to know exactly which traits, trait values, and functions we are interested in. We will use moose, *Alces alces*, as an example. The moose is the largest extant species of cervid mammal (deer and their relatives). Moose are strikingly dimorphic. Males are approximately 30% larger than females, and many (but by no means all) grow large palmate antlers. The antlers, like the horns of dung beetles, are used in intraspecific displays and contests over mating opportunities. Moose shed their antlers annually and, if all goes well, replace them with larger ones for the next mating season. In European moose (*Alces alces alces*), antler size and shape 'improve' as bulls approach reproductive age, then decline in older senescent bulls (Nygrén *et al.* 2007). Thus, the trait that interests us is a male's antlers. The trait value is a measure of antler size, and the function is the individual's ability to win contests against other males. Next, we imagine that we know the distribution of possible trait values (antler sizes) in the population, and that we can associate each with a measure of its function (fighting success).[26] Then we can easily generate the functional relationship between the 'purpose' of the trait and its value (note that we have not made, at this point, any assumptions about the fitness of the function). Many traits, such as the size of moose antlers, are likely to perform more than one function. We can imagine that antlers also aid in defence against predators. In principle, we could derive and plot that relationship also, and gain a deeper understanding of adaptive evolution.

---

[26] This example is interesting because the 'function' of achieving victory depends on the trait value of the opponent. The probability of encountering a particular opponent varies with population density and habitat.

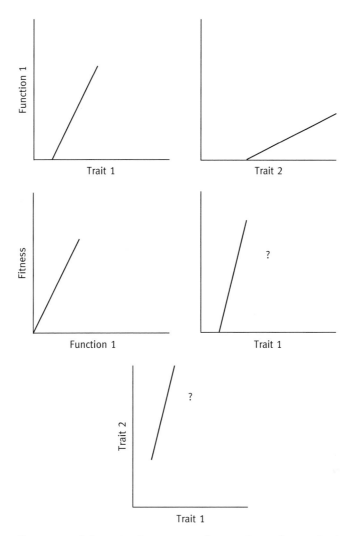

Figure 4.11. An illustration of the trait→fitness maps for members of a species in which fitness depends on two interdependent traits. In this example we imagine that we have complete knowledge of the trait→function and function→fitness maps. Each trait acts to increase the value of the function (e.g. antler size and body size increasing mating opportunities in cervid mammals). But even with that knowledge we cannot be certain about the relationship between either trait and fitness, or between the traits themselves (our ignorance is indicated by question marks). Each trait might, for example, also influence other functions with complex or opposite effects on fitness. Genetic and developmental constraints might also alter the expected relationship between the traits irrespective of their 'total' contributions to function and fitness. Each relationship is assumed linear for illustration purposes only.

In summary, we imagined that we identified all of the relevant trait values that influence fighting success and predator defence. Knowing this, we could then explain the adaptive value of moose antlers of different sizes. Our ability to model antler evolution assumes, however, that we:

1. searched the various places where the populations that interest us live (the habitat component of 'environment').
2. examined each population.
3. determined the various possible genotypes for which there are different values of antler size.

But to have done this, we have examined only the products of past evolution. In many cases this will yield a sufficient explanation for evolution. If we want to completely understand adaptive evolution, however, we may also wish to think beyond what we actually observe, and imagine what we might possibly observe in a different context. In other words, we will need to explore the total set of possibilities (bauplan) for antler size.

'A thorough evaluation of the structure matrix requires that we explore not only what is feasible, but what is possible'

How can we imagine what is possible when evolution yields only what is feasible? We must delve deeper into the structure matrix. Thus when we explore patterns of antler size we find that they fit an allometric relationship with body size. Larger animals possess larger antlers than small animals, but the relationship between the animal's body size and antler size is constant (Fig. 4.12). Within a species, this relationship specifies the reaction norm for antlers, the set of evolutionarily feasible strategies available for adaptation. Among species, the allometry represents the bauplan, or potential strategy set, possible for the fit of antler form and function by cervid mammals. At each scale we can assess potential evolution by 'sliding' up and down the allometric relationship. Other allometries reflecting different physical realities (e.g. storage and digestibility limits on the ability to process the low-quality food consumed by most members of the deer family) could help us determine the limits of cervid body size that we need to explore. Any other values would be possible only if the species has diverged onto another bauplan with different 'rules'. To do so, it will have broken the constraints of its past adaptation. There are two possibilities:

1. It is no longer a cervid (obeys the same general rules, but in a different way).
2. The physical rules have changed (we are in a different reality).

'Many traits are likely to perform more than a single function'

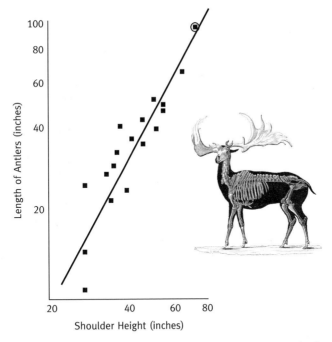

Figure 4.12. The allometric relationship between antler size of cervid mammals (deer) and their body size. In principle, any cervid could evolve to fit this relationship provided that it does not exceed other physical and physiological constraints. The circled point is from the extinct Irish elk, *Megaloceros giganteus*. Inset drawing from Wikipedia commons (http://upload.wikimedia.org/wikipedia/commons/3/3e/Megaloceros_1856.png, accessed 17 October 2010). After Dobzhansky *et al.* (1977) and Gould (1973).

Our task of predicting adaptation is further complicated whenever the trait that we are interested in serves multiple functions. If the trait has opposite effects on each function, that is, if an increase in the trait's value improves one function while it reduces another, then the organism may be faced with trade-offs. But the presence of a trade-off also depends on the relationships between the functions and between each function and fitness (Fig. 4.13).[27] It is also possible that the trait has the same effect on each function (e.g. increases 'performance') but that the functions are antagonistic (an increase in one function increases fitness, whereas an increase in the other reduces fitness).

'Allometric growth of sexual ornaments and weapons emerges through the separate effects of the sexual traits and body size on fitness'

---

[27] Fig. 4.13 represents one possible description of the underlying structure responsible for pronounced size dimorphism in male common dung beetles.

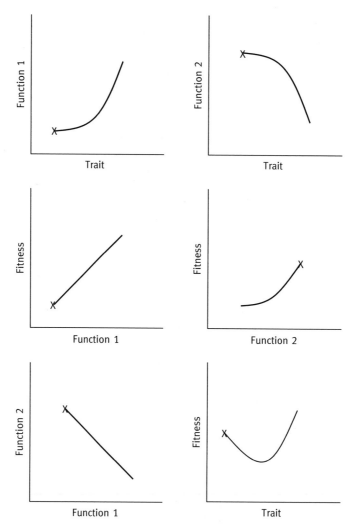

Figure 4.13. A set of illustrations demonstrating how traits that affect two functions can lead to trade-offs and, in this case, a stable polymorphism. A representative phenotype is indicated by X. The role that each trait and function plays in creating trade-offs and in adaptation will depend on the trait's value that has opposing effects on the two functions, and a U-shaped indirect effect on fitness. There are two possible evolutionary optima. Adaptation toward one or the other optimum will depend on whether all, or only some, trait values are available for adaptive evolution.

The University of New Mexico's Astrid Kodric-Brown and her colleagues (Kodric-Brown *et al.* 2006) have shown how allometric relationships of body size with sexually dimorphic ornaments and weapons, such as moose antlers, yield insight into the evolution of trade-offs. Building on a model developed by Bondurianky and Day

(2003), Kodric-Brown's team defined the relative size of sexual ornaments to body size as

$$\frac{y}{x} = ax^{b-1}$$

This is obtained simply by dividing the allometric equation (Equation 4.1) by body size, x. This relationship can be linearized by plotting y/x against the logarithm of body size (Fig. 4.14). Organisms are assumed to have limited energy available for growth and to trade off energy allocated to increasing the size of the ornament against that allocated to body size. Individuals are also assumed to allocate energy in such a way as to maximize fitness. Thus, early in life, fitness will be maximized by investing energy primarily to increase body mass. As individuals approach sexual maturity, fitness will be maximized by switching the resource allocation toward sexual ornaments and weapons. When one overlays the allocation strategies on top of the trade-offs, the optimal life history is revealed as an allometric scaling between the relative size of the ornament and body size (Fig. 4.14).

It would be convenient if we could encapsulate the various forms of trade-offs, reinforcement, allometries, and modularities under the rubric of pleiotropy. To do so

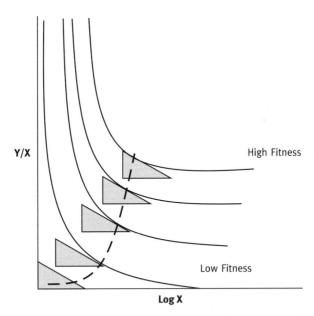

Figure 4.14. The Kodric-Brown *et al.* model for the evolution of allometric scaling of sexual ornaments and weapons. Small triangles represent the trade-off between the relative size of the sexual ornament (ordinate) against body size (abscissa). Contours reflect the relative fitness value of the ornament and body size at different ages. The optimal strategy at any age occurs when the fitness contour is tangential to the trade-off (hypoteneuse of the small triangles). The dashed line traces the optimal allometric strategy through different age classes. After Kodric-Brown *et al.* (2006).

could obscure their adaptive significance. Indeed, one can argue very convincingly that genetic pleiotropy for many traits emerges indirectly through linkage disequilibrium. A complex of highly beneficial and interacting genes are transmitted together. While it is easy to understand the advantage of non-independent assortment and linkage of traits that reinforce one another, it is more difficult to imagine how antagonistic traits may become linked.

One possibility is, as in the Kodric-Brown model, that the functions performed by the traits influence fitness at different times. Stearns and Hoekstra (2000) describe such a pleiotropic trade-off associated with human aging. Sex hormones (testosterone and oestrogen) are essential for successful reproduction, but long-term exposure of males to testosterone is associated with prostrate cancer and in older women osteoporosis is associated with estrogen. Genes (or gene complexes) responsible for the production of the hormones are advantageous in young adults even though they are associated with reduced survival late in life.

Let us evaluate whether this pleiotropic effect could emerge through linkage disequi-librium. Imagine that the genes responsible for the long-term effects of hormones on other tissues are initially independent of those responsible for hormone production. Now imagine that each gene is variable. So in some individuals, high levels of hormone production will be associated with low levels of 'protection' from non-target effects. These individuals will have low survival because hormonal disorders occur too early in life. In other individuals, low levels of hormone production will be associated with high levels of protection. These individuals will have low fertility. The unfavourable alleles will be eliminated from the population, but only at the expense of also eliminating otherwise favourable ones.

Now consider a mutant in which the two traits are linked. Unfavourable combina-tions of the genes (low production and low protection) will be eliminated together. Favourable combinations (high production and high protection) will be retained. Such super organisms may not be possible if the protection gene cannot fully compensate for high hormone production. The linked complex would then always generate an antago-nistically pleiotropic effect.

Of course we do not know whether antagonistic pleiotropy in human sex hormones evolved in this manner or not. The apparent pleiotropy might even be caused by different effects associated with a single structural gene. Our point is that we can easily conceive a set of events under which antagonistic pleiotropy could emerge through adaptively linked antagonistic genes. Once linked, they would function as a single pleiotropic gene.

'Improvement in function can occur without directional adaptation on traits'

Antagonistic pleiotropy emphasizes the diversity of possible relationships that can exist between the value of a trait and its function. If both are continuous, then we might find that an increase in the value of the trait is associated with an increase in its function. In many cases, however, we are likely to find that more is not always better. Function will be inhibited by costs. In our moose example, increased antler size might always increase the ability to win contests and secure mating opportunities, but only if the animal can carry and manipulate them properly. Other traits, such as body size, also come into play. Those traits may be correlated with the trait of interest (antler size), and they may also have either an indirect or direct influence on function.

So we can anticipate, for many traits, that the function is similar for two or more values of the trait. A small, male moose that can allocate much of his time searching for mates and avoiding conflict may have as many mating opportunities as a much larger male spending most of his time guarding mates and fending off rivals. Such an effect could result in equal values of fitness for different values of the trait. Let us imagine for the sake of the argument that the function→fitness map is linear. If adaptation was operating on this single function, we would expect improved function through time. But the directional adaptation for improved function is achieved, nevertheless, by adaptive evolution of the trait toward different values (small versus large males or small versus large antlers).

'*Some traits have larger effects than others*'

It is important to note that we have assumed, implicitly, that our description of 'structure' has explored only the 'partial' effects of each pairwise relationship between traits, between traits and their function, between functions, and between function and fitness. Thus to predict the evolution of horn length in dung beetles, we imagine that we are considering only the marginal increase in fitness associated with functions related to longer horns. We often describe this marginal effect as though we are able to hold all other traits and functions constant. What we actually mean, however, is that we are examining only the residual differences in fitness associated with horn length while all other factors vary. It is as though we conducted a replicated breeding experiment where we manipulated the mating success of males with different lengths of horns, but controlled nothing else. Any change in mean horn length in the population would be properly attributed to the experimental manipulation of mating success. Part of the response, but not all, would be related to the sign and shape of relationships between traits and function, among functions, and between function and fitness. But a major component of the response will also depend on how 'steep' and how variable those relationships happen to be.

Let us explore both effects. Imagine two traits influencing a single function. Higher values of each trait increase function, and higher values of the function increase fitness (Fig. 4.11). Imagine further that an increase in the value of Trait 1 has a higher influence on the function than does an increase in the value of Trait 2. So the influence on fitness will be greater for Trait 1 and, other things being equal, we can expect it to change more quickly through adaptation.

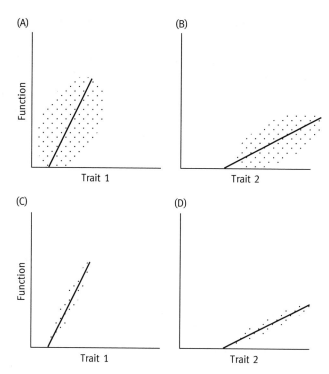

Figure 4.15. A set of illustrations demonstrating how variability in the trait→function map can alter our ability to predict changes in trait distributions through time. In panels A and C, the relationship between the trait and its function is steeper than in panels B and D, but the relationship is much less variable in panels C and D than in A and B. Adaptation depends on both characteristics.

'Traits with a tight connection to function will evolve more rapidly than traits with highly variable effects on the same function'

What will happen if the influence of the two traits on the shared function is more variable for one trait than it is for the other? We provide an example in Fig. 4.15. The slopes of the trait→function map are identical to those in Fig. 4.11, but Trait 1 has much more scatter around the relationship than does Trait 2.[28] The scatter could arise from many different genetic, developmental, and environmental effects and influences. Evolution is blind to all of them. Fitness simply emerges from its relationship with function. But if we map fitness onto values of the two traits, we will find much more ambiguity for Trait 1 than for Trait 2. Many more of the possible values for Trait 1 will

[28] The scatter about a regression line is summarized statistically by covariance. Covariance, which we first introduced in Chapter 2, is crucial to our understanding of adaptation and will be discussed formally in Chapter 6.

yield the same value of the function (and thus fitness) than will the possible values of Trait 2.

Scatter in the trait→function map highlights one of the many sources of ignorance encapsulated in the structure matrix, which reduce our ability to predict changes in the distribution of trait values. Some traits are more closely related to function and fitness than are others. Some traits have different relationships with function than others. Some traits have simple and direct maps to genetics and development, while others are complex. In some cases we know a great deal about the genetics and inheritance of certain traits, and little about their function. For others, we know a lot about function, but little about inheritance or how it influences fitness.

Where traits fail to map onto function

So far, our treatment of structure assumes that we identified traits with clear functions. We also noted that traits influencing one function may have no effect on another, and some characters are so variable that their potential effect on function disappears. But we can also think of traits that are essentially invariant (Fig. 4.16). Any change in the structure of a key metabolic enzyme, for example, may destroy its function. So, as we learned in Chapter 3, working organisms would possess no variance for the trait, and perhaps no underlying genetic variance either. In other instances, the trait is invariant even though its underlying genetic architecture is highly variable. And, in many cases, the trait is also insensitive to changes in environmental conditions.

'Invariant traits may lack genetic variability, or be canalized by phenotypic expression around a constant value'

We noted in Chapter 3 that such constant or 'robust' traits began to attract the attention of evolutionists in the 1940s.[29] Despite their importance to evolutionary understanding these ideas were slow to gain ground, in part because underlying mechanisms were poorly understood. We now know that several different processes can account for this so-called canalization of traits. At its most basic level, canalization can be defined as any process that reduces variation in phenotypic (trait) expression with altered conditions (Flatt 2005). The mechanism can be genetic (the trait's value remains constant even though the genetic background has changed) or environmental (the trait's value is invariant even though the environment has changed). Genetically canalized traits arise through epistasis, dominance, and pleiotropy. More generally, genetically canalized traits occur through a lack of independence among alleles, genes, and other traits. A genetic change (usually an increase in genetic variability) in one gene that influences the trait may not be expressed because other genes also influence its expression.

---

[29] Most notably the University of Edinburgh's Conrad Waddington and Ivan Schmalhausen at the University of Kiev.

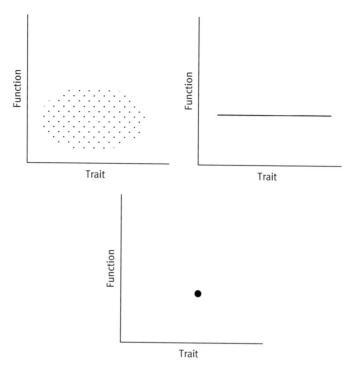

Figure 4.16. An idealized illustration of traits that have no effect on function. In panel A, a particular value of the highly variable trait influences function more for some individuals than it does for others. In panel B, the trait has many possible values, but the effect on function is constant. In panel C, the trait exists as a single value (exaggerated dot) with no variance because it either lacks genetic variability or because it is canalized towards a fixed value.

Dominant alleles mask the effects of recessive mutants, and the expression of an otherwise highly variable trait may be hindered because the genes that control it also affect other traits. If alternative traits are near their adaptive equilibrium, it may be impossible for other linked traits to evolve.

Traits can also be canalized through $G \times E$ interactions that influence phenotypic plasticity. Changes in genotypic expression among environments produce plastic (variable) traits. A graph documenting these changes represents the trait's reaction norm (Fig. 4.17). Reaction norms can be parallel to one another (different genotypes yield the same relative trait value in different environments) or non-parallel ($G \times E$ interaction; different genotypes vary in the way the trait is expressed in different environments). The absence of any change (one flat overlapping reaction norm) is environmental canalization. So environmental canalization can be considered a special case of phenotypic plasticity where the phenotype's expression is invariant to changes in environment (Flatt 2005). The importance of this observation is that it provides a framework for investigating the adaptive evolution of canalized traits in the context of reaction norms

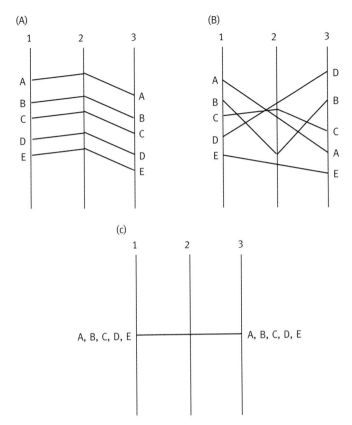

Figure 4.17. An illustration of phenotypic plasticity revealed by reaction norms. Lines join the values of the trait expressed for single genotypes (letters) exposed to three different environments (numbers). Panel A illustrates parallel reaction norms. The relative values of the traits are preserved in different environments. Panel B illustrates a $G \times E$ interaction (the reaction norms are not parallel to one another). Panel C illustrates the special and extreme case of both genetic and environmental canalization (all genotypes produce the same value of the trait in all environments).

(differences in expression of the same genotype in different environments). The reaction norms remind us that patterns in the structure matrix itself represent traits available to adaptive evolution.

Reflection

This chapter demonstrates that an understanding of structure is crucial in our efforts to evaluate adaptive options in evolution. One of its most important lessons is that a seamless connection from genetics to trait distributions exists only for traits with the simplest maps onto function and fitness. We can anticipate that values for the vast majority of traits are not nearly so simple and that they will reflect not only genetic, environmental, and $G \times E$ interactions, but also that their relationships with other traits, function, and fitness will be complex. It would be incorrect to assume that the complexity eliminates our ability to predict adaptive responses. Instead, now that we have a firm grasp of structure and its manifold possibilities, we can begin to explore the role of scale on adaptive evolution.

Yet it is clear for most traits that we have but a rudimentary understanding of structure. And it should also be clear that if our structural map is incorrect, then so too will be our understanding of, and ability to predict, the products of adaptation. It is for these reasons that we propose, like Valone and Mitchell, Vincent and Brown, and many others, that it is often best to wrap genetics and development into the warm, protective, but sometimes fuzzy blanket of 'evolutionarily feasible strategies'. We can then use our knowledge of population and evolutionary dynamics to search for evolutionarily stable strategies emerging from adaptation. However, that approach, as powerful and seductive as it is, cannot override the mechanics, function, and structure inherent in evolution.

Fortunately, we will discover that our interpretations are self-correcting. Rather than defining a strategy as an 'inherited phenotype' (Vincent and Brown 2005) we defined it in terms of evolutionarily feasible options. Evolutionary feasibility is defined by the structure matrix. Since we are unlikely to ever completely understand that matrix, and especially so when we attempt to model the strategies of several species simultaneously, we must further distinguish between feasible and real evolutionary strategies. Feasible strategies are those for which we imagine that we understand enough of their structure to model their adaptation.[30] How will we know whether we possess enough knowledge? We use reverse logic. We imagine that we have the requisite knowledge and build a model that yields stability around the supposed strategy's current value.[31] We then perturb the strategy away from its imagined evolutionary stability. If the experimental system subsequently converges on the original predicted equilibrium under the same sets of conditions existing at the start of the experiment, then we will know that the strategy is real. If it fails to converge, then we know that our logic, our structure matrix, or both, are wrong.

Our ability to determine feasible strategies depends critically on the scales at which the functions of strategies map onto fitness. We now turn our attention toward that crucial topic.

---

[30] A feasible evolutionary strategy is mirrored by Vincent and Brown's (2005) concept of a 'species archetype'. The archetype is defined as the evolutionarily stable strategy that emerges from the joint analysis of population and strategy dynamics (collectively called 'Darwinian dynamics' by Vincent and Brown). But the species archetype is defined by the sets of strategies, dynamics, and environments (structure) in the model and need not be realized in nature.

[31] Recall Mitchell and Valone's argument that strategies should exist close to their optima.

5

Scale

Overview

The pattern and course of evolution varies with scale. Structure varies through space and time, function depends on the level of organization, and mechanics vary with structure, across levels of adaptation, and with the questions that interest us. Although it is crucial to include these various dimensions into our understanding of evolution (and ecology), it is even more crucial that we do not use the complexity of scales (and their association with structure) to make excuses about our limited ability to model evolution.

Our summary of structure (Chapter 4) noted limitations to a gene-centred worldview of evolution. The limitations of that perspective in representing the total evolutionary process are magnified by scale. But so too are all other perspectives. The key to dealing with scale is to match models and worldviews with the questions that we ask. In order to do so, we must possess clear and unambiguous insights into the dimensions of evolution.

Many of these insights emerge by jointly considering the grain-size of the environment, and the scale of its use.[1] We learned in Chapter 3 that grain was introduced to evolutionary biology by Richard Levins in a precocious series of papers in the 1960s. When organisms exploit very different ecological opportunities (e.g. habitats), the grain of their environment is coarse. If different individuals spend their lifetimes in one or the other opportunity, their use of the environment is also coarse. But if they exploit each opportunity in proportion to its occurrence, their niche is fine-grained.

Levins used this ingenious classification to assess the evolution of specialist versus generalist phenotypes. But grain size has numerous additional implications to our study of evolution. Grain also determines how we model fitness, the importance of

---

[1] Our interest is in assessing grain and scale in their evolutionary context. The terms have quite different meanings in landscape ecology, where 'scale' is typically decomposed into 'extent' (the maximum area under study) and where 'grain' is used in at least two different ways (1, resolution; the smallest area from which data can be gathered or inferred, or 2, the relative size of homogeneous landscape elements). Mayer and Cameron (2003) review use of the terms and their importance to landscape ecology.

gene flow, whether all individuals in a population adapt similarly or not, whether different subpopulations are exposed to different adaptive gradients, and the shape of adaptive landscapes.

Many of our insights into grain and its effects on evolution can be attained by careful attention to habitat and habitat selection. Indeed, theories of habitat selection followed closely on the heels of Levins' theory and represent another important origin for evolutionarily stable strategies. Merging these two constructs sets the stage for our more detailed ecological and strategy analysis in Chapter 6.

Although it is important to appreciate our limited ability to draw complete gene→ecosystem maps, research on a famous model system demonstrates that we can nevertheless use a gene and developmental perspective to gain considerable insights into the ecological and evolutionary significance of some traits, as long as the mappings onto function and fitness are relatively simple. These maps correlate well with models that assume fitness consequences for all genes, but are difficult to reconcile with evidence that many genes have little effect on fitness in simple organisms.

Introduction: backward-looking adaptation

If you live in or have visited eastern North America, you might have been thrilled to glimpse the iridescent flash of metallic red on a hovering, male ruby-throated hummingbird. You may have been amazed to watch it manoeuvre deftly among the flowers of a columbine, to balance in mid-air as it probed each tubular corolla for nectar before darting to another. Perhaps you witnessed the male's dizzying backwards then forwards courtship flight. If so, we suspect that you marvelled at this tiny vertebrate's speed, its rapid wing-beat, its agility, and its apparent ease at maintaining hovering flight. Who would dare criticize you if you were to state that the hummingbird's adaptations for flight approach perfection?

'Adaptation is more innovation than it is invention'

But perfection through evolution, like beauty, lies in the eyes of the beholder. Against what standard should one compare 'perfection'? Hummingbirds and hawkmoths make their living in similar ways by feeding on nectar. They converge in diet, body-size, and hovering ability. Hawkmoths, like many other insects, are wonderful flying machines. They achieve equal aerodynamic lift from both the downbeat and upbeat of their wings. Hummingbirds were thought to do the same, but a team led by Oregon State University's Douglas Warrick corrected our misconception. Hummingbirds, constrained by their vertebrate body plan, can support only 25% of their weight on the upstroke beat (Warrick *et al.* 2005). In this sense, hummingbirds are not as efficient at hovering as are hawkmoths. The rigid bones and muscles along the proximal edge of a bird's wing create a fixed airfoil that is less efficient than the reversible camber afforded by the flexible wings of insects. Hummingbirds are not perfect flying machines.

'Adaptations are time-lagged responses to the mapping of fitness onto a trait's function'

The hummingbird's wing reminds us that adaptive evolution occurs not so much through invention (mutation) as through improvisation. Though the adaptations of hovering flight fulfil related functions in hawkmoths and hummingbirds, they arose from unique morphology along dramatically different phylogenetic lines. As hovering ability evolved in hummingbirds, it did so within the organizational rules embedded in the hummingbird structure matrix. Any change in the value and frequency of traits linked to improved hovering occurred only in response to their effects on the function of hovering, and then only through the mapping of hovering onto fitness. So the hummingbird wing demonstrates that the adaptations we observe at any instant in time not only trail the fitness consequences associated with a trait's function, but also include a historical lag representing past adaptations.

These distinctions reinforce lessons learned from our earlier discussion of backward-looking organic evolution versus forward-looking intelligent design. An intelligent designer driving along a twisting mountain road can see how the road changes ahead. Warning signs allow her to anticipate such features as curves, hills, and narrow shoulders. Our intelligent driver can thereby adjust her speed and steering to yield an efficient and safe path along the highway (the path will be imperfect because drivers vary in their ability to trace the roadway, and particularly so when inebriated, distracted, facing reduced visibility, or encountering deteriorated road conditions). Adaptation, on the other hand, is like a driver who can view progress along the road only through the rear-view mirror. If the car is moving slowly, and if the bends are not too sharp, a careful backward-looking driver will be able to respond to each turn and twist in the road without calamity. The car's wobbling path, though not as efficient as that of the forward-looking driver, will nevertheless direct it safely from one point to another. A trace of the vehicle's path, except for the wobbles, will match that of forward-looking drivers. The two routes may even be indistinguishable along stretches of straight highway. Both drivers face equal risks from stochastic effects, such as wildlife darting into the vehicle's path or rocks catapulting onto the road from the cliff above. No wonder then that adaptive evolution mirrors intelligent design and yields a splendid, but imperfect, fit between form and function.

But if our rearward-looking driver proceeds too quickly, or over- or under-steers, she will career toward disaster. So too will evolving populations. Slow, gradual, consistent adaptation allows traits to track the changing target of a variable environment. But if the environment changes too rapidly, or if the structure matrix fails to match the 'speed' of environmental change, populations will lurch toward extinction.

We can use this metaphor to reveal other lessons about adaptive evolution. Some biologists would have us believe that, with enough understanding, we should be able to map the expression of traits in real organisms onto their underlying genes. And, as we showed in Chapter 3, we agree, for traits with a simple one-to-one mapping between genes, structure, function, and fitness. So, in our vehicle analogy we should be able to find a one-to-one correspondence between the vehicle's blueprints and measures of such things as the vehicle's gross weight, wheelbase, and turning radius. But if we aim to predict the vehicle's path along a tortuous mountain highway, knowledge of other factors such as the age, experience, and state of the driver, the road conditions, and the vehicle's speed and maintenance are likely to be far more instructive than knowing the vehicle's design. We are not suggesting that design is unimportant—design can inform us about the vehicle's performance—but it cannot fully compensate for the high variability among drivers with different skills. The scales of variability do not match. We can contrast the design features of different vehicles to assess their innate differences in performance and we can contrast drivers in much the same way. But unless drivers with different skills are strongly associated with vehicles of specific designs, we cannot use one to predict the other.

'Successful models of evolution match traits with the scale of their adaptation'

Much the same is true of genes. If we attempt to predict complex, quantitative traits and strategies from genetics alone, the scales will not match. We do not mean, of course, that one can or should ignore genetics. Models by Washington State's Richard Gomulkiewicz and colleagues (2010) demonstrate that the assumptions we make about the genetic connections to fitness can have dramatic effects on the ability of species to invade new environments or withstand rapid environmental change. The models show, if one fixes the variance in fitness, that the probability of a population adapting to harsh environments is inversely proportional to the number of loci contributing to that constant variance. Each locus added to the model thus contributes less to fitness, thereby slowing its rate of adaptive evolution. If, on the other hand, one fixes the selection gradient for every locus, then the pace of evolution is advanced with each additional locus. The expected frequency of deleterious alleles declines with every additional locus, so a smaller change in the frequency at any locus has greater overall effect on fitness. The worldview expressed through these models is that the genetic architecture of fitness is crucially important to adaptive evolution.

An alternative worldview recognizes that the assumptions reflect different structures. A constant variance in fitness implies, for example, that one or more underlying quantitative traits perform redundant functions. We may or may not be able to link expression of a trait and its fitness to its genetic roots in the bigger picture of adaptive evolution operating on interacting genes, traits, and functions in variable environments. The reverse is also true. Though we can often understand how different environments influence the expression of traits,[2] our picture of cause and effect becomes increasingly fuzzy as we attempt to trace the traits' genetic origins.

---

[2] Recall the discussion of reaction norms in earlier chapters.

The abstract models of Gomulkiewicz *et al.* (2010) yield insights because they imagine a direct connection to fitness that circumvents the complexities of function and structure. There is no attempt to link genetics with traits, and it is thus possible to explore the length of time that a population may require in order to adapt to rapidly changed conditions or new opportunities. So the successful study of adaptation is very much an issue of matching the scale of our interest with scales of variation and what, exactly, we aim to understand. The theorist's brilliant abstraction is, too frequently, the empiricist's albatross.

At a very fine scale we can often associate differences in genes with differences in regulation, gene function, gene products, and, in some dramatic cases, with differences in fitness. Our ability to do this confirms that we understand underlying mechanical processes of adaptive evolution. But simple mechanics fail to predict the values of many other traits the expression of which depends on dynamic interactions among genes, individuals, and environments. The evolution of these traits can be understood only by matching our models with their density and frequency-dependent scales of adaptation. Success in doing so does not mean that we can recover the ultimate underlying genetic/developmental map responsible for the traits' value, let alone its function, in any single circumstance.

'The map of evolution varies with scale'

Theoretical models represent many different maps of evolution. With few exceptions, each model portrays a different scale in the evolutionary process. And though each is intricately related to the others, we can only rarely move across scales. In a sense, then, the study of evolution mimics the problem faced by cartographers in their choice of scale for different maps. A biologist struggling to map traits and strategies onto the mechanics and dynamics of evolution is very much like a surveyor trying to match the scale of a physical map with the processes producing its patterns. The size, path, and current of large rivers cutting across the landscape depend on such things as the lie of the land, the nature of the substrate, and on the long-term dynamics of the watershed and its hydrological cycle. If we marked and identified water molecules at the river's source, we could, presumably, trace their path toward the river's mouth. The trace would, at a sufficiently large scale, outline the river's course and give us insight into the large-scale processes creating patterns in the watershed. That trace, however, is a collective, emergent property of the molecules, and it is the trace that gives us insight, not the molecules themselves. If we reduced the scale of our interest, we could use the trace to discover and understand such things as eddies and vortices in the river's current. The disappearance of marked molecules could provide information on withdrawal and evaporation. But the behaviour of the separate molecules would inform us only about processes operating in the neighbourhood of the molecules themselves.

It would be a mistake to push our river and vehicle analogies too far. Genes are not water molecules and DNA is much more than a blueprint. But in the same way, evolution is much more than genes, nucleic acids, and narrow-sense heritability. Evolution occurs simultaneously along multiple non-independent dimensions at a variety of organizational, temporal, and spatial scales.

Shortcuts in modelling evolution

The dimensions of evolution tell us that our models can never be more than caricatures of its multi-faceted complexity. So how are we to know which models to use and what scale is appropriate for our analysis? When, and at what scales, will our mechanical models of evolution (e.g. Equation 2.12) yield correct predictions? Are there limits to our ability to cross scales, or do we 'simply' need to pack our models with extra dimensions and their geometically increasing complexity? Or is it better to convert to a strategic analysis free of genetics?

The answers emerge from the ways that genes, traits, environments, and function interact. Generally speaking, we do not understand those interactions, so perhaps we should mount an international research programme to flesh out the full structure matrix.[3] What would we gain? We would discover some traits with 'simple' gene→trait→function mappings that should yield adaptations predicted by our classical equations in population and quantitative genetics. We would also discover that many of these traits are highly conserved and lack the variability necessary for further adaptive evolution. But we would be perplexed by genes that, when deleted with complete loss-of-function, appear to have little effect on either population growth or fitness (Bell 2008, 2010). A deeper understanding of structure could definitely allow us to make broader use of genomics in such applied areas as disease control and horizontal gene transfer, but it may not produce many new insights about adaptive evolution.

We would also learn that many of the traits and strategies that interest ecologists emerge from a complicated structure in which genes, traits, and functions interact with density, state, and frequency dependence imposed by environments varying across several different scales in time and space. We have argued, as have Vincent and Brown (2005), that we can avoid many of these inevitable complexities by modelling the fitness-mapping functions of evolutionarily feasible and ecologically acceptable strategies. Analysis of the ensuing evolutionary game (Chapter 6) allows us to explore the dynamics of evolution. The game is solved by using a maximum principle that identifies ecologically and evolutionarily stable equilibria (or the basins of attraction that bound non-equilibrium dynamics).[4] The singularities emerging from the 'grand equilibrium', when every adaptive peak is occupied by a strategy with zero fitness,

---

[3] We suggest that readers contemplate how much of the structure matrix will be revealed by techniques such as QTL mapping and our global initiatives on genomics and proteomics.

[4] Joseph Apaloo and colleagues (2009) review the confusing terminology of evolutionary games and demonstrate that evolutionary stability must necessarily arise if a strategy simultaneously resists invasion from other nearby strategies (an evolutionarily stable strategy, ESS) and can invade those nearby strategies (a neighbourhood invader strategy, NIS).

represents an endpoint for evolution that can only be disrupted by a different fitness-mapping function.

'Evolution is endless and everlasting'

Scales of variability in natural systems limit adaptation's ability to ever achieve the grand equilibrium. Changing environments alter the dynamics of populations, their density and frequency-dependent effects, and the ecological acceptance of traits and strategies. The adaptive landscape in a variable environment is fluid. It flows and undulates under strategies anchored to their bauplan like navigation buoys in a lake. Viewed in this light, Vincent and Brown's (2005) species archetype is ephemeral, a glorious sphinx rising then disappearing in the drifting sands of time.

But of course it is not just environments that change. The genetic and developmental architecture of traits and strategies varies as well. Traits change, their genetic variances and covariances change, and their functions are modified. Each has the potential to alter strategies and the map of existing strategies onto fitness. Changing the fitness-mapping function is analogous to moving the anchors and adjusting the lengths of the tethers that position the adaptive buoys of evolution. If the tether for any single strategy is too short, fitness can never rise high enough to float on the adaptive landscape. If the tether is too long, the highly variable strategy can drift with the currents of change, but can also be ripped from its moorings and wrecked in the rocks, shoals, and surf of evolution.

So evolution is an endless, everlasting process. Most of its 'winners', like sports heroes, are short-lived, cast aside initially by (slightly) more successful strategies, whose cumulative effects (as well as infrequent and extraordinary macromutations or environmental changes that have potential to revolutionize the relationships among traits, function, and fitness) create new bauplans in the adaptive race of evolution. Often, we can track the race phylogenetically through the emergence of shared derived characters that reflect the evolutionary history of bauplans. Each synapomorphy[5] represents a 'branching point' that differentiates one taxon from another. Many of these branching points will represent different adaptive solutions by populations and species belonging to the same bauplan. But many others will mark a divergence in the fitness-mapping function, and the replacement of one bauplan by another.

Sadly, our ability to reconstruct phylogenetic relationships and their resident bauplans is often hindered by evolutionary reversals and convergence of traits. Reversals and convergence can be caused either by trait values evolving from different bauplans or by strategy shifts within a single bauplan. These homoplasies[6] mean that the gradual

---

[5] The term 'synapomorphy' is frequently used by systematists as a synonym for 'shared derived character'.

[6] Homoplasy is a term used by systematists to represent the occurrence, in two or more taxa, of a similar character or trait value that did not arise through shared ancestry.

adaptive evolution responsible for much of the diversity of life does not necessarily leave a unique signal in the phylogenetic relationships among taxa. The unfortunate consequence is that we may not be able to use the history of life to tell us reliably where one bauplan ends and another begins.

'The study of evolution must match the scale of process with the scale of interest'

One of the reasons for this evolutionary frustration lies within the structure matrix. The mechanics of evolution specify the feasible sets of evolutionary strategies. The analysis of evolutionary strategies is thus simplified because it considers only those genetic, developmental, and other changes in the structure matrix that modify the fitness-mapping function. But as we have noted before, the complexity of the structure matrix limits our ability to map changes in its elements onto fitness. Scale, or more correctly the matching of scales, saves the day. If one is interested in finding evolutionarily feasible and ecologically acceptable strategies, then the analysis must be focused on dynamics. If the interest lies in the mechanics of the evolutionary process, then the analysis is properly focused on genetics. The objective of evolutionary analysis, for the vast majority of traits, must not and cannot be to trace the path from gene to adaptive strategy. The scales of mechanics do not, for all but the simplest gene→trait→function mappings, match those of the dynamic processes acting on strategies.

Size and allometry

One of the most striking patterns in all of biodiversity is that organisms are packaged in different sizes. Even within taxa, body sizes typically range over several orders of magnitude. How does such variation evolve? What are its evolutionary consequences?

'Allometric relationships with body size are connected to underlying physical principles'

All organisms must secure, transform, transport, and allocate energy. These basic facts suggest that underlying physical principles might explain size differences amongst organisms according to the general allometric equation

$$Y = Y_0 M^b$$

where Y is one of many variables influenced by body size, Y_0 is the allometric coefficient, M is body mass, and b is the allometric scaling exponent (Chapter 4). The University of New Mexico's James Brown and colleagues champion the view that underlying physical properties and constraints govern the general observation that scaling exponents are multiples of a quarter, such as the three-quarter scaling of whole organism metabolic rates generally referred to as Kleiber's law.[7] With physicist Geoffrey West, Brown's team predicted three-quarter scaling if organisms' transport systems obey similar branching patterns, minimize the energy required for transport, and have identical limits on the smallest parts of the transport network (West *et al.* 1997). Combined with the temperature dependence of biochemical reactions and the limits on transformation imposed by stoichiometry, body size emerges as a key component of Brown's controversial metabolic theory of ecology (MTE; Brown *et al.* 2004). Numerous macroecological patterns ranging from developmental and reproductive rates to abundance and biomass turnover rates scale allometrically with body size. At issue is not so much whether allometric relationships yield patterns, but rather whether those patterns scale consistently among organisms of different types.

Anthropologist Isabella Capellini and co-authors (Capellini *et al.* 2010) note that many assessments of allometric scaling have failed to include proper phylogenetic controls. Related groups of organisms inherit their ancestors' traits, hence comparative analyses searching for general trends must first account for patterns arising through common descent. When Capellini *et al.* applied the appropriate controls to several mammalian taxa, allometric exponents for metabolic rates varied dramatically among phylogenetic lineages. Basal metabolic rates of rodents fit an exponent (0.71) significantly less than the theoretical three-quarter scaling law, and insectivores fit an exponent (0.587) less than the alternative two-thirds scaling expected from surface-to-mass ratios. Capellini and colleagues conclude that there is no convincing evidence of a universal scaling exponent, hence theories that depend on a predominant exponent 'have little explanatory power' (Capellini *et al.* 2010, p. 2783). Although the jury is still out on whether its precepts are valid and whether it is a theory or a model (del Rio, 2008), MTE has yielded numerous novel patterns that continue to shape the way biologists view the world (e.g. Price *et al.* 2010). There is no denying the general principle that organisms must adhere to the properties and laws of physics and chemistry.

However, it is also true that even though many ecologically and evolutionarily relevant characteristics vary allometrically with body size, there are important and notable exceptions in the scales in space and time that organisms exploit and thus the scale of their environment. The largest birds are not those with the greatest long-distance migrations, and parasites of similar sizes can have widely different exposures to hosts and environments.

Brown and his colleagues (1993) used somewhat related models to predict optimal body sizes. According to this metabolic theory, organisms maximize reproductive power, the rate at which energy is converted into offspring. Reproductive power is the compromise between two rates with opposing allometric scaling. The rate at which

---

[7] Max Kleiber (1893–1976) emigrated from Switzerland in 1929 to join the Department of Animal Husbandry at UC Davis where he became a world leader in the fields of animal nutrition and metabolism.

organisms of different sizes acquire energy from the environment increases as the 0.75 power of body size, but the rate at which they can convert it into offspring scales as the –0.25 power. So small organisms can channel resources into offspring quickly, but have limited capacity to acquire them. Large organisms can harvest an abundance of resources but are slow to convert them into offspring. This theory, too, has its supporters and detractors. But again, regardless of mechanism, the concept of an optimal size for organisms of a given body plan has an alluring and enduring quality.

'The range of body sizes in any given taxon is the consequence of density and frequency-dependent evolution'

The real issues, of course, are why do organisms of all taxa vary widely in body size and what does that tell us about the scale of evolution? Brown's explanation is that the model's assumptions fail in resource or biotically limited environments. Competition among similar-sized competing species reduces fitness for the modal classes such that the remaining ecological opportunities lie at more extreme body sizes. As species diversify, the range of body sizes increases. So the variance in body size that emerges through evolution is not so much about underlying metabolic processes as it is about the density and frequency dependence of competing strategies. We resolve the implications of density- and frequency-dependent evolution in Chapter 6.

'Although there are exceptions, the scale of space and time tends to increase with body size'

The key point for evolutionary analyses of problems other than the evolution of body size is to recognize that size is important and that its various allometric scales influence the spatial, temporal, and contextual exposure of organisms to their environment. Generally speaking, larger organisms extract resources at larger scales and live longer than smaller organisms with similar body plans. This means, of course, that the map of their environmental heterogeneity is different from that of their smaller cousins. It is this relative heterogeneity that we must understand in order to appreciate the role of body size in the scale of evolution.

Grain: how the scale of environment influences evolution

The way in which we map fitness onto strategies and traits depends critically on the scale at which organisms distribute themselves along environmental gradients. There are two extremes: fine-grained individuals use different environments in direct proportion to their frequency,[8] while coarse-grained individuals spend their entire lifetime in a

---

[8] Readers interested in the use of fine- and coarse-grain in an evolutionary context may wish to consult two of Levins' classic contributions, published in 1962 and 1968.

single environment. There are, of course, numerous other options between these two polar alternatives.[9]

An evolutionary analyst needs, therefore, to explore how environmental grain influences adaptation. She could, in principle, choose any environmental gradient to accomplish this task. We find it convenient, nevertheless, to think of the gradient as representing different habitats. We do this for two purposes:

1. Theories of habitat selection are relatively easy to visualize.
2. All organisms necessarily occupy space.

We showed in Chapter 3 that adaptation in populations occupying two or more habitats depends on how similar the habitats are,[10] and whether individuals use them in a coarse- or fine-grained manner. Habitat similarity and grain size can be thought of as issues of scale. We learned that similar habitats yield convex fitness sets and adaptation toward generalist individuals with intermediate trait values. Dissimilar habitats yield quite different fitness expectations. The fitness set for dissimilar habitats is convex and often leads to the evolution of habitat specialists, but with potential for a stable polymorphism or a mixture of pure evolutionary strategies (coexistence of specialists in each habitat).[11]

Our initial analysis included the frequency of the two habitats exploited by the population, but not population and ecological dynamics.[12] Our conclusions on adaptation were thus preliminary because we did not solve the complete dynamic game of evolution in heterogeneous environments. So we now return to the simplified two-habitat model that we first explored in Chapter 3 to assess a more complete model of fine- versus coarse-grained scale on adaptive evolution.

The relationships between the values of traits, functions, and fitness must, by definition, differ between the two habitats in our model. We explore two versions. In the first version we examine evolution in a geographical landscape composed only of Habitats 1 and 2. We imagine that the frequency distribution between fitness and a trait's value in the two habitats is identical, except in the location of its mean (as in Figs 3.6 and 3.7).

---

[9] The scale of 'grain' must always be assessed in the context of the species' life cycle and population structure. A species in which non-reproductive individuals occupy a single habitat accruing resources for reproduction, then mix thoroughly as breeding adults, would be appropriately considered 'fine-grained' because fitness would be a simple weighted average of each habitat's contribution to reproductive resources.

[10] Habitats are defined by the species that use them. Use depends on fitness. This means that each habitat will have a different trait→function→fitness map to others. This statement is, perhaps, the least ambiguous definition one can give for 'habitat'.

[11] A pure evolutionary strategy occurs when an individual opts for a particular strategy under defined conditions (e.g. if density is low, then occupy only Habitat 2). The contrasting alternative is a mixed evolutionary strategy, where an individual plays two or more options according to either a fixed or variable probability (e.g. occupy Habitat 2 with probability p, and occupy Habitat 1 with probability $1-p$).

[12] We did evaluate some of the consequences of density-dependent habitat selection on the evolution of clutch-size.

Trait values that maximize fitness in Habitat 2 are larger than those that maximize fitness in Habitat 1.[13] In the second version we explore adaptation in the landscape with an altered Habitat 2. We imagine that the fitness-mapping function in Habitat 2 is not only shifted away from Habitat 1, but that the expected fitness in that habitat is also greater than the fitness in Habitat 1. Our models assume that individuals can obtain all resources for growth, survival, and reproduction (including mates) within a single habitat.

We begin by further assuming that the density-independent adaptive function is linear (individuals exploit the two habitats in a fine-grained manner). The fine-grained generalist exploiting two similar habitats has a higher expectation of fitness than do the extreme specialists (Fig. 5.1). Although this conclusion is general, adaptation favours more specialized individuals when the average fitness payoff is greater in some habitats than others. Specialists also reap greater payoffs when individuals exploit quite different habitats that yield a convex fitness set.

> *'Adaptive evolution of habitat specialists and generalists depends on whether habitats are similar or dissimilar, and whether the adaptive landscape is rigid or flexible'*

How should we include density and frequency dependence in this model? We illustrate three possibilities and contrast their effects for each landscape. First, we assume that the relationship between fitness and density is similar for all trait values in all habitats (Fig. 5.2). Hence we assume that each individual loses exactly the same amount of fitness with every increase in density.[14] Density, in this example, causes the rigid adaptive landscape (the fitness-mapping function) to sink at the same rate across the trait space. Density has no influence on the shape of the fitness set. Extreme trait values with low but positive fitness in sparse populations yield negative fitness in dense populations.[15] These trait values, which would normally be eliminated from a population occupying a single habitat at high density, may persist because they maintain positive fitness in a different habitat. Fig. 5.2 illustrates that when the maximum fitness is identical in the two habitats, adaptation along a concave fitness set will yield a single generalist. Adaptation along convex fitness sets will yield a single specialist. And when maximum fitness differs between the habitats, adaptation along both convex and concave fitness sets yields a specialist for the habitat with high fitness.

---

[13] Recall from Chapter 3 that the mean difference and variance in fitness distributions determine whether the fitness set is convex or concave.

[14] This assumption also implies that each individual has an equivalent competitive effect on all others, irrespective of its trait value.

[15] Our statement of negative fitness corresponds with fitness models assuming continuous reproduction (e.g. r). Fitness would be positive, but less than unity, in models based on discrete periods of reproduction (e.g. λ). Regardless, the outcome is the same. The frequency of individuals with the trait would decline in dense populations.

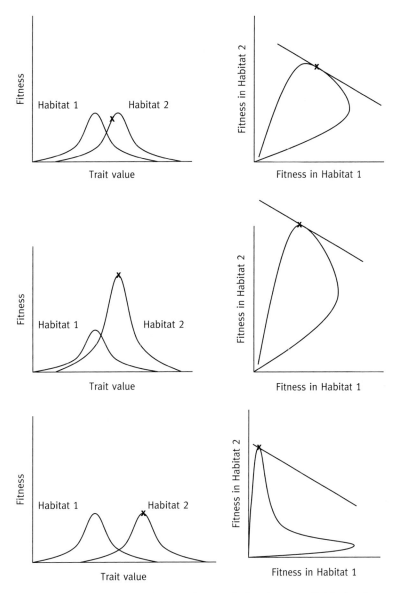

Figure 5.1. Illustrations of adaptive evolution of a trait belonging to individuals who occupy two different habitats in a fine-grained environment, when fitness is independent of population density. Panels on the left illustrate three different fitness-mapping functions for the variable trait. Panels on the right illustrate the single adaptive outcome of evolution corresponding to the trait value where the adaptive function is tangential to the negatively-sloped boundary of the fitness set. The symbol 'x' corresponds to the fitness associated with the trait value maximizing fitness in the mix of habitats. Scenarios from top to bottom represent, respectively, equal fitness potential in two similar habitats, unequal fitness between two similar habitats, and equal fitness between two dissimilar habitats.

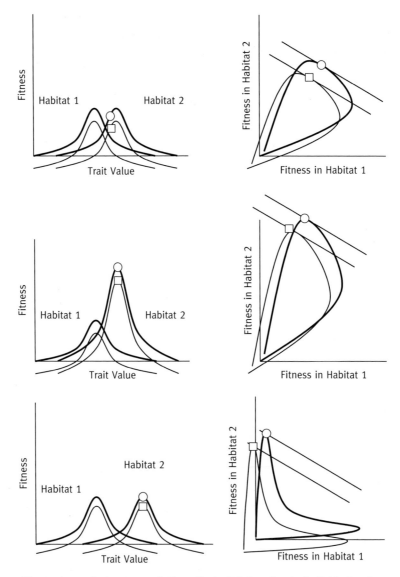

Figure 5.2. Illustrations of adaptive evolution of a trait belonging to individuals who occupy two different habitats in a fine-grained environment, when fitness declines equally with increases in population density. Panels on the left illustrate three different fitness-mapping functions for the variable trait. Panels on the right (not necessarily to the same scale) illustrate the single adaptive outcome of evolution. Bold lines correspond to low density, light lines to higher density. Symbols 'o' and '□' correspond to the trait values maximizing fitness under each scenario at low (o) and higher density (□). Fitness axes cross at zero. Scenarios from top to bottom represent, respectively, equal fitness potential in two similar habitats, unequal fitness between two similar habitats, and equal fitness between two dissimilar habitats.

In our second 'simulation' we again assume a sinking adaptive landscape where the density-dependent decline in fitness affects all individuals within a habitat similarly. But we now assume that the effect is greater in one habitat than in the other. The fitness-mapping functions of this flexible landscape sink at different rates with increased density. So, in this scenario, the fitness set changes shape with changes in population density. If the fitness set is concave, the point of tangency with the adaptive function on the outer 'active edge' of the fitness set rotates gradually with changes in population density. There is thus a gradual density-dependent shift in the trait value that yields the highest fitness. But if the fitness set is convex, adaptation (in this fine-grained case) bifurcates from selection of one specialist to another (Fig. 5.3).

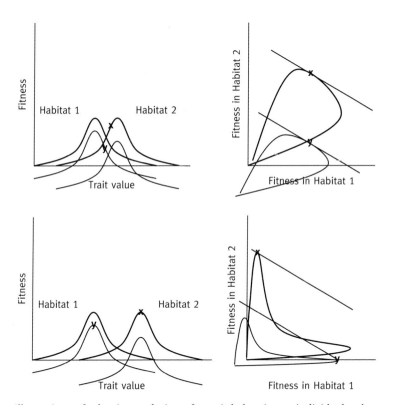

Figure 5.3. Illustrations of adaptive evolution of a trait belonging to individuals who occupy two different habitats in a fine-grained environment, when fitness declines more quickly with density in one habitat than in the other. Panels on the right illustrate adaptive evolution of different trait values with increasing population size. Bold lines correspond to low density, light lines to higher density. Symbols 'x' and 'y' correspond to the trait values maximizing fitness under each scenario at low (x) and higher density (y). Fitness axes cross at zero. Even though trait value y yields high fitness in Habitat 1 in dense populations, it may not be optimal because it can yield negative fitness in Habitat 2. The top panels correspond to adaptive evolution in similar habitats producing concave fitness sets. The bottom panels correspond to adaptive evolution in dissimilar habitats that produce convex fitness sets.

Based on what we have learned so far, changes in density can effect no change in trait value, or cause either gradual or rapid reversible changes in trait evolution. But we have ignored density-dependent behavioural strategies of habitat selection. What pattern of trait evolution will emerge if individuals can assess their expected fitness, select habitats that maximize fitness, and are free to occupy the habitat that they choose, an ideal-free distribution, IFD (Fretwell and Lucas 1969)?

> *'Behavioural strategies of habitat selection can trump the evolution*
> *of traits that would otherwise favour habitat specialists'*

Imagine that the population is composed of several different individuals possessing each trait value. Which habitat should these individuals occupy? If they have higher fitness in Habitat 1, then they should attempt to use only that habitat. But as more and more individuals occupy Habitat 1, fitness there declines, until at some point an individual can gain equal fitness in a different habitat. Either habitat is then equally acceptable and each should be occupied. If there are even more individuals seeking habitat, the number of individuals in each habitat will attain a dynamic equilibrium such that the expected fitness in each habitat is the same. Otherwise an individual would move from the lower-fitness habitat to the higher one. In this way, the evolutionarily stable strategy of habitat selection creates an IFD of individuals among habitats because each individual has the same expected fitness payoff as do all others sharing that trait value.[16] Note that this distribution occurs across all population sizes and does not require that the population dynamics reside at equilibrium with carrying capacity.[17]

We will again explore two possibilities. First, we evaluate the consequences for trait evolution when we assume that the IFD is indeed evolutionarily stable. Then we assess the simultaneous adaptation of both the trait and the habitat-selection strategy to ensure that we are examining evolutionarily stable dynamics.

How will habitat selection operate? The answer lies in its mechanics and structure. Imagine a set of individuals with trait values that yield high fitness in Habitat 1 and lower fitness in Habitat 2. Those individuals should congregate in Habitat 1, then move to Habitat 2 at high density. But at the same time, individuals with trait values yielding higher fitness in Habitat 2 are congregating there, and lowering fitness. So, if the frequencies of individuals with the two trait values are equal, the only individuals that can actually achieve an IFD while occupying both habitats are those with trait values that yield identical fitness in each one.

---

[16] Ideal habitat selection represents a hierarchy of strategies. At one scale, individuals either possess the potential for ideal habitat selection or they do not. At a finer scale, the distribution of individuals among habitats at different densities represents the optimal strategy set corresponding to the evolutionarily stable solution that emerges from ideal habitat selection.

[17] The distribution of individuals in this stable population would, of course, also obey the principles of the habitat-selection game and rest at a stable ideal-free distribution.

*'Adaptation of ideal-free habitat selectors can always yield a habitat generalist
even if the generalist strategy resides at a fitness minimum'*

We can again use the techniques we learned in Chapter 3 to search for the adaptive
solution (Fig. 5.4). If habitat use is fine-grained, then the adaptive function is given by

$$A = p^* w_1 + q^* w_2 \qquad (5.1)$$

where p^* and q^* represent the proportions of the population occupying Habitats 1 and
2 ($p^* + q^* = 1$; the asterisks denote that we are including both differences in area of
the habitat as well as differences in population density caused by the IFD). But since
$w_2 = w_1 = w$ at the IFD, then

$$A = w(p^* + q^*) = w$$

Thus, for any given value of A, when both habitats are occupied at the IFD, the adaptive
function is a constant. The fitness set, on the other hand, is compressed by density-
dependent habitat choice onto a straight line with slope of unity. Each point along the
$w_2 = w_1$ line represents the density and trait-dependent fitness of individuals obeying
an IFD. It can be generated from both convex and concave fitness sets. Points farther
from the origin correspond to an IFD at lower density than points close to the origin. If
fitness declines with population size similarly in both habitats, then the adaptive
landscape is rigid across habitats, and both will be occupied by ideal-free habitat
selectors at all population sizes.

The ability to select habitat according to density can be viewed as an 'eat your cake
and have it too' strategy because it appears to yield the same fitness payoff for all
individuals, regardless of their trait value. The fitness-mapping function is flattened,
and there is no advantage for possessing one trait value over another.[18] The behaviour
thus creates a fitness stalemate that neutralizes adaptive evolution toward habitat
preference.

The stalemate can be broken in at least six different ways:

1. If some individuals are dominant over others, they can force the subordinates to
'overpopulate' sub-optimal habitat.[19] The number of individuals occupying the best
habitat will thus 'undermatch' density with resources.

---

[18] There could be an advantage for traits that improve assessments of density and habitat quality, as
well as ability to disperse from one habitat to another.
[19] An ideal-free distribution assumes that all individuals are capable of 'scrambling' for resources.
The alternative, where individuals interfere directly in the habitat choices of others, is usually referred to
as either an ideal despotic- or ideal-dominance distribution.

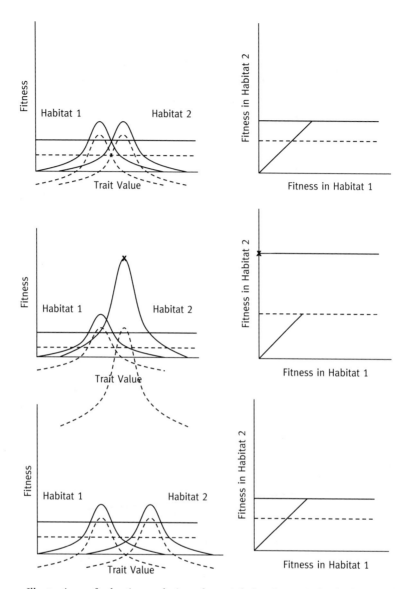

Figure 5.4. Illustrations of adaptive evolution of a trait belonging to individuals who occupy two different habitats according to an IFD. Panels on the left illustrate a sinking adaptive landscape with increasing population density. Bell-shaped fitness mappings, in these examples, represent the potential differences that exist among individuals with different trait values. Dashed curves correspond to the potential fitness differences expected among individuals with different trait values at increased population size. Horizontal lines reflect sinking adaptive ideal-free landscapes, where habitat-selection behaviour has equalized fitness amongst all individuals. Panels on the right illustrate adaptive evolution along the collapsed ideal-free fitness sets. Scenarios from top to bottom represent, respectively, a sinking rigid adaptive landscape for two similar habitats with a concave fitness set, a sinking flexible adaptive landscape for two similar habitats in which the fitness maximum at low density is much greater in one habitat than in the other, and a sinking rigid adaptive landscape for two dissimilar habitats with a convex fitness set. Fitness differences among individuals will be retained at low densities when only a single habitat is occupied (middle scenario) unless an IFD also equalizes fitness in smaller-scale patches within the habitat.

2. Undermatching can also emerge from 'centrally planned' kin systems (such as may occur in many social, colonial, and modular organisms), where inclusive fitness is maximized by underexploiting rich patches while overexploiting poorer ones (Brown 1998, Morris *et al.* 2001). These 'inclusive fitness distributions' will be evolutionarily stable whenever the inclusive benefit achieved by relatively few, highly-efficient foragers in rich patches exceeds that obtained by relatively more, but less-efficient individuals exploiting poor patches.

3. Species with constrained dispersal, such as those with life stages that depend on physical transport (e.g. wind- or vector-dispersed micro-organisms, plants, and invertebrates; aquatic and marine larvae) may often overpopulate suboptimal habitats.

4. Individuals may vary in their competitive effect. Parker and Sutherland (1986) developed a well-known solution to this problem by imagining an IFD that equalized the total competitive effect (e.g. resource consumption) across habitats rather than just the density of individuals. Under this model, some individuals attain higher fitness than do others. Differences in fitness amongst individuals opens the door for adaptation.

5. The door will be opened wide when individuals with different fitness expectations are more likely to mate with one another than with other individuals in the population. Assortative mating associated with habitat choice is increasingly recognized as a mechanism that repels populations away from the evolutionary nodes represented by fitness minima (Rosenzweig 1995, Kawecki 2004).

6. A sixth way that an ideal-free fitness stalemate can be broken requires fluctuating populations and a habitat (Habitat 2 in our second version) that yields higher density-independent fitness than does the other (Habitat 1). Individuals obeying an IFD will occupy only the habitat with high fitness at low population size. In this instance the adaptive function becomes simply

$$A = w_2$$

because only a single habitat is occupied ($q^* = 1; p^* = 0$). In our example, the horizontal adaptive function favours the Habitat 2 specialist, and since individuals are capable of habitat selection, the fitness set and adaptive landscape are flexible. Fitness will decline with density only in Habitat 2 at low population sizes because it is the only occupied habitat. When population size becomes large enough such that an additional habitat is occupied, the fitness set snaps immediately to a slope of unity. Adaptation will switch from the Habitat-2 specialist to the fitness stalemate and, at larger population sizes, all individuals will have equal fitness expectations regardless of their trait value.

'The ability of ideal habitat selection to equalize fitness among phenotypes depends on the frequency of phenotypes exploiting each habitat'

In order to appreciate these effects it is important to differentiate between the 'behavioural fitness set' that emerges from ideal-free habitat selection (slope of unity) and that dictated by the trait distribution among phenotypes (which reflects the expectations of fitness in each habitat as determined by the range of phenotypes available for adaptation). The distribution of trait values determines the shape of the fitness set in the absence of habitat selection. Phenotypes thus vary in the trade-off of fitness in one habitat with that in another. The mean fitness of each phenotype depends on the mix of habitats in the environment. Under ideal habitat selection there is, for each population size, an optimal distribution of individuals among habitats. This distribution will determine, for each phenotype, the value of the adaptive function. If all phenotypes can allocate their exposure to habitats such that fitness is equal in both, there will be no habitat-determined adaptation of one phenotype over another (the fitness set for all phenotypes has slope unity). But if some phenotypes are incapable of matching habitat use with fitness (as might occur if their choices are compromised by the distributions of others), then phenotypes will vary in fitness and adaptation will favour those with maximum fitness. In the game of life, plastic behaviour can, but does not necessarily, trump differences that exist in other traits.

How does environmental grain influence the effect of habitat selection? The adaptive function in a coarse-grained environment is given by the hyperbola-like function (e.g. Equation 3.5)

$$log\ A = p^*(log\ w_1) + q^*(log\ w_2)$$

Yet if we assume an ideal-free distribution where both habitats are occupied at all densities, there is no fitness advantage to be gained by occupying one habitat over the other, and the adaptive function, for any given level of fitness, is a constant. Once again, we learn that whenever both habitats are occupied at an IFD all individuals receive equal payoffs, which would appear to stymie further evolution of habitat preference.

The implication of zero fitness advantage among individuals with different fitness-enhancing traits is so counterintuitive that we need to ask whether the ideal-free solution is evolutionarily stable (Box 5.1). We have already noted, for example, that if some individuals possess traits that allow them to inhibit habitat occupation by others, the fitness stalemate can be broken.[20] But there may be other solutions.

'Habitat preference can continue to evolve if different phenotypes occupy habitats in different frequencies'

---

[20] The evolution of a dominance distribution assumes that dominant individuals gain more fitness by excluding subordinates than they lose in aggressive encounters.

Our models of the IFD assume that all phenotypes occupy habitat with equal frequency. This also assumes, implicitly, that the functions associated with habitat selection are independent of phenotype. Imagine that an initially rare mutant phenotype trades lower performance of a function in one habitat for a higher performance in the other. The mutant would have a different habitat preference than its ancestors, and a population of such mutants would occupy the two habitats in different frequencies than the ancestral population. Whether such a mutant can invade depends on whether the IFD population lies at a behavioural, ecological, or evolutionary equilibrium (see Chapter 6).

For the moment, let us assume that the mutant achieves higher fitness at a given density than does the average resident at the behavioural IFD equilibrium. The mutant gains more fitness by its altered preference toward habitat i than it loses by less performance on habitat j. Will it invade? A mutant invading a population, in which the IFD lies distant to the equal trade-offs in performance, will alter the frequency of habitat occupation. By doing so, the mutant will increase the mean fitness in the population. The University of Florida's brilliant Robert Holt demonstrated, given a range of phenotypes, that the strategy of habitat selection will evolve until the trade-off in fitness is equal in the different habitats (Holt 2003). Our conclusion, that the IFD limits further habitat specialization, thus assumes implicitly that the population has attained the evolutionarily stable habitat distribution.

> *'When habitat selection is without cost, there is no strategic limit to habitat specialization'*

In order to better understand specialization we reassess the conditions that lead to an IFD. Look again at any of the fitness functions in Figs 5.1–5.4. Recall our assumption that individuals can meet all of their life requirements in either habitat. Under these conditions, the maximum fitness potential of any jack-of-all-trades generalist can never be greater than that of the specialist.[21] So if there is no cost to occupying only a single habitat, the generalist strategy can never yield more fitness than the specialist and will almost always yield less. This important observation tells us that there is no strategic limit to habitat specialization. Or, stated another way, the number of habitats is limited only by the number of species. In general, this prediction holds true. No species occupies all habitats, and all species are more abundant in some habitats than they are in others. Yet it is also true that many species occupy a variety of different habitats, and in a way that is consistent with an IFD.[22]

---

[21] The jack-of-all-trades generalist is the one with equal fitness in both habitats. Rosenzweig (1987) introduced the acronym JOAT to assess adaptive evolution of habitat generalists versus specialists.

[22] Interested readers can begin to gain an appreciation for this huge literature from Rosenzweig (1991), Kacelnik *et al.* (1992), Kennedy and Gray (1993), Morris (1994, 2003a,b), and Doncaster (2000).

'Ideal habitat selection emerges from the mechanics, function, structure, scale, and dynamics of adaptation'

Clearly, then, there are costs to habitat selection that inhibit the evolution of extreme specialists. The costs must necessarily be rooted in the mechanics, function, structure, scale, and dynamics of evolution. Thus, for example, we can imagine that specialist strategies are limited by genetic and developmental mechanisms that maintain a variety of different trait values in any single population. Trade-offs among traits and functions, as well as a variety of constraints, can reduce the fitness potential of specialists. Different habitats may also represent trade-offs among essential resources or functions such that individuals cannot persist by living in only one habitat. And when specialists can live in a single habitat, trade-offs in function among habitats (such as between food and safety) may allow a generalist using many habitats to attain higher fitness than the specialist using only a subset of those available. Specialist strategies are not available when the patch structure of the environment is so fine that individuals cannot persist within a single habitat patch. Finally, specialist strategies can also be limited by ecological dynamics that cap the potential population size of specialists or cause its dynamics to fluctuate toward low numbers.

'The adaptive landscape reveals the form, speed, and direction of adaptation'

Before we leave our discussion of habitat selection and its influence on specialization, look again at Figs B5.1.1 and B5.1.2 (in Box 5.1). There are two general patterns and one 'exception':

1. Both landscapes sink as population size increases (density-dependence).
2. Both landscapes change shape and become more rounded at high density.
3. The strategy set depicted in Fig. B5.1.1 is 'fixed' (a single strategy of habitat selection) whereas that in Fig. B5.1.2 is variable (different strategies of habitat selection at different population sizes;[23] the strategy maximizing fitness (frequency of individuals occupying Habitat 2) varies with population size.

The two landscapes have important lessons for density-dependent evolution. The shape of the landscape reveals whether or not adaptation is directional or stabilizing. Let us concentrate on the contorted landscape depicted in Fig. B5.1.2. The best strategy at low density (occupy only Habitat 2) shifts with increasing population size. Adaptation, in this instance, is directional, but the 'direction' varies with density. The strategy of habitat occupation shifts quickly across a rather narrow range of population densities. But note that the landscape shifts shape from being tilted at low density to rounded

---

[23] The suite of different strategies (proportional use of habitat) represents the strategy set of ideal habitat selection. This set is given by the system's habitat isodar (Morris 1988), which also can be thought of as the reaction norm of habitat selection.

Box 5.1. Is the ideal-free distribution evolutionarily stable?

We can begin to explore the stability of an IFD by drawing adaptive landscapes for habitat selection. To do this, we must first know the relationship between fitness and density in alternative habitats. To keep our example simple we imagine that this relationship is linear. The linearity assumption also means that the density-dependent effect on fitness is independent of other traits but not necessarily the frequency of alternative habitat-selecting strategies. Each individual in the population has an equivalent negative effect on fitness. Next, we imagine that this competitive effect differs among habitats and, again to keep our example simple, that individuals choose between only two habitats. The model assumes that habitat choice and movement between habitats does not reduce fitness (cost-free habitat selection). We contrast two scenarios.

In the first scenario, maximum fitness is identical in each habitat (Fig. B5.1.1). The top panel illustrates our assumptions. Fitness diverges with increased population size. Individuals can achieve an IFD (each individual has the same expectation of fitness) at different population sizes by moving from one habitat to another until fitness is equalized. The proportion of individuals living in each habitat will be constant at the IFD because the two lines diverge linearly from a fixed point. This proportion is illustrated in the density-dependent adaptive landscape in the bottom panel (each strategy of habitat occupation is evaluated independently; there is no frequency-dependence). This adaptive landscape is a graph of the mean fitness emerging from all possible combinations of densities at different population sizes. As demonstrated by Robert Holt's model in the main text, different phenotypes with different fitness functions would possess slightly different adaptive landscapes. The IFD lies along the contour of maximum fitness. No other behavioural habitat-selection strategy achieves higher fitness. The IFD of the optimum phenotype, given these assumptions, is evolutionarily stable.[24]

In the second scenario we imagine that fitness at low density is greater in Habitat 2 than it is in Habitat 1 (Fig. B5.1.2). Again, we let individuals move from one habitat to the other to equalize fitness at different population sizes. The fitness functions diverge from different points, so the ideal-free proportion living in each habitat changes with population size. When we overlay these densities onto the adaptive landscape, we observe that they do not lie along the contour of maximum fitness.[25] Thus, alternative strategies of habitat selection may invade our ideal-free system. The fitness difference between the maximum achievable and that produced by

continues

---

[24] A graph of the densities corresponding to the ideal distribution lying on the surface of the adaptive landscape represents the system's 'habitat isodar' (Morris 1988), the densities corresponding to an equal expectation of fitness in each habitat.

[25] It is easy to confirm the maximum fitness contour on the adaptive landscape. Draw a line parallel to the x,y-plane (or use a ruler) and move it across the landscape so that it lies tangential to the highest fitness value at different population sizes. These points should lie along the bold fitness contour.

Box 5.1. (Continued)

ideal-free habitat selection is greater at intermediate densities than it is when density is low or high. Thus, to determine the strategy that maximizes fitness, we would also need to know the fitness costs of each strategy relative to those of ideal-free habitat selection, and how those costs vary with density.

Some readers may wonder why we do not include an explicit analysis of convergence and invasion stability. There are two reasons. First, much of this analysis is implicit in the density dependence of fitness sets. Second, we assume that the relationship between fitness and density in each habitat is fixed. An alternative strategy, with different density-dependent fitness functions, or one in which fitness depends on the frequency of alternative strategies, may indeed be able to invade. This new strategy would yield a different adaptive landscape. But our general conclusions regarding the stability of an IFD would still apply.

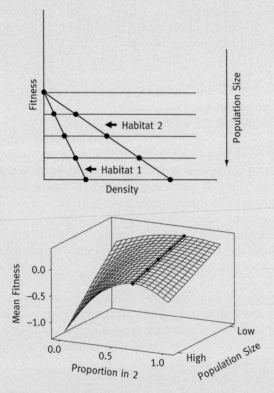

Figure B5.1.1. An illustration of linear fitness functions and the resulting adaptive landscape of habitat selection when maximum fitness is the same in two different habitats. An IFD of individuals at different population sizes is represented by the intersections of horizontal lines with the negatively sloped fitness functions (top panel; fitness is equal in each habitat but density differs). This distribution is then plotted on the adaptive landscape (bottom panel) where we graph mean fitness for all possible density combinations in the two habitats (different frequencies). Note that the IFD follows the contour of maximum fitness (bold line). Ideal-free habitat selection is evolutionarily stable. After Morris (2003a).

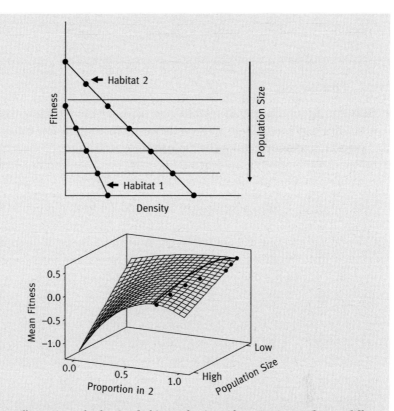

Figure B5.1.2. An illustration of adaptive habitat selection when maximum fitness differs between two habitats. The IFD of individuals at different population sizes (intersections of horizontal lines of equal fitness with the negatively sloped fitness functions; top panel) is plotted on the adaptive landscape of habitat selection (bottom panel). Note that the IFD (dots) does not lie along the contour of maximum fitness (bold line), and is then subject to invasion by alternative strategies that yield a reduced frequency in the preferred habitat. Whether or not invasion will actually occur requires a proper eco-evolutionary or adaptive-dynamics analysis. After Morris (2003a).

at high density. Thus although the directional selection exists across all population densities (the proportional occupation of Habitat 2 declines), stabilizing selection becomes ever more important as densities increase.

The landscape in both Figs B5.1.1 and B5.1.2 is flatter at low density than it is at high density and, since the rate of adaptation is directly proportional to the slope of the selection gradient, adaptation toward the best strategy of habitat selection will be much slower at low than at high density. When density is low, individuals can live in either habitat and achieve similar fitness. But when density is high, a strategy that allocates individuals away from the peak of the landscape will suffer from low fitness.

*'Density-dependent habitat selection can purge populations
of accumulated mutation load'* [26]

Populations at low density are particularly prone to accumulating non-adaptive strategies of habitat use:

1. Selection at low density is relaxed (the landscape is relatively flat), and multiple strategies may accumulate because they exhibit relatively low fitness disadvantage.
2. Non-adaptive strategies may become fixed by drift alone.

At high density, however, the effect of drift is reduced, and non-adaptive strategies will be removed by steep selection gradients. The lesson extends well beyond theories of habitat selection. Fitness advantage in any particular habitat is bound to be influenced by many, if not most, genes.[27] So the minor fitness disadvantages among habitats at low density favour accumulation of numerous mutations. Some of these may be removed by genetic drift, but drift can similarly eliminate favourable alleles and gene combinations that reduce a population's adaptedness. If aptitude for living in and using habitat is influenced by numerous genes, then many of those mutations will be revealed at higher densities, where they can be purged by intense stabilizing adaptation.

These conclusions depend on evolutionary stability and underlying structure. Mutants with different trait values than their ancestors are likely to occupy a different adaptive landscape of habitat selection. If the mutation is of small effect, the mutant and parental landscapes will be similar and mutants will be exposed to cleansing selection at high density. If the mutation is of large effect, however, density-dependence may not mirror that of ancestors, and selection against mutants at any given density could be either relaxed or enhanced relative to wild-type individuals.

The interaction between habitat selection, the frequency of habitats, and grain size is linked rather tightly to a population's genetic structure.[28] Adaptive movement of individuals along fitness gradients will tend to homogenize otherwise structured populations. The effectiveness of habitat selection to stir the genetic pot will depend on the scale and distribution of habitats. One interesting outcome bears on the question of habitat selection's influence in purging mutation load. Structured populations with

[26] 'Mutation load' is the reduction in selective value for a population compared to what the population would possess if all individuals had the most favoured genotype (no mutations).

[27] Florida State University's David Houle (1991) has argued rather convincingly that 'every locus in the genome must be capable of affecting fitness, if only by its inactivation' (p. 641). This view may appear as stark contrast with loss-of-function gene deletions in yeast that have little effect on normal growth (Bell 2010), but single-gene deletions may not be an effective way to assess epistatic effects.

[28] A structured population is one in which allele frequencies vary from one group of individuals, or one part of a species' distribution, to another. Structure is frequently estimated by the degree of genetic differentiation (level of heterozygosity of neutral alleles) among subpopulations compared to the total population (F_{ST}). A high value of F_{ST} implies a more genetically subdivided population than does a low value. The calculation of F_{ST} may require weighting by population size. Whitlock (2002) provides a thoughtful example.

concomitantly higher levels of inbreeding will tend to produce higher frequencies of homozygotes possessing deleterious mutations and thus expose them to adaptive removal. Whitlock (2002) demonstrated that this effect is most pronounced under so-called hard selection, where the regulation of density occurs at the scale of the 'global population'. One way to think of hard selection is to imagine that habitats produce variable numbers of individuals (and phenotypes) who then compete for future opportunities with all individuals from all habitats combined (as might occur in some migratory species or when individuals raised in a mixture of different habitats join together to form mating aggregations). Soft selection occurs when adaptation takes place within local habitats (and, more generally, demes), and where the contribution of individuals from each deme has no effect on the regulation of the population as a whole.[29] Thus, under soft selection, each phenotype competes only with other members in its deme (or habitat). Deleterious mutants can cumulate and persist because they are tested only against other similar individuals rather than being exposed to the full range of phenotypes existing in different demes (and habitats).

The scaling of habitat selection thus influences local adaptation and mutation load in three inter-correlated ways. Habitat selection implies (1) spatially-structured small 'populations' that (2) tend to differentiate and thus increase the frequency of homozygotes. The genetic differentiation, and its concomitant mutation load, will be maintained with (3) relatively low rates of inter-habitat migration. But if gene flow among habitats is high, then phenotypes and strategies will be more exposed to global adaptation, which purges deleterious mutants.

' The effectiveness of habitat selection to purge mutation load depends on population dynamics, gene flow, the form of adaptation, and demography'

The consequences of population subdivision thus depend on the dynamics of populations, the timing of population regulation, and the degree to which individuals remain in single habitats or move among them. If population dynamics and dispersal are such that gene flow among habitats is relatively low, the mean genetic quality and absolute fitness of the population will be much lower than it would be with higher rates of dispersal. A model developed by the University of Toronto's Aneil Agrawal (2010) shows that this effect also depends on demography. Agrawal begins by assuming a direct correspondence between total resource consumption by a deme and the production of offspring by its members. He then imagines that juvenile mortality decreases the numbers of both mutants and wild-type individuals. Mortality on young individuals reduces the competitive effect that their phenotype could have on other individuals, if they had survived. If mutants tend to waste less resources by dying (e.g. perish earlier than their similarly ill-fated wild-type cousins), then the average competitive effects of

---

[29] The terms 'hard' and 'soft' selection have been used in many different contexts. Readers will find a lucid account of much of this otherwise confusing literature in an elegant article by Ravigné *et al.* (2004).

mutants will be less than for wild-type individuals. Demes with many mutants will waste fewer resources and possess higher mean fitness (and a greater number of adults) than will demes with fewer mutants. This rather peculiar form of 'supersoft' selection thus acts to reduce the mean genetic quality of the global population.

'Gene flow among habitats, and thus the "hardness" of adaptation, depends on the relationships between fitness and density'

Agrawal's model is still rather abstract ecologically. The model imagines genetically structured populations but does not specify the scaling conditions that might lead to deme formation and subsequent hard-to-soft selection. Theories of habitat selection can help to provide the missing ecological context. Look again at the diverging linear fitness functions and adaptive landscape in Fig. B5.1.1. The evolutionarily stable strategy of habitat selection is traced by the bold straight line lying on top of the landscape. The proportion of individuals living within each habitat is constant at all population sizes. If we assume initial conditions of equal fitness and synchronous growth in both habitats, the densities in each habitat will increase in parallel, and the relative contributions of each habitat to the global population will be constant. If the dynamics are synchronized, the frequencies of individuals in the two habitats will remain constant, dispersal will be minimal, and adaptation will occur at the level of a single habitat (selection is mostly soft). Now look at the fitness functions in Fig. B5.1.2. Although they also diverge, the maximum fitness at low density is greater in Habitat 2 than it is in Habitat 1. The trace of the best strategies of habitat selection on the adaptive landscape is curved. The optimum frequency of individuals living in each habitat changes with density, as does the contribution of individuals to the global population. The expectation of equal fitness in each habitat can thus be maintained only by dispersal that exposes phenotypes to alternative habitats (relatively hard selection). Although theories of habitat selection thus provide insights into a population's genetic and spatial structure, detailed assessment of hard versus soft selection must also account for other sources of potential mixing, as may occur through feeding or mating aggregations, habitat-independent dispersal, and seasonal migration.

'The evolution of habitat specialists versus generalists depends on fitness trade-offs and the frequency of habitats'

An underappreciated message from theories of habitat selection is that the frequency of individuals living in different habitats varies with the abundance of those habitats. Imagine, for example, a species specialized on Habitat 2 (e.g. Fig. B5.1.1). The peak of its adaptive landscape represents its best strategy of habitat selection and dictates the density of individuals living in the two habitats. In this particular case, three individuals occupy a unit area of Habitat 2 for every single individual occupying an equal area in Habitat 1. If we assume that individuals can indeed occupy all areas of both habitats while incurring minimal cost, then the majority of individuals will live in Habitat 1 whenever it is more than three times as abundant as Habitat 2. Let us now imagine a mutant strategy that increases the efficiency of garnering resources in Habitat 1, at an equal expense of lowering efficiency in Habitat 2 (a 1:1 trade-off). If we assume that Habitat 1 is indeed more than three times as abundant as Habitat 2, then mean fitness will increase and the strategy has a reasonable chance of successful invasion. If the mutant strategy acts only to modify the effect of density on fitness (increases carrying capacity in Habitat 1, reduces carrying capacity in Habitat 2), then the population will become more generalized in habitat use. If the mutation also increases fitness at low density, then the population will begin to evolve specialization on Habitat 1. At low density it should occupy only that habitat (fitness intercept greater than for Habitat 2), but then switch its preference to Habitat 2 at high density (as long as the carrying capacity of Habitat 2 exceeds that in Habitat 1—the fitness functions cross over one another). An alternative mutation that improves fitness in Habitat 2 will, under these assumptions, yield lower mean fitness. Increased specialization toward Habitat 2 would increase mean fitness in a different population, however, if Habitat 1 was less than three times as abundant as Habitat 2.

More generally, in a population exploiting only habitats i and j, a mutant strategy m will be capable of successful invasion whenever

$$p^* w_{i,m} > q^* w_{j,m}$$

for fine-grained species and

$$p^* (log\ w_{i,m}) > q^* (log\ w_{j,m})$$

for coarse-grained species (this derivation originates from Chapter 3, Equation 3.5).[30] Although these simple inequalities are general, we remind readers that the strategy may often vary with density (e.g. Fig. B5.1.2). The critical message is that the scales in space and time at which the population perceives and exploits its environments, as well as the density of the population, interact with the frequency of environments to dictate future evolution. Such knowledge should be incredibly important to managers and conservationists who wish to predict the long-term consequences of their management and conservation practices.

Holt (2003) and Hebrew University's Dan Cohen (2006) have made similar pleas. Cohen notes that the selection operating on any locus, trait, or strategy in a mixed population depends on its contribution to the population's mean fitness (Fig. 5.5). This rather simple observation has numerous profound effects. A trait value that is highly adaptive in a small subset of habitats or conditions, but yields moderate increments to

---

[30] Whether the strategy actually invades or not would require a full analysis of the evolutionary and population dynamics (see Chapter 6).

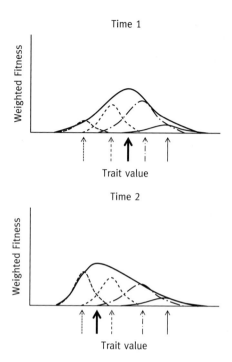

Figure 5.5. Comparison between the contributions to fitness of local trait distributions associated with a variety of habitats (light curves), their local optima (small arrows), and the mixed population's fitness (bold curve) and optimal trait value (large arrow). The optimal value may not correspond to that of any single habitat. A change in the frequency of habitats or their quality relative to individuals with different trait values can cause a shift in the optimal value for the population at large. After Cohen (2006).

fitness elsewhere, will have little chance of increasing in frequency. A study taking place in the set of conditions where the trait value yields high fitness might wrongly conclude that the value is adaptive. If those conditions are widespread, however, then the value of the trait will increase, even if it has lower fitness than other values elsewhere. But if the population occupies many habitats or opportunities, then it is unlikely that any single trait value will yield high fitness in all of them. Thus, the optimal trait value for the population may often never be optimal in a single habitat or set of conditions.

Cohen's model has numerous implications for our understanding of species invasions, and the effects of climate and habitat change on evolution. An invading species' likelihood of success depends on how fitness is weighted for the population as a whole. Similarly, a change in area or quality of a habitat alters its contribution to the population's mean fitness (Fig. 5.5). Such changes could either shift the mean phenotype or, if fitness depression is large enough, force the species to extinction even though there are habitats where it appears to be doing well.

It is a mistake, however, to think of scale only in the context of space and time. We must also contemplate how adaptation operates across organizational scales, and how it resolves the inevitable conflicts of interest that exist among genes, traits, functions, individuals, and groups.

Multi-level adaptation

*'Adaptation occurs at any level of organization where heritable
variation influences the struggle for existence'*

Most treatments of adaptation from a 'gene's perspective' assume that traits are phenotypes measured on individuals, that their function benefits only the individual in which they occur (or close relatives), and that individuals with different trait values compete in such a way that the function confers fitness. What is wrong with this view?

We paraphrase an answer by Texas Tech University's Sean Rice (2004). Imagine a population of haploid individuals composed of siblings possessing alternative alleles that make them either cooperate (P) or be selfish (S).[31] The degree of relatedness (r, the proportion of the genome shared through common descent) between siblings is 0.5. Each individual produces $\lambda = 1$ offspring if it has no interaction with other individuals in the population. Each cooperating individual interacts with each of its siblings. When it does so, it provides a benefit ($B = 1$; its sibling produces an additional offspring) but at a cost to itself ($C = 0.25$; each cooperating individual in this model is an altruist because the fitness benefit it extends to others reduces its own individual fitness). Selfish individuals do not reciprocate. The P allele will thus increase in abundance because the benefit to relatives (rB) is greater (twice in our example) than the cost (C). Absolute fitness of the genes present in cooperating individuals, weighted by the benefit received by relatives, is greater than the fitness that they would receive without interacting.

But does this mean that cooperating individuals will increase in frequency? Imagine that the population is composed of seven individuals, four of which are P (the other three must be S). Since each cooperator interacts with each of its siblings, its total cost is $0.25 \times 6 = 1.5$, whereas it receives a total of three more offspring from the interactions with each successive cooperating sibling. Thus, as we noted above, the total number of individuals with the P allele in the next generation has increased from four to ten. But each selfish individual has also reaped the benefit from each cooperating sibling at no cost whatsoever (each produces five selfish offspring; fifteen in total). In actual fact, then, the frequency of the P allele has actually decreased substantially from $4/7$ ($\simeq 0.57$) to $10/25$ ($= 0.4$). If we now assume that the population is regulated such that all offspring face an equal probability of juvenile mortality, the selfish allele will eventually displace the cooperative one. How then do cooperative alleles increase in frequency? Is cooperation adaptive?

---

[31] The assumption of haploid genetics simplifies the problem without altering its conceptual value.

> *'Adaptation within groups favours selfishness; adaptation among groups favours cooperation'*

The cooperation/conflict riddle is solved by invoking David Sloan Wilson's (1975) concept of 'trait groups'.[32] We illustrate the concept by imagining that instead of one group of interacting individuals, there are i such groups, each with a different frequency of the cooperator allele ($0 \leq p_i \leq 1$). Groups remain distinct while reproducing, then all offspring join a common pool before forming new groups. Each cooperating individual in group i will thus produce $\lambda - C(N-1) + (Bp_i)(N-1)$ descendants bearing the P allele each generation, whereas selfish individuals in the same group produce $\lambda + (Bp_i)N$ descendants with the S allele. Let us imagine, for example, that in addition to our trait-group family of seven siblings with four being cooperators, the deme includes another trait-group family of seven siblings, all of whom are selfish (that thus produce a total of $\lambda N = 7$ offspring). Since all offspring join the same pool of descendants, the total proportion of cooperating alleles has indeed increased (from $4/14 \simeq 0.29$ to $10/32 \simeq 0.31$). If all offspring are again faced with equal probabilities of juvenile mortality, then the cooperator allele will increase in frequency because the trait group with cooperators produced more descendants than did the trait group composed of only selfish individuals. Adaptation within a group containing cooperators favours selfish individuals whereas adaptation occurring among groups favours cooperators.

> *'Multi-level adaptation requires multiple trait groups'*

When we assess adaptation, we are particularly interested in whether a trait can increase when rare (see Chapter 6). If we thus assume that the cooperation allele is initially rare, then most selfish genotypes will exist in groups with only selfish individuals (fitness $\simeq \lambda$). If all groups are of size N, then cooperation will increase in frequency only if $\{\lambda - C(N-1) + (Bp_i)(N-1)\} > \lambda$, that is, if $Bp_i > C$. As Rice (2004) notes, this general approximation for the adaptive evolution of altruism occurs not through kin selection acting on related individuals, but instead because there is large variation amongst groups in the proportion of cooperative alleles. Adaptation among groups that favour cooperation occurs at a different level than does adaptation within (multi-level adaptation).

One effective way to do the accounting of multi-level adaptation is through Price's equation (see Chapter 2)

$$\Delta \bar{z}_g = (\mathrm{cov}[w_g, z_g]) + E[w_g \bar{\delta}_g]$$

---

[32] A trait group is a small group of 'interacting' individuals that share a particular trait value. Another useful definition is that such a group would share a strategy (see Chapter 6).

where the subscripts remind us that we are evaluating the change in mean phenotype of the group from one generation to the next. The first right-hand term represents the covariance between fitness and the value of the trait in the group. The final term includes all changes in the value of the group phenotype caused by all remaining processes, including countervailing adaptation for individual advantage within groups (Rice 2004). As we just learned, adaptation for individual advantage occurs through the covariance between the fitness of individuals and the value of the trait within groups. Thus adaptation of the trait occurs at different levels because there is a struggle for existence taking place at each level (each contributes to the deme in our example), and the struggle is influenced by the heritability of the trait at each successive level.

'Adaptation at one level is often opposed by adaptation at a lower level'

David Sloan Wilson and Harvard's Edward O. Wilson (2008) liken the hierarchical structure of adaptation to Russian matryshoka dolls. Each level of adaptation is nested inside a higher one. The hierarchical structure yields the important principle that adaptation at any level requires a process of natural selection at that level and tends to be undermined by natural selection acting at lower levels (Wilson and Wilson 2007). But Wilson and Wilson (2007) go further. They argue that higher-level adaptation must be evaluated case by case. Is this necessarily true? Might it instead be possible to use the 'map of evolution' to build a classification system for multi-level selection?

'Adaptation is invisible to group structure unless the functions of traits depend on density or frequency'

The answer depends on the function and structure of the trait. Whenever a trait's function is independent of density and the frequency of other trait values, the problem of adaptation collapses to an optimization problem. Within the constraints of its history and the trade-offs associated with its mechanics and structure, optimization determines the trait value (or values) that maximizes fitness.

We return to Fig. 5.1 to illustrate our point. Each panel represents a different trade-off reflected in the negatively sloped boundary of its fitness set. The trait's function and the map of its value onto fitness are independent of the density of similar individuals as well as the density and frequency of individuals with other trait values. The optimum phenotype(s) maximizes the environment's adaptive function. The independence of trait values dictates that their fitness contribution is independent of the composition of groups. There is no conflict between adaptation within and between groups.

Let us now revisit Fig. 5.2. The optimum trait value depends on density. If different groups exist at different densities, then the within-group optima will vary and the pattern of adaptation will depend on the frequency of groups (in Chapter 6 we will learn that this pattern defines the density-dependent strategy set emerging from ecological and evolutionary dynamics).

Fig. 5.3 introduces an additional complexity to the density-dependent adaptation we explored in Fig. 5.2. Note that, as population size varies, the fitness distributions (and the fitness set) change shape. Shape-changing could be caused by habitat differences in the value of fitness-associated trait values (as in the figure), by variation in density-dependence of each trait value's function or by a more complicated interaction with habitat. Regardless, the optimum trait value will vary among groups. The difference from Fig. 5.2 is that group identity no longer depends only on density.

The function and fitness associated with a particular trait value may also depend on (interact with) individuals possessing other trait values within the group. The interactions can be of different kinds and occur at multiple 'levels'. Individuals possessing different trait values may, for example, interact cooperatively, antagonistically, or be engaged in a combined cooperative/antagonistic conflict (as frequently occurs between males and females in sexual reproduction). The fitness of those synergies and antagonisms is likely to depend on the frequency of each type both within and among groups.

There is, moreover, a fifth and very important possibility. The frequency of the habitats (and more generally the environment) may change and thereby alter the slope (or shape) of the adaptive function. Even greater complexity emerges if the function of the trait value varies among groups.[33] Each step of our classification thus increases the dimensionality and complexity of multi-level adaptation. Optimization approaches are appropriate at the simplest scale, where trait values are independent of one another, density, and environment. Such traits are likely to be very closely linked with fitness and may possess minimal variation. All other options require careful consideration of, and solutions based on, ecological and evolutionary dynamics (see Chapter 6). The challenges of understanding adaptation increase with each dimension. Each step in the hierarchy reduces our ability to understand evolution from the gene's 'eye view'.

'The dichotomy between micro- and macro-evolution disappears when they are viewed as different levels of adaptation'

Evolutionary biologists typically differentiate the gradual accumulation of favourable trait values (so-called micro-evolution) from the broad taxonomic patterns emerging through speciation in the phylogenetic record (macro-evolution). According to the gradual view, slowly accumulating changes in adaptive trait distributions together with reduced gene flow allow populations, species, and higher taxa to diverge from their ancestors (but also to converge in form and function with other lineages). These gradual effects, over the great expanse of time, produce the illusion in the

---

[33] All of these dimensions plague bureaucratic structures in institutions such as universities.

phylogenetic record of occasionally rapid bursts of evolutionary change, where new forms emerge and radiate. This type of evolution, where rapid divergences interrupt long periods of time over which taxa show little appreciable change in trait values, was termed 'punctuated equilibria' by Niles Eldridge and Steven J. Gould (1972). Their provocative and still-controversial view of macro-evolution argues that speciation takes place mainly at the margins of geographical ranges and tolerances, where small isolated populations evolve toward locally determined maxima in the fitness landscape. With time, these 'peripheral isolates' not only diverge from their ancestors, but also become ever more reproductively isolated from other populations within the species' range. Speciation occurs in isolation. Once formed, the new species may expand its range and overlap with that of its antecedents. Thus when we reconstruct a phylogeny from fossils collected in a single stratigraphic sequence, new species emerge rapidly when they immigrate into the 'fossil record', which is captured at one point in space. The resulting pattern yields a record of stasis, while resident populations remain in equilibrium with their selective environment, punctuated by invading daughter species produced allopatrically over relatively short periods compared to the duration of the parental lineage.

Does punctuated equilibrium in particular, and macroevolution in general, represent a fundamentally different process, pattern, event, or concept than those we model in this book? We think not. We believe that their different scales in space and time fit comfortably within the pillars of evolution. Darwin's worldview of slow-paced micro-evolutionary events operating within and among populations is sufficient explanation for most of the diversity of life. It includes opportunity for local adaptation, inhibited in some cases by gene flow from large populations, and unimpeded in geographical isolates. But there is no denying that species and clades diversify and go extinct, and they tend to do so at somewhat different rates. Descendants inherit their phylogenetic placement from successful ancestors. Can evolution at such a grand scale fit into the concept of multi-level adaptation?

The answer is 'yes', provided that we can identify relevant traits or strategies and assess their function at the proper scale. This is most easily done if we imagine that each species represents a separate strategy, such as mean body size. The functions of an average body size emerge through its allometric scaling. Adaptation at the species scale will occur if the functions, such as average rates of resource procurement, mean reproductive rates, carrying capacity, and so on, act to prolong the species' persistence or increase its probability of fostering a radiating clade (fitness). Adaptation will lead to an optimum solution if the species' strategies acquire fitness independent of the number of other species present and the frequency of their strategies. Dynamic solutions (Chapter 6) will be necessary if the strategies' success depends on the numbers and frequency of other coexisting species.

Prescriptions: avoiding the fallacies of simplicity and complexity

We can begin to see the importance of an expanded view of evolution in the impending extinctions of the world's fish stocks.[34] The collapse of global fisheries alerts us to the difficulties associated with the modern synthesis' gene-to-population perspective of evolution. On the surface, that worldview has served us well. Does selective fishing change gene frequencies? Yes. Does harvesting alter the genetic structure of populations? Yes. Do the traits expressed in individuals change with harvest? Yes. Do these changes have a genetic basis? Yes. Can we map the entire genome of harvested species? Yes. Can we map gene function? Yes. Can we trace these effects onto morphometric and other traits of individuals? In some cases, yes. Can we use the modern synthesis to predict evolutionary change? Yes. But can we use its lock-step connection with genetics to assess the ecological and evolutionary dynamics of those changes? No. The modern synthesis lacks integration with ecological dynamics.

Some are likely to argue that the integration simply takes time. Rapid advances in the sciences of genetics and development will add flesh to the bones of the structure matrix and allow us to understand the dynamics of evolution from a gene→trait-centred perspective. Despite our substantial advances in understanding of the mechanics of evolution and our increasing ability to link genetics with function, we are still a very long way from a full integration with ecological dynamics.

'Scale and structure limit our ability to draw the gene→trait→function→fitness map'

The modern synthesis is able to explore evolution within and among populations not because it conquers issues of scale, but because it ignores them. The genetic models of Fisher, Wright, Haldane, Kimura, and others explored changes in allelic frequencies within and among populations, but the units of adaptation, drift, and mutation were centred on genes. So too is the variance-covariance matrix of population and quantitative genetics. In this worldview, the life, death, and dispersal of individuals is subsumed in models focused on genetics.

The Leslie/Lefkovitch and community matrices of ecology lie at the opposite end of the spectrum.[35] Individuals are lumped by age or state-dependent classes and are used to project future population sizes. Ecological stability is assessed by projecting the joint dynamics of interacting species. There is little opportunity in this worldview to invoke adaptation.

---

[34] Evidence, consequences, and prospects of this international problem can be found in a series of papers by Dalhousie University's Ransom Myers and Boris Worm (e.g. Myers and Worm 2003, 2005, Worm *et al.* 2006, 2009).

[35] Much of this material is covered in Caswell (2001).

But we know, as did Darwin, Wallace, and countless other naturalists, that the temporal, spatial, and organizational scales of ecology and evolution overlap. Gene and trait frequencies vary on the same scales as do the dynamics of populations. So our challenge is to develop a worldview that identifies the best way to either integrate, or identify the limits of, genetic, developmental, and ecological approaches to understanding evolution.

In many respects, each of these disciplines fits nicely into the mechanics (genetics), dynamics (ecology), or structure (development) of evolutionary analysis. And although subdisciplines of ecological genetics, 'evo-devo' and 'eco-devo', explicitly conjoin ecology with genetics, genetics with development, and ecology with development, respectively, serious problems emerge when we try to link all three with function and scale. The question that we need to answer is whether this reflects only the current limits of our knowledge or whether there are natural limits to each approach.

The answer lies in the structure matrix. We can link genetics, development, and ecology together in a seamless evolutionary map only when:

1. genes map uniquely or additively onto traits.
2. traits map uniquely or additively onto function.
3. function maps uniquely or additively onto fitness.
4. the mappings are constant among environments.

And what, under these conditions, is likely to emerge? Genes and traits that are so crucial to the functioning of living creatures that they lack variation.

But genes often fail to map cleanly onto traits, many traits have multiple functions, and most traits interact to modify fitness. How much value are we likely to gain by trying to reveal each of those complex mappings? The answer lies in how much value we place on the trait(s). We might pay particular attention to the mappings of traits linked, for example, with disease, disease resistance, antibiotic and pesticide resistance, and the growth and yield characteristics of domestic plants and animals. Some of these traits and trait-mappings will be wonderful and valuable model systems yielding insights into the structure matrix. But we must avoid the trap of thinking that any success we achieve from these maps necessarily represents the best and 'simplest' way to understand evolution.

'Evolution must follow the rules of its mechanics, structure, function, scale, and dynamics'

We must be equally alert to the pitfalls of evolutionary- and adaptive-dynamics approaches to evolutionary understanding. Although we can model the dynamics of evolution independent of genetics and development, the evolutionary process is not simply dynamics. Evolution is constrained to follow the 'rules' of mechanics, structure, function, and scale. But the rules themselves evolve, as do the dynamics of populations and communities.

Complexities in the structure matrix limit our ability to follow evolutionary processes from genes to evolutionarily stable strategies in dynamic ecosystems. But we must be careful that we do not use complexity as a crutch that limits our ability to understand evolution. We need instead to learn how apparent complexity can aid us in identifying the appropriate scales that promote answers to interesting evolutionary questions. While we do that, we must also avoid complexity's evil twin of oversimplifying the mechanics, structure, function, scale, and dynamics of evolution. So we must know precisely the questions for which we seek answers. The most crucial questions can often be revealed by thinking carefully about the assumptions and predictions emerging from a particular worldview.

Evolutionary dynamics imagines, for example, that the traits and strategies of interest can be modelled along a fluid, adaptive landscape that rises and falls with density and frequency dependence. An evolutionary equilibrium for organisms belonging to a single bauplan emerges when the values of the traits or strategies converge on domains of attraction that resist invasion from other options within the bauplan.[36] Stated another way, the evolutionary equilibrium imagines a 'stabilized' adaptive landscape that can still rise and fall, but with fixed peaks and valleys. Evolutionary equilibria can similarly be calculated for members from several bauplans that represent the stabilization of intersecting landscapes. Evolutionary dynamics wiggles out of its rigid steady-state worldview in two different ways. It incorporates the possibility of alternating and displaced strategies in non-equilibrium systems (the adaptive landscape includes travelling and standing waves), and it allows bauplans to evolve.

In order to do its work of predicting the strategic outcomes of adaptation, evolutionary dynamics makes numerous assumptions. Some of these include:

1. eliminating complications associated with genetics and development by assuming that the trait values or strategy sets reflect only those that are evolutionarily feasible.[37]
2. assuming that traits and strategies are perfectly heritable and independent except for indirect interactions that emerge through dynamics.
3. allowing strategies and bauplans to 'mutate'.
4. imagining that all trait values and strategies within the feasible set are available for adaptation.

Each specific model carries additional assumptions related to its structure, parameter set, and parameter values.

It is not the specific assumptions that should concern us, but rather the 'big' questions that emerge from them. Thus we might ask: Is it appropriate to model traits

---

[36] If the domain of attraction corresponds to that of the entire bauplan, there is a single globally stable equilibrium where selection gradients vanish to zero (a singularity).

[37] The concept of evolutionarily feasible strategies is central to Vincent and Brown's (2005) version of strategy dynamics.

conferring fitness advantages independently of one another? To answer the question, we must conduct research at a different scale than the one that gave rise to the assumption.

'Adaptation in Galapagos finches reveals a tight correspondence between trait, function, and directional evolution'

Princeton's Peter and Rosemary Grant studied the 14 finch species inhabiting the Galapagos archipelago for more than three decades. Their research reveals a text-book model of adaptive radiation driven by ecological interactions. The birds radiated from a common ancestor in the relatively short time of a few million years. The avifauna diversified and now exploit a variety of ecological niches closely associated with a wide divergence of beak sizes and forms.

Early work by Grant's team on the island of Daphne Major revealed dramatic directional selection to drought in the medium ground finch *Geospiza fortis* (Boag and Grant 1981, Grant 1986). Plant cover and productivity varies dramatically, as floods and droughts alternate with the El Niño Southern Oscillation (ENSO). Under normal conditions the finches feed preferentially on abundant small seeds. But during an extreme drought in 1977, the birds depleted the supply of small seeds and only the largest birds with deep bills could break open alternative hard fruits. The smaller birds died of starvation and average beak depth increased in the population. Beak depth in these finches is highly heritable, so the increase in beak depth represented an adaptive evolutionary response to changing climate.

Beak size returned slowly to its long-term mean value during subsequent years. The island was then invaded by the large ground finch, *G. magnirostris*, in 1982. The large cactus finch is much more capable at cracking open large seeds and forages on them more efficiently than the largest individuals of *G. fortis*. Its population increased consistently until another severe drought in 2004. The Grants observed a strikingly different pattern of beak divergence to the 2004 drought in *G. fortis* compared to that in 1977 (Grant and Grant 2006). This time, in competition with the expanding population of large cactus finches, the surviving adults were smaller than average. In a period of only 30 years, the beak size of *G. fortis* has resided on three different adaptive peaks. In each instance there is strong support for an ecological cause associated with climate-induced fluctuations in the population and community dynamics of Galapagos finches.

So beak depth in Galapagos finches would seem to be a highly heritable, labile, and independent fitness-related trait consistent with those assumed by analyses of evolutionary dynamics. Thus we might ask: Does the mode of expression of beak depth in Galapagos finches also reveal the independent control apparent in its rapid response to adaptive variation? Harvard's Arhat Abzhanov and colleagues (including the Grants) provide compelling evidence that the genetic and developmental control of beak length in a closely related Galapagos finch does indeed allow independent evolution of beak shape.

Abzhanov's team searched for differential gene expression in developing chicks with a complementary DNA microarray (Abzhanov *et al.* 2006). Genes that yielded increased expression relative to controls (upregulation), as well as those that yielded reduced expression (downregulation) were sequenced. The sequence data documented that a gene coding for a molecule involved in Ca^{++} signalling (called calmodulin, CaM) was expressed at much higher levels in the long-billed cactus finch (*G. scandens*) than in the control. And *in-situ* hybridization experiments on finch embryos confirmed that CaM was expressed in the appropriate embryonic region corresponding to beak elongation. The expression was much greater in the long-billed cactus finch than in the deep-beaked ground finches.

The team has also demonstrated that a different factor (BMP4) is involved in the independent developmental control of beak depth and width in Galapagos finches. Thus the joint expression of the two genes appears to be capable of a full range of beak morphologies from the shallow, narrow, and long beak of *G. scandens* to the robust deep, wide, and short beak of *G. magnirostris*. It is still too early to conclude that there is a simple one-to-one correspondence between gene expression and beak morphology in Galapagos finches. But the Galapagos-finch model does teach us that highly labile continuous traits can be under relatively simple genetic/developmental regulation that promotes rapid adaptive responses in real populations. And where such mechanisms exist, the breeder's equation can actually predict the response to selection with reasonable accuracy (Grant and Grant 2006).

The emerging story on the far more complex development of sexually dimorphic traits in dung beetles and other insects (see Chapter 4) reminds us, however, that adaptation is not perfect, it is simply 'good enough'. The good news, for those who prefer a simplified view of evolution, is that numerous mechanisms may be available to uncouple fitness-related traits from developmental and phylogenetic constraints, and possibly from trade-offs with other traits that compromise adaptive evolution. The bad news, for those who would like to explore all of evolution from a genetic perspective, is that those numerous mechanisms reinforce the importance of addressing different evolutionary questions at different scales of inquiry. Evolution is indeed an ongoing, endless, everlasting process.

Reflection

We now know that at least some ecologically significant traits can be inherited independently through relatively simple gene regulation. We also have evidence that adaptation can decouple previously correlated traits.[38] Evolutionary biologists need to reflect carefully on how that knowledge influences their worldview. We have argued

---

[38] Genetic variation and developmental plasticity may often interact to create novel traits or trait values that can then respond to adaptation. A putative example can be found in the sex reversal of horn development caused by pupal remodeling in *Onthophagus sagittarius* (Moczek 2006b).

that it reinforces the perspective that evolutionary analysis depends on scale. Different scales allow us to ask, and more importantly answer, different types of questions. If constraints and trade-offs among traits can be decoupled, for example, we are justified in using evolutionary dynamics to predict the evolution of traits within their ecological context.

How does scale impact those among us who are interested in revealing the gene→ ecosystem map or, less ambitiously, the genetic basis of 'ecologically-significant traits and responses' (ecological genomics)? We suspect that the scale of evolution will cause both objectives to fall far short of the mark. Attempts to map the functional significance of genes in an ecological context presuppose that we already understand how the trait maps onto fitness, how that map varies in different environments, how it changes with the density and frequency dependence of population and community dynamics, and how fitness is rewarded in different environmental and landscape contexts. We suspect that there will be some rather special cases where single traits can be located on simplified maps from genes→traits→function→fitness→adaptation (as may be the case for beak size in some Galapagos finches). Superb naturalists and evolutionary biologists interested in the rules of adaptation might be drawn to such systems. But it would be risky, if not foolhardy, to imagine that these models provide a general description of adaptive evolution in complex, heterogeneous environments.

The promise of gene→ecosystem maps fails to recognize the dimensionality of evolution. The University of Tennessee's Sergey Gavrilets (e.g. 1997) argues cogently that the dimensionality of genotypes greatly exceeds that of evolutionarily significant fitness differences among organisms. If the number of genotypes is much larger than the number of fitness values, then individuals representing many different gene combinations will accrue similar fitness.[39] It is thus impossible to draw unique maps from most genes to fitness because there will be many redundant mappings among the class of potential genotypes.

Some readers might counter, quite convincingly, that the existence of relatively simple genetic controls on the regulation of ecologically significant traits nevertheless justifies use of quantitative genetic approaches to evolution. And they could point to Peter and Rosemary Grant's success at using the breeder's equation to predict (albeit *post hoc*) the adaptive response by Galapagos finches to reduced resource supply. They would not be deterred that adaptation in many species likely involves multiple traits rather than a single trait such as beak depth. Evolutionary change in multiple traits can be predicted by Lande's G-matrix (Box 3.2) which can be thought of as a multivariate analogue of the breeder's equation (Lande 1979, Lande and Arnold 1983). The G-matrix promises more. If the G-matrix is more or less constant through long periods of time, then the covariance among traits in living species should reflect the matrix of the ancestors. The assumption appears to hold for field crickets, where genetic

---

[39] The number of possible genetic combinations will often exceed population size, which acts to limit redundancy among genotypes.

relationships between five morphological traits were similar among seven different species (Bégin and Roff 2004). Thus, the crickets diverged from one another in accordance with their shared ancestral G-matrix.

The importance of this observation depends on perspective. The worldview represented by Lande's equation tells us that a constant or slowly changing G-matrix constrains subsequent evolution to fit within a pre-specified phylogenetic mould. To those who ascribe to the worldview represented by evolutionary dynamics, a constant G-matrix specifies a single bauplan within which we can search for adaptive evolution.

6

Dynamics

DENSITY- AND FREQUENCY-DEPENDENT CHANGES
IN TRAIT DISTRIBUTIONS

Overview

Evolution is about change. To be fit of form and function requires constant adjustments to the environment. In the previous chapters, we have put much emphasis on the inner workings, the constraints, and the possible outcomes of evolution, and how to identify and understand adaptation at various spatial and temporal scales. Here, we are going to focus explicitly on the change in traits and trait values and the ever-changing environment in which this takes place. Adaptation to a more-or-less constant abiotic circumstance involves moving along a more-or-less constant selection gradient irrespective of the composition of the population, the density of other individuals, or the presence or absence of predators, competitors, or any other important components of the biotic environment. The physical environment is, however, not entirely constant and there is a fair amount of environmental stochasticity, at least at some scale. No organism lives in isolation from other organisms. They all feed on something (and there may be competition for those essential resources) and everybody is food for someone else, at least at some stage of life (or when dead). So, there are interactions among organisms. Those interactions can be weak and temporary, or strong and ever present. In order to understand adaptation, we have to be able to identify those interactions and determine which of them are relevant parts of the evolutionary feedback environment.

Our goal in this chapter is to study the dynamics of single populations, understand their ups and downs, and examine how those changes influence the course of evolution. We are then going to introduce interactions from a few different angles. First, we open the Pandora's box of *G*-function analysis and the world of adaptive dynamics. As a special case of particularly tight interactions and their consequences, we will have a brief look at Red Queen dynamics. Red Queen dynamics teaches how the process of adaptation in two (or more) species unfolds in tandem, sometimes resulting in evolutionary cycles, sometimes in the cessation of the interaction (decoupling).

One aspect of environmental variability is spatial heterogeneity. Ever since Alfred Russel Wallace's, and later, Sewall Wright's days (although almost a century apart), the spatial structure of the environment has caught the attention of evolutionary biologists.

Here, we will bring attention to just a few aspects of this infinitely rich topic. We will highlight the opportunities for evolutionary novelties, but also show how difficult it can be to adapt to novel environments.

Temporal variability imposes other challenges for adaptation. What works in one year does not necessarily work in another, so strategies that work under a large set of conditions, as opposed to conservative ones that attempt to play the same game regardless of circumstances, might be favoured. We pay particular attention to the concept of bet-hedging, the idea that hedging one's bets in the face of an uncertain future could be a successful strategy. Finally, we will have a little closer look at trophic interactions and how different aspects of the interaction between resources and consumers may influence the strength and direction of selection.

Since evolution by its very nature *is* dynamics, this could be the only chapter in this book. We do, however, prefer to see it as one of the pillars because without the others it would not have the power to stand up and help understand the final and most synthesizing chapter on adaptation. But first to the dynamics of populations and communities.

Introduction

Sunshine is a critical resource for plants. Trees striving for access to sunlight that grow tall and shade other individuals monopolize the desired resource. Ideally, an individual tree would not have to grow tall at all but could instead grow laterally and invest all available resources in photosynthesizing tissue instead of supportive tissues like stems, branches and trunks. But all individuals would ideally do the same and the only way to get an upper hand is to grow a little taller than all others and then spread out the canopy. All neighbouring trees are striving to do the same—hence the race for sunlight by growing ever taller. The idyllic scattering of light, swaying of branches, and fluttering of leaves that renews our souls along a forest path conceals an intense and brutal struggle for existence in the economy of nature.

Physical constraints set an upper limit to how tall a plant can grow. The same is true for lateral growth. Supportive tissue is necessary to keep the photosynthesizing parts in a horizontal position facing the sun, and tubing must be maintained to transport water, nutrients, and photosynthates. If there are very few plants around, a tall individual wastes energy and resources that could otherwise be invested in leaves and productive tissues. But plants do not live alone and neighbouring plants compete for the same sunlight with the same constraints. The more dense the population, the more profitable it would be to grow taller instead of wider so as to capture the sunlight and shade the others. Thus, the most successful growth strategy depends on density—the more plants per square unit, the more it pays to grow tall. The growth strategy also depends on frequency. The most profitable growth strategy from the individual plant's perspective will depend on what the other plants are doing. The individuals are playing a game of growth. If the opponent is growing a little taller, so should the other plant; if the opponent is not shunting its resources toward growth, but is instead allocating energy to activities that might enhance reproduction or survival, then the other plant should not waste energy on growth either. This stylized example illustrates a fundamental principle of life:

'Life is a game—strategies for growth, reproduction, and survival are played against each other and the evolutionary solutions are contingent on the frequency and density of alternative strategies'

The plant growth example illustrates another important aspect of the game of life. The growth strategy is, in reality, a complex collection of biological processes and observable properties of a plant that constitutes its phenotype. The phenotype is real in as much that it is what we assign as observable aspects of the organism. The 'strategy' of growth is, however, an abstract construct encompassing all the hidden or obvious information about the organism's genetics, developmental programme, physiology, morphology, or behaviour. Each possible phenotype may be represented as an (evolutionary) strategy but the notion of a strategy is silent about the underlying biology. We use strategies as shortcuts and proxies for candidate solutions to the evolutionary play. It follows that an individual plays many strategies simultaneously—as many as the number of games we can identify or that are relevant to the organism's interactions with its environment.[1] The imaginary plant does not only play the growth game, but also, for example, one or more reproductive, survival, and dispersal games.

We can imagine two ways to play the games of life. Static players use strategies that are genetically and developmentally hardwired. The phenotype is invariant across environments, including the density- and frequency-dependent feedback from other individuals. Dynamic players, on the other hand, possess phenotypically plastic strategies that allow the organism to make, for example, growth patterns, demographic responses, and behaviours contingent on the current environment. So, in a sparse population of plants, more lateral and less vertical growth should be initiated, whereas the reverse should happen in a denser population (or in environments differing in soil or wind conditions, for instance). This plasticity can, of course, be a strategy itself. Plasticity is an adaptive solution to a variable environment.

'Strategies are abstractions that produce measurable phenotypes. Phenotypic plasticity is itself an adaptive strategy that can be measured by its reaction norm'

---

[1] A game is an evolutionary (frequency-dependent) challenge to an organism, for example choosing habitat or corolla shape and colour. One or more strategies can solve that problem.

Growth and decline

The struggle for sunlight (and other essential resources) leads to differential survival and reproduction among individuals in plant populations. Although there are no winners in the games of life (Chapter 1), staying in the game means that survival and reproduction have both been maximized and that, for any individual i, we can evaluate its success by comparing the product $R_x S_x$ with all others. This measure of individual success comes from the Euler–Lotka equation

$$\sum_{x=1}^{k} R_x S_x \lambda^{-x} = 1 \tag{6.1}$$

where x is age (in a population with maximum age k) and λ is population growth rate (Caswell 2001). Equation 6.1 is derived from the assumption of a population with stable age structure where each age class (x) is characterized by its specific survival (S_x) and fecundity (R_x). If there is only one age class (as assumed in our plant example), it is easy to rewrite Equation 6.1 so that $RS = \lambda$, i.e. the product of survival and reproduction equals growth rate. The strategy with the highest growth rate stays in the game. If all individuals in the population play the same strategy (that is, the population is monomorphic) then all plants grow in the same way and receive identical pay-offs in reproduction and survival. Individuals may, however, differ in the ways in which they respond to increased density of other plants (Fig. 6.1). The strategy pay-off depends on

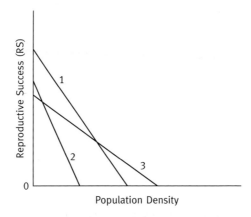

Figure 6.1. Individuals' strategy pay-offs (RS) plotted against density (straight lines). As density increases, the pay-offs go down, but differently for each strategy. The strategy that stays in the game depends on the current density. If the area or volume occupied by the population saturates such that no more individuals can be added to the population, the density does not change any further and the strategy with the highest pay-off (here, the strategy numbered '3') will replace strategies with lower pay-offs (1 and 2).

density. Since all strategies are responding negatively to density, the average pay-off also decreases monotonically, so the average strategy's growth rate is no longer positive.

'The mean absolute fitness in a population is the average per capita growth rate; the absolute fitness of a strategy is its mean growth rate'

If we are interested in the averages only (as we often are when studying population dynamics), we can write the change in the average (*per capita*) population growth rate as a function of population density (*N*) as

$$\frac{1}{N}\frac{dN}{dt} = <f(N)> \qquad (6.2)$$

where the angle brackets indicate average. The *per capita* population growth rate is equivalent to mean absolute fitness, i.e. the average *per capita* growth rate of all strategies in the population.

The *per capita* growth rate of a strategy can now be used for further analyses of strategy dynamics and it can in fact take us all the way to a general model of evolutionary dynamics. But before we embark on that journey we have to work out in somewhat more detail the density- and frequency-dependent influences on births and deaths and how they map onto each strategy's absolute fitness in the population.

Density dependence and demography

Density dependence is a key concept in ecology and evolutionary biology. The idea builds on the fact that we cannot add more than a finite number of individuals into an area or volume, and long before the physical limits are reached the likelihood of giving birth to new individuals or of dying has been affected by the increased number of individuals sharing the environment and its resources. In fact, the classic tenet is resource competition, and here is how it works. First, assume that we can assign mean values to the number of births an individual produces and to the probability of its death. Working only with the population averages has obvious limitations, but we will initially accept this approximation. When the density of the population is low each individual has more or less full access to the resources available in the environment and there is little interaction with other individuals. Resource acquisition is at its maximum and, given that reproduction depends on resource supply, maximum fecundity (set by whatever physiological constraints) should be realized. As we add more and more individuals to that environment, each accrues a smaller and smaller share of the resources, such that maximum fecundity can no longer be achieved. The expected (average) number of births per individual would therefore go down as more and more individuals attempt to acquire the resources necessary for reproduction. Fig. 6.2 illustrates what happens.

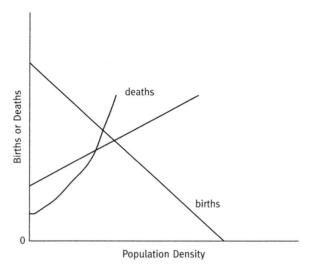

Figure 6.2. *Per capita* births and deaths as functions of population density. The figure illustrates a linear decline in *per capita* birth rate with increasing population density, together with two examples of increasing *per capita* death rates with increasing population density. The intersections of the birth and death functions correspond to the equilibrium density where the population has ceased to grow.

We can use the same arguments for the average risk of death. As the density increases, each individual gathers a smaller and smaller share of the resources in the environment and, for example, faces a higher risk of starvation. The function that relates population density[2] to demography (births and deaths) can have many shapes, and Fig. 6.2 shows a few examples.

In a closed population (or in a population where immigration and emigration marginally effects the internal dynamics), all dynamics are fully described by births and deaths. We can therefore write down a simple mapping of the population size from one time to another:

$$N_{t+1} = N_t + bN_t - dN_t \tag{6.3}$$

where N is density, and the index t indicates time (such that we move from one point in time t to another point $t + 1$ and we set the length of that time step so that it matches some relevant time scale for the organism. It is often convenient, but not necessarily correct, to think of time steps in years). We can rewrite the right-hand side of Equation 6.3 as $N_t(1 + b - d)$ and we note that the terms within the parentheses represent the

---

[2] Note that 'density' is often used as a proxy for the level of resource competition. If the area (volume) and also the total amount (and renewal rate) of resources are kept constant, then changing the number of individuals in the population also changes effective density. A view that adheres more closely to biological reality is to use *per capita* availability of resources, unless density *per se* is of interest.

per capita population growth rate. We multiply this number by the current population density (N_t) to yield the population density (N_{t+1}) at the next point in time. The *per capita* population growth rate is often symbolized as λ. If $\lambda > 1$, the population increases, if $\lambda < 1$ it decreases, and if $\lambda = 1$ then there is no change in population size from one time step to another[3].

In our treatment thus far, *per capita* births (b) and deaths (d) are constants, but as we saw earlier, they are more likely functions of density ($b \rightarrow b(N)$ and $d \rightarrow d(N)$). Assuming that those functions are linear, an approximation which we use here for sheer convenience, we can write Equation 6.3 as

$$N_{t+1} = N_t + (b_0 - \beta N_t)N_t - (d_0 + \delta N_t)N_t \qquad (6.4)$$

Four demographic parameters have now been introduced: the maximum *per capita* birth rate (b_0), the rate by which *per capita* births decline with density (β), the minimum *per capita* death rate (d_0), and the rate by which *per capita* deaths increase with density (δ). When population density is low, $b(N)$ greatly exceeds $d(N)$, so λ is high (mean absolute fitness is high) and the population grows in size. As it grows, $b(N)$ becomes smaller and $d(N)$ becomes bigger, λ is reduced and the population does not grow as quickly. When the population has become sufficiently large, we reach the point when $b(N) = d(N)$ (see Fig. 6.2), λ has become 1 and the population has ceased to grow. Should the population for some reason exceed that critical density, $d(N)$ is greater than $b(N)$, $\lambda < 1$ and the population declines. Hence, the population density at which $b(N) = d(N)$ is an equilibrium point. Any density deviations from this point are brought back to the equilibrium by the $b(N)$ and $d(N)$ functions. Setting $b(N) = d(N)$ and using the linear form of these functions specified earlier we can, after some rather straightforward algebra, find that the population density N satisfying this relation is $\frac{b_0 - d_0}{\beta + \delta}$. A simple evolutionary analysis of this model is given in Box 6.1.[4]

'The consequences of density on birth and death rates varies among phenotypes and with the state of individual organisms'

Before we end the simplest case of single-population growth without any population structure, a further example in the same vein as above will illustrate how we then move

---

[3] This discrete mapping from one point in time to the next by multiplying the state variable with a constant is analogous to what population geneticists do when calculating changes in gene frequencies. Herein lies the fundamental observation that among alternative 'types' (alleles, genes, populations, strategies) the one with the highest λ will lead the race, i.e. have the highest fitness. Viewed as a race, the instantaneous change in each strategy's position relative to others is, in fact, the very *definition of fitness* (see Chapter 2).

[4] The expression $\frac{b_0 - d_0}{\beta + \delta}$ and the 'carrying capacity', K, in the traditional logistic equation for density-dependent population growth have identical meaning. Note that $b_0 - d_0$ is identical to the maximum *per capita* population growth rate in the logistic formulation and we see that r (the instantaneous rate of increase) is embedded in K (it is the numerator in the above expression).

Box 6.1. The carrying capacity game

The equilibrium population density $N^* = \frac{b_0 - d_0}{\beta + \delta}$, or 'carrying capacity' as it is called in the more familiar logistic equation version, is the dynamic endpoint when a (monomorphic) population has reached ecological equilibrium. We may now ask whether there is room for an alternative strategy using different values of the demographic parameters b_0, d_0, β, and δ. In other words, we ask whether the resident strategy with the above parameter values can be invaded by an alternative strategy characterized with different parameter values. In invasion analyses we assume that the resident strategy is at equilibrium and that the invader (a mutant or immigrant from outside the resident population) is initially rare. If the invading strategy is initially rare, then there would be no or very little density feedback from its own kind, but, since it is presumably an alternative that is very similar to the resident strategy, it would experience full density feedback from the resident. A successful invasion must meet the condition that the *per capita* growth rate (fitness, λ) of that strategy is greater than 1 (otherwise it would not increase in density). Using Equation 6.4 and the above equilibrium population density we can now write the invasion criterion such that the fitness of the invader, λ' must be greater than one:

$$\lambda' = 1 + (b_0' - \beta' N^*) - (d_0' + \delta' N^*) > 1 \Rightarrow 1 - \left(\frac{b_0 - d_0}{\beta + \delta}\right)(\delta' + \beta') + b_0' - d_0' > 0$$

with the invader parameters indicated by '. In order to fulfill this criterion, the invader should minimize β', δ' and d_0' but maximize b_0'. In other words, its equilibrium population density ('carrying capacity') should be maximized. Thus, we reach the general and important conclusion that, in a single-population game, the strategy with the highest equilibrium population density will always win.

into models with somewhat more sophisticated demography. The starting point will be Equation 6.4, but with a slight modification. Recall that both births and deaths were in a sense happening simultaneously (this is a rather incorrect statement because the flow of time is actually not represented in the discrete jumps implied by Equation 6.4). Let us instead imagine the following ordering of events: we start out with a population of size N_t and the individuals now reproduce at a rate $b(N)$ *per capita* such that by the end of the reproductive season we have $N_t + b(N_t)N_t = (1 + b(N_t))N_t$ individuals. Before the end of the time step (a year, say) all individuals experience a *per capita* death rate $d(N)$, where now N is $(1 + b(N_t))N_t$, i.e. all the newborn and their parents, so that the *per capita* death rate becomes $d_0 + \delta((1 + b(N_t))N_t)$. For the full dynamics we now have

$$N_{t+1} = N_t + (b_0 - \beta N_t)N_t - \left(d_0 + \delta\left(\left(1 + (b_0 - \beta N_t)\right)N_t\right)\right)\left(1 + (b_0 - \beta N_t)\right)N_t \quad (6.5)$$

This terrible equation illustrates a simple form of seasonality. Individuals first reproduce, then that whole segment of the population is taken into an episode of density-dependent death, after which the cycle starts over again. There is, therefore, a built-in delay in the density feedback. We wait until all the newborn and their parents are ready for tough times when most of the mortality takes place (the autumn and winter, say). It is also possible to interpret this more complicated procedure in terms of population structure, although it is not explicitly done so in Equation 6.5. The term N_t can be said to represent the 'adults' (the ones reproducing) whereas the term $(1 + b(N_t))N_t$ represents the 'juveniles' (until they become adults at the next point in time). Temporally structured models like Equation 6.5 are less well designed for dealing with more sophisticated structures of the population, but they illustrate an important principle, namely that the *density-dependent feedback, and therefore an important component of the fitness function, does not act uniformly and linearly across all individuals in the population.*

Adaptive dynamics and the G-function

In order to model and understand adaptation, we must be able to map fitness onto the myriad feasible strategies available for evolution. We start by writing down what is often called the equation for replicator dynamics

$$\frac{dp_i}{dt} = p_i(r_i - \bar{r}) \quad (6.6)$$

where p_i is the frequency of strategy i, r_i is the growth rate of strategy i players (remembering that this is a function of all strategy frequencies in the population), and $\bar{r}$ is the mean growth rate of all strategies. The derivation and discussion of this fundamental equation in evolutionary biology can be found in, for example, Hofbauer and Sigmund (1998) and Rice (2004). Confirming our intuition, Equation 6.6 says that the frequency of strategy i will increase (decrease) if its growth rate is greater (lesser) than the average growth rate of all existing strategies in the population. The use of replicator dynamics gives limited insights into evolutionary dynamics because it can only tell us the fate of strategies that are already present and does not allow for the possibility that new strategies emerge, either by mutations or invasions from elsewhere. For that purpose, we have to expand the replicator dynamics to include adaptive dynamics (Box 6.2).[5] The following treatment is borrowed from the work by Vincent

---

[5] The term 'adaptive dynamics' is here used in a casual sense and subsumes the many variants of models of evolutionary dynamics that explicitly include both density and frequency dependence, such as those of Metz *et al.* (1996).

Box 6.2. The canonical equation of adaptive dynamics

The principles of adaptive dynamics—how trait or, more abstractly, strategy values change with both population density and the frequency of traits (or strategies) in the population—have been captured succinctly by the so called canonical equation of adaptive dynamics (Dieckmann and Law 1996). This is one version of it:

$$\Delta \bar{z} = \frac{1}{2} N \mu \sigma^2 \frac{\partial \ln w(z, \bar{z})}{\partial z} \Big|_{z=\bar{z}} \qquad (B6.2.1)$$

Here, $\Delta \bar{z}$ is the change in mean trait value, N is population density, μ is mutation rate per individual, and σ^2 is the variance of mutational effect (and the ½ term is there because the equation was derived for haploid organisms). $w(z, \bar{z})$ is the fitness of a rare mutant with trait value z in a population with mean trait value $\bar{z}$. The fitness function w has further implicit arguments representing the population density. Equation B6.2.1 is in many respects structurally very similar to Lande's model (Lande 1976) based on quantitative genetics. The mechanics of evolution is taken care of by the mutation rate (μ) and the variance of the mutational effects. The variance term generates new alternative strategies (trait values) that then breed true (there are no epistatic, pleiotropic, or developmental interactions).

The canonical equation is one version of a more general family of models originating from quantitative genetics that describes evolution as *gradient dynamics*—strategies that climb the adaptive landscape according to the slope (gradient) of the possibly multidimensional landscape at the point of the mean resident strategy value. Sometimes σ^2 is called the speed term of evolution because it can be said to be related to the genetic variance in the population. Under these conditions, the canonical equation matches Fisher's fundamental theorem of natural selection that the speed of evolution (change in phenotypic trait value) is directly proportional to the additive genetic variance.

Note how the canonical equation of adaptive dynamics differs from the G-function formulation. The canonical equation is explicit about changes in trait value (or strategy value) whereas the G-function formulation describes the adaptive landscape with its maxima and minima.

and Brown (2005). We recommend that readers interested in a deeper understanding of adaptive dynamics and G-functions consult Vincent and Brown's book.

'An evolutionarily stable strategy (ESS) is one that maximizes the G-function'

The first step is to identify what Brown, Vincent and Cohen (Vincent *et al.* 1993, Cohen *et al.* 1999, Vincent and Brown 2005) call the G-function (the 'fitness-generating function' that we first encountered in Chapter 3). Fitness is defined, as above, as the mean absolute fitness of a strategy; that is, the expected *per capita* growth rate of an individual playing strategy *i*. As before, the strategy can be a behavioural scheme, an aspect of morphology, a rule for habitat selection, or any combination of such traits. The basic assumption is that strategies are 'clones', i.e. breed true, so that as a strategy grows (according to its absolute fitness), it produces more of the same without the quirks of sexual reproduction.[6] An example of a fitness-generating function is

$$\frac{1}{n_i}\frac{dn_i}{dt} = G_i = r_i \left(1 - \frac{\sum_j \alpha_{ij} n_j}{K_i} \right) \tag{6.7}$$

where n_i is the number of individuals using (or density of) strategy (or phenotype) *i*, r_i is the *i*th strategy's maximum *per capita* growth rate, α_{ij} is the interaction coefficient weighing the impact of the presence of strategy *j* on strategy *i*'s growth rate, and K_i is the carrying capacity (equilibrium population size) of strategy *i*. Equation 6.7 is the Lotka–Volterra equation for interspecific competition. The idea is now to assume that evolution starts with a situation where the population is monomorphic, i.e. consists of one strategy only, and we ask whether an alternative strategy can invade such a population, outcompete the resident strategy, and thus replace it. If successful, the new strategy is now the resident, and we again ask whether an alternative strategy would be able to invade and replace it, and so on. The strategy that resists all such attempts by other strategies to invade and replace the resident is the evolutionarily stable strategy (ESS).[7] It is assumed that the ecological (e.g. population) dynamics runs faster than evolution (there is separation of time scales), which means that the population quickly reaches its dynamic equilibrium before a new invasion attempt is made. This assumption has sometimes been questioned—see Vincent and Brown 2005 and references therein.

For a strategy to be an ESS two conditions must be met. First, the *G*-function must be an extreme point, i.e.:

$$\frac{\partial}{\partial x} G(x|x^*, n^*)|_{x=x^*} = 0, \tag{6.8}$$

And, second, the second derivative of Equation 6.8 must be less than zero, ensuring that it is a maximum. Note that we have changed the notation slightly compared to Equation 6.7: in Equation 6.8 we now have the strategy *values*, *x*, not just the abstract

---

[6] This assumption can often be invoked without loss of generality unless there is an explicit need to deal with sexual reproduction, such as in the reproductive isolation part of speciation. See for example Abrams (2001), Dieckmann and Doebeli (1999), and van Doorn *et al.* (2004).

[7] The concept of an ESS has been described in many different ways. Apaloo and colleagues (2009) provide a detailed list of terms and definitions, and propose a resolution to the problem.

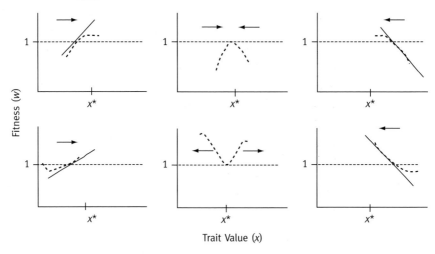

Figure 6.3. The evolution toward a fitness maximum (top row of panels) and toward a fitness minimum (bottom row). The top row of panels show the fitness function (solid curve) and the fitness gradient (dashed line) for trait value x. At trait value x^* the fitness function has a single peak and the selection gradient is zero. Any deviations from x^* in trait value has lower fitness than the ESS solution x^*. The bottom row shows the evolution toward a fitness minimum. The selection gradients to the right and left of the trait value x^* converge towards x^*, but at x^*, although the fitness gradient is zero, the selection is disruptive and any value deviating from x^* has higher fitness. The latter situation is a branching point (see p. 194).

notation in Equation 6.7 that strategies compete with each other. The *G*-function in Equation 6.8 represents the fitness of a rare individual playing strategy x, given that the rest of the population is playing strategy x^* with a population size of n^* (the equilibrium population size). Equation 6.8 says that a point x^* along the strategy axis of all x is either a maximum or a minimum (so that the derivative of the *G*-function is zero), and the second derivative condition ensures that the function is maximum. So if strategy x^* is resident, no alternative strategy can achieve higher fitness (Fig. 6.3).[8]

> *'The fitness-generating function (G-function) maps strategy (trait) values, the distribution of strategy values, and population density onto mean absolute fitness (per capita population growth rate)'*

Fig. 6.3 illustrates how fitness varies with trait (strategy) value. Starting at any given point along the x-axis, we seek to learn whether fitness will increase or decrease by deviating (mutating) the trait value (strategy). So, the slope of the *G*-function at any

---

[8] The *G*-function is silent on how the trait maps onto function.

given point is a fitness gradient. If the slope is positive, then trait values to the right of that point have higher fitness and should increase in frequency. If the slope is negative, then trait values to the left of that point have higher fitness and should increase in frequency. The steepness of the slope also illustrates how quickly trait values can adapt in either direction.[9] Thus, the G-function also reveals the selection gradient.

Fig. 6.3 also illustrates evolution of the strategy (trait) value. Here, we see how the G-function progresses during the course of evolution towards either a function with a peak (indicating the ESS) or a function with a minimum (branching point, see the 'Evolutionary branching' section later in this chapter). The strategy game is played whenever the G-function crosses the line of zero fitness. Trait values to the right (positive slope at the intersection) or to the left (negative slope at the intersection) will increase in frequency (the number of individuals playing those strategies become more common). The game ends when the maximum of the G-function is tangential to the zero-fitness line. No strategy to the right or to the left of the peak can do any better than the one with the maximum value, and that strategy does not increase in density either because its *per capita* growth rate is zero. If the G-function has a minimum that is tangential to the zero fitness line, then a resident strategy right at that minimum is stable in the sense that:

1. there is no change in population size unless any strategy with a deviant trait value (to the left or right) appears, and
2. the population actually evolved towards that minimum.

This latter case sounds counter to any intuitive notion of evolution. How can a population actually evolve to minimize fitness? This problem has attracted considerable attention in the literature and it has been shown that fitness minima indeed can be convergence stable (i.e. adaptive evolution takes the system there).

The adaptive landscape

Evolution as a fitness-maximizing process was firmly established with the publication of *The genetical theory of natural selection* by R. A. Fisher (1930). Soon after, Sewall Wright (Wright 1931, 1969) showed that the problem could be illustrated pedagogically by envisioning a 'landscape' with plains, peaks, and valleys. The 'horizontal' extension of the landscape is defined by traits (or alleles and their corresponding trait values) and the 'elevation' by fitness. Mountain peaks in the landscape represent fitness maxima, and the troughs and valleys fitness minima. Adaptive evolution would take any combination of traits away from the valleys and move them upslope towards the peaks.

'Hill climbing in the adaptive landscape is the fundamental process in adaptive evolution'

---

[9] The slope of the fitness gradient is often referred to as the 'strength' of natural selection.

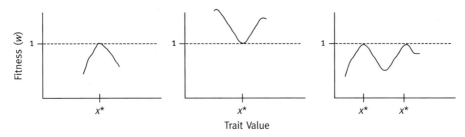

Figure 6.4. Three alternative fixed points on an adaptive landscape—the solid fitness-function (*G*-function) curve—here with fitness (*w*) plotted against trait value (*x*). The evolutionarily stable strategy can either be a fitness peak such that no alternative strategy on either side of the fitness maximum can invade, or it can be a fitness minimum. Both points are here drawn to be convergence stable. There can also be more than one solution. The far right panel shows a solution with two fitness peaks, and thus two different equilibrium trait values (i.e. either a stable polymorphism or speciation).

Adaptive evolution is hill climbing in this landscape. Given enough time, traits or trait combinations would be selected such that different peaks in the landscape would be 'inhabited' by different locally adapted phenotypes. Unlike real hill climbing though, steep upward slopes would be climbed quickly (strong selection) whereas travel across relatively flat regions in the landscape would take longer because fitness gains and losses in any direction from the current location would be marginal. Entirely flat stretches would give selection no sense of direction, and random genetic drift and gene flow would dictate the course of evolution. Should, for whatever reason, a partic- ular peak be attained, evolution would stop and the combination of traits and their values representing this peak would not change over time. Once on a peak, evolution cannot travel downwards. This metaphor has been part of evolutionary biology ever since Wright first presented it.

Plotting the *G*-function onto strategy values is a way of drawing the adaptive landscape, but unlike Wright's adaptive landscape, the *G*-function landscape is not static. In Wright's landscape it is difficult, if not impossible, to get from one adaptive peak to another, even if they are separated by an ever so shallow valley, because descending a slope is impossible, at least through adaptation alone.[10] It is different with the *G*-function: here the landscape is no longer static but depends on both the population density and the frequency of strategies in the population. Increased popu- lation density pushes the landscape downwards (Fig. 6.3). Frequency-dependent selec- tion changes the shape of the landscape. As evolution proceeds towards the current peak of the landscape, the contours may change so the peak itself is moving as the population evolves towards it. Figure 6.4 illustrates the three principal outcomes.

---

[10] Sewall Wright (1931, 1932) proposed a complicated and controversial three-stage process for peak shifting in static landscapes called the 'shifting balance hypothesis'.

First, the adaptive landscape ends up with a single peak from which there is no escape. Fitness of the strategy corresponding to the peak is zero (or one, if the dynamics is rescaled to discrete time so that no change occurs when the G-function takes on the value of unity) and lower (negative) for all other strategies. This point on the G-function is stable (any attempts to move away from it are punished because such strategies have negative fitness) and unbeatable, so it is an ESS. The point is also convergence stable because the system converged to this point through adaptive evolution.

The second possibility is, as indicated earlier, that the end result is not a fitness maximum, but indeed a minimum. The minimum is convergence stable because evolution actually took the system there through continuous adaptive changes in trait values. But this strategy solution cannot resist invasion because alternative strategies to the left or to the right of the minimum have higher fitness than the resident strategy and divergence to new strategies is possible (see the 'Evolutionary branching' section later in this chapter). This may lead to the third possible outcome, namely multiple peaks. A single resident strategy has split into two or more alternative strategies. Two strategies emerging from one common ancestor strategy may sound like adaptive speciation and, in principle, that is precisely what it is, or at least can be. It is, however, a matter of controversy whether adaptive dynamics as outlined here actually can lead to true speciation or whether the two ESS solutions thus created would rather represent 'morphs' or alternative strategies within a species. The core of the debate concerns the details of the strategy mechanics (inheritance, the generation of genetic variance, positive and negative assortative mating, and reproductive isolation).[11]

There is a fourth scenario of quite some importance. Unlike the situation above, in which a stable solution actually exists and when both the ecological and evolutionary dynamics come to rest, we must also consider the possibility of instability. We may be especially interested in the route to extinction because we know that populations (including entire species) do go extinct. So let us imagine that we have a population for which deaths exceed births at any density: fitness would be less than zero for all strategy values, but the adaptive landscape still has troughs and peaks, and evolution does not stop just because the population is declining—it still obeys gradient dynamics—and strategies will be selected that maximize fitness (striving for the peaks in the landscape). Attaining a peak in this negative landscape is clearly adaptive but it is not enough to take the population out of its route to extinction. This is sometimes (but perhaps erroneously) called a maladaptation.[12] We illustrate this problem in Fig. 6.5. The population starts out with positive fitness for the resident strategy (so it is increasing in density) but the positive slope of the adaptive landscape generates selection for higher trait values. The population evolves in that direction but in doing so fitness goes down.

---

[11] The *Journal of Evolutionary Biology* (vol. 18, pp. 1139–219) published a series of back-to-back papers in 2005 on this controversy.

[12] We evaluate the significance of maladaptive evolution (as distinct from the noun 'maladaptation') in Chapter 7.

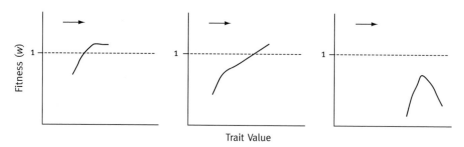

Figure 6.5. Climbing a sinking landscape. As adaptation progresses, the mean trait value moves closer and closer to the fitness peak at the same time as the peak is sinking, potentially below positive fitness (and the population eventually goes extinct). Adaptive evolution pushes the fitness function down as the peak is approached. This adaptation to the demise of the population is truly maladaptive.

Eventually the peak of the landscape is reached, as it should through adaptive evolution, with the unfortunate twist that the peak is located in the negative fitness region and the population evolves to extinction.

Evolutionary branching

Frequency- and density-dependent selection can lead to unexpected results. We saw earlier in the chapter that organisms can travel towards the adaptive peak, yet become extinct. Adaptive evolution can also take the population to a fitness minimum. A convergence stable fitness minimum is a feature of the adaptive landscape such that the ESS is located not at the peak of the adaptive landscape, but at the (local) minimum (Figs 6.3 and 6.6). The dynamic equilibrium is reached (no population growth or decline), but the adaptive landscape shows us that any strategy (or trait) deviating from the ESS has higher fitness than the resident strategy. This is opposite to the expectation of lower fitness associated with adaptive peaks.

This counterintuitive result has received quite some attention from theorists because it has some potentially very important ramifications. The fitness minimum is convergence stable, i.e. the population is forced there by climbing positive fitness gradients, but it is wide open for invasion. Any strategy deviating from the ESS on either side of it (higher or lower value of the strategy or trait) has higher fitness. This is potentially a branching point. Depending on the exact nature of the adaptive landscape and the underlying properties of the population or community dynamics,[13] a fitness minimum can lead to disruptive selection. Fitness is higher on either side of the point at which the population is residing, so alternative strategies, generated by random mutation

---

[13] The properties of fitness minima have been explored theoretically by, among others, Abrams *et al.* (1993), Doebeli and Dieckmann (2000), Abrams (2001), Vincent and Brown (2005), and van Doorn and Dieckmann (2006).

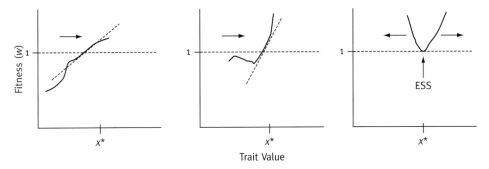

Figure 6.6. Adaptation toward an evolutionary branching point. The fitness landscape changes as adaptation is directed toward a fixed point. This fixed point is, however, a fitness minimum which opens up opportunities for disruptive selection (branching). 'ESS' indicates where the fixed point is located along the trait axis. The curve is the G-function function and x^* indicates where the equilibrium is located. The dashed line tangential to the fitness function at point x is the selection gradient at x.

(or migration in an open population), can move the strategy away from the former ESS (Fig. 6.6). Under the right circumstances (see, for example, Vincent and Brown 2005), two alternative strategies diverge from each other in a changing adaptive landscape that has positive fitness gradients pointing in different directions. Eventually, adaptation forces sequential strategies to migrate onto two separate peaks on either side of the original minimum. The population that was originally defined with one strategy has branched out into two separate ones. One ESS has become two. The monomorphic population formed through stabilizing selection has become dimorphic through disruptive selection. Two competing strategies emerged from one. This, and the many other possible outcomes from strategy games, can be illustrated by so-called pairwise invasibility plots (PIP, see Box 6.3).

One situation where fitness minima represent branching points occurs when the resource distribution is very wide in relation to the niche width. Let us assume there is one trait axis determining how efficiently resources are acquired in relation to the distribution of resources (e.g. beak size in relation to the seed-size distribution). Initially, there would be rapid evolution of trait value toward the peak of the resource distribution. There will be a fierce intraspecific struggle for resources close to that peak so one might expect that strategies deviating slightly away from it (in terms of trait value) avoid intense competition. If the resource distribution is wide enough, the price paid by deviating would not be very high, but the gain from avoiding competition could be considerable. Fitness would be higher on either side of the resource peak and the stabilising selection that drew the population to the fitness minimum would have changed to being disruptive. Eventually, the one kind of forager (or 'species' or 'morph'), with an intermediate beak size matching the peak of the resource distribution, will split into two, one with a beak size somewhat smaller than the intermediate one,

Box 6.3. Pairwise invasibility plots

A convenient way of illustrating the invasion potential and stability of adaptive dynamics systems is the pairwise invasibility plot (PIP; Metz *et al.* 1992, Geritz *et al.* 1998). In a PIP, the abscissa is the phenotypic value (trait value) of the resident strategy. The ordinate is the trait value of a possible mutant and the diagonal combines all trait values that are equal for residents and mutants. Beginning at a point of possible equilibrium (on the diagonal), for each and every resident trait value we ask whether a mutant with a higher or lower trait value can invade (occupy the region with positive fitness), take over, and become the resident strategy. The panel to the left in Fig. B6.3.1 shows a case where the mutant can, from both lower and higher trait values, eventually arrive at a singular point (small circle) where no further change is possible. For resident trait values smaller than that point, a mutant with higher trait values can invade, and for resident trait values higher than that point, lower mutant values invade. Any deviations from the singular point are impossible to invade since they always fall in the negative (invasion) fitness region. This is a convergent stable ESS (cf. top row panels in Fig. 6.3).

The panel to the right illustrates a branching point. It is convergent stable in the same manner as the left-hand panel, but deviations from the singular point now fall into positive (invasion) fitness regions, *in both directions* (up and down). Mutants with higher *or* lower trait values can invade from the singular point. This is a convergent stable (attainable through adaptive evolution) branching point (cf. Fig 6.6 and bottom row panels in Fig. 6.3).

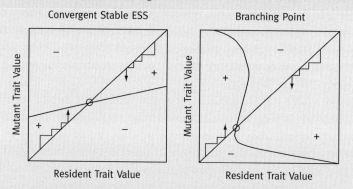

Fig. B6.3.1. Two example pairwise invasibility plots (PIP). Along the abscissa are the values of the resident strategy (or trait), on the ordinate the strategy (or trait) values of potential invaders. The diagonal is the line of equal strategy values for the resident and the mutant and on which a possible equilibrium must lie. The regions with a plus sign are regions where the mutant has higher fitness than the resident, and the regions with a minus sign correspond to those where the reverse holds. Step arrows show hypothetical trajectories of change in trait value. See the box text for further explanation.

another with a beak size somewhat bigger.[14] This is what we try to illustrate in Box. 6.3 (Fig. B6.3.1). There is a convergent stable fixed point at an intermediate trait value, so smaller and bigger beak size will be continuously replaced by beaks of ever more intermediate size, but *after converging on the same intermediate size*, there will be disruptive selection. The adaptive landscape is not constant and what was once a peak to climb is now a trough.

> *'Evolutionary dynamics can yield either an adaptive peak*
> *or a fitness minimum capable of adaptive branching'*

The outcome of evolutionary branching can be interpreted in two different ways. We can think of it as two coexisting alternative ESS strategies within a population. Individuals of intermediate size might be less successful than those that are either small (specializing on one end of the resource spectrum, say) or big (specializing on the other end of the resource spectrum). Such dimorphisms are widespread in nature (think about different colour morphs or our example of fish morphotypes in Chapter 4) but whether or not they are the result of evolutionary branching is not always clear, since we only rarely have been able to study the disruptive process in action. Usually we observe only the possible outcome.

> *'A branching point in the adaptive landscape can potentially*
> *be the starting point for sympatric speciation'*

An intriguing alternative to dimorphism is *bona fide* speciation. The branching point and the subsequent consequences of the disruptive processes are the starting point for ecological separation. Whether such branching toward ecological opportunity also leads to reproductive isolation (a prerequisite for speciation) is an open question and has been much debated. Some argue that the branching point can indeed be the seed for sympatric speciation (for example Dieckmann and Doebeli 1999). This would require, however, that the disruption into two strategies is associated with mechanisms that also lead to reduced gene flow and reproductive isolation. It has been suggested, for example, that assortative mating could do the job if, by chance, mate-preference traits are associated with the ecological trait undergoing adaptive evolution.

One potential (and mostly semantic) problem with this scenario is that the ecological separation created by the disruptive selection at the branching point often leads to niche and spatial separation. Some would now say that we no longer have two truly sympatric, but rather parapatric, or even allopatric morphs.[15] This raises the question

---

[14] Might such a process explain the curious and striking dimorphism in bill size exhibited by Africa's black-bellied seedcrackers (Bates Smith 1993)?

[15] Allopatry refers to two or more populations that are isolated spatially (occupy different areas) whereas parapatry refers to some, but incomplete, spatial segregation.

of whether true sympatric speciation is possible at all. One's view on this matter is an issue of scale. Complete geographical overlap does not necessarily imply full or even partial (micro-) habitat overlap so the resolution of the scale at which potential separation occurs is ambiguous. Whether true sympatric speciation is common or rare in nature remains an open question, but evolutionary branching points necessarily play an important role whenever the initiation of disruptive selection is to be understood.

The adaptive dynamics framework is in many respects a coevolutionary theory. The densities of conspecifics and competitors or predators contribute to the strength and direction of selection gradients, and the frequencies of existing traits (strategies) do the same. The course of evolution and the resulting adaptations are contingent on the strategies that the focal one interacts with: they co-evolve. An adaptation by one competitor that relaxes competition is counteracted by a corresponding adaptation in the other. The next section will take a closer look at some of the consequences of coevolution.

Red Queen dynamics

'Now, HERE, you see, it takes all the running you can do, to keep in the same place.', says the Red Queen in Lewis Carroll's *Through the Looking Glass*, when Alice wonders why they have to run so fast just to stay where they are.[16] This passage, as so many others in Carroll's two novels about Alice, has served as a metaphor for an evolutionary principle first proposed by the University of Chicago evolutionary biologist Leigh van Valen[17]. van Valen had discovered in 1973 what he called a 'new evolutionary law' (van Valen 1973). He showed that there is a constant probability of extinction for any lineage (at the family level) through the history of life and interpreted that as the inability of organisms to 'improve' their performance on a relative scale. Any improvement (in some fitness terms) in one lineage is counteracted by improvements in others so that there will be a continuous race in order to not to be eliminated by competitors.

The ideas behind van Valen's macroevolutionary arms race have since been used in attempts to understand many coevolutionary problems. There is a constant need for 'improvements'. If one competitor becomes a little better at capturing light, say, it takes new adaptations for others to do the same in order to keep up and not be outcompeted. In predator–prey systems, strong selection for prey evasion or protection is counteracted by corresponding evolution of increased capture success by the predators. An infectious disease that has hacked the immunological code of the host forces it to find new ways of stopping the virulence of the attacker that in turn would select for novel lock picking of the host's defence system. It is easy to come up with a number of similar

---

[16] Quotation from Chapter II in *Through the Looking Glass* (http://www.gutenberg.org/files/12/12-h/12-h.htm). Lewis Carroll was the *nom de plume* of mathematician Charles Lutwidge Dodgson.

[17] Coincidentally, Leigh van Valen passed away the very day this section of the book was written.

examples of the Red Queen running just to stay in place. The metaphor is very appealing, but is it a good one?

In the 1980s and 1990s, theoretical ecologist Peter Abrams wrote a series of papers showing how the arms race often can come to an end.[18] One key is density dependence. If prey evolve greater escape ability or protection, thereby reducing capture rate by the predator, the equilibrium population density of the prey should increase. With increased prey abundance, the predator would no longer need hyper-efficient capture traits and the *per capita* rate of consumption would remain the same, thus reducing the selection gradient for evolving prey-capture improvements.

Arms races can also quickly become decoupled. When the race is escalating to a point where further improvements become too costly, the predator may switch its attention to alternative prey or alternative habitats. Rather than the exhausting gradual climb toward heights in the current adaptive landscape that take forever to reach, evolution may lead the predator to more easily scaled adaptive peaks with steeper slopes and more rapid adaptation.[19] Such decouplings could break current evolutionary constraints. If a predator abandons one prey type for another, adaptations in the former prey can now take new routes entirely. Predation (at least from its former enemy) is no longer part of its evolutionary feedback environment and entirely new peaks in the fitness landscape are now potentially available.

One classic area in evolutionary biology where the Red Queen has made herself particularly relevant is the evolution of sex. In 1980, the notoriously creative evolutionary thinker William Hamilton (Hamilton 1980) suggested that rapid evolution in parasites (including microparasites such as viruses and bacteria) would call for an equally rapid evolution of defences against them. The problem is that parasites operate at a much faster timescale than their hosts typically do, and the generation time can often be orders of magnitude shorter in the parasites. Sexual reproduction, despite its two-fold cost of producing males instead of clonal females,[20] could be one way of overcoming this problem. If the parasites are adapting rapidly to a clonal host, there is no way the host can counteract and keep pace with the parasite. Sex, however, is a way of constantly reshuffling genomes from independent individuals thereby facilitating the creation of a more diverse population with individuals that are different from the ones the parasite adapted to. Constantly changing the genome would create the necessary genetic variation for the host to keep up with the never-ending running by the parasitic Red Queen.

---

[18] See for example, Abrams (1986a,b) and Abrams and Matsuda (1994).

[19] Similar processes typify human arms races, where emerging security threats can decouple old enemies and lead the 'victors' as well as the 'losers' towards new strategies. Too often, however, nations are bound in cycles seeking international dominance.

[20] See Olofsson and Lundberg (2007) for the *ecological* conditions for the twofold cost to be of any significance and Lively (2010) for a review of the Red Queen's role in the evolution of sexual reproduction.

Our last example of Red Queen dynamics concerns evolutionary cycles. This problem is rather closely related to the evolution of sex problem, but can be generalized beyond that. Imagine that there is host population susceptible to the infection of a particular parasite, which here, for simplicity, has two genotypes. Suppose further that there is a trade-off between the resistance to one parasite genotype versus resistance to the other. If parasites with Genotype 1, say, are much more common than the other one, there would be strong selection for host individuals that are resistant to that genotype (and by the trade-off argument, they cannot be equally resistant to both). This would give parasites with Genotype 2 a great advantage because the host population would consist primarily of individuals resistant to Genotype 1. Genotype 2 parasites can now spread in the host population. This would select for host individuals more resistant to Genotype 2, reducing the prevalence of the parasite. This is different from the decoupling scenario. The two interactors are locked in a cyclic race with no 'winner' and no 'loser'.

Spatial dynamics

Most models of population and community dynamics imagine well-mixed and homogeneous populations. The assumption is patently false. No matter at what scale we observe nature, space is not entirely homogeneous. The physical environment in which organisms live varies across all spatial scales. Nutrient levels, moisture, cover, food abundance, and predation risk all change as one travels from one place to another. For any given organism and scale, these environmental mosaics and gradients can conveniently be lumped into larger landscape elements, often called habitat patches. Spatial heterogeneity inevitably leads to an uneven distribution of individuals across space, with some places inhabited by very few individuals and others by many. These patchy distributions can have far-reaching consequences for the ecology and adaptive evolution of the population.[21] First, there is population size itself. If the local population is sufficiently small, then demographic stochasticity, chance events affecting mortality or reproduction,[22] comes into play. Populations with few individuals are also more prone to extinction. As we learned in Chapter 2, for example, small population size enhances random genetic drift and the rate of fixation of mutations. Population size can thus have rather large genetic and ecological effects that either promote or stall adaptive evolution.

The uneven distribution of individuals is the result of the size and distribution of different habitat patches. Spatial structure also makes some habitats more rewarding in terms of survival and reproduction than others. If a habitat is of sufficient quality, the

---

[21] Recall the effects of habitat selection that we explored in Chapter 5.

[22] Demographic stochasticity can, for example, create severely biased sex and age ratios (e.g. events that affect only males or females, only adult reproductive individuals, or differentially influence cohort recruitment through time) that result in net negative population growth. Such chance events tend to average out in large and widely distributed populations.

population inhabiting it can reach a positive carrying capacity (which may be small or large). But if the habitat is of lower quality, reproduction or survival may be too low to sustain the population through time, regardless of how large it is. Ecologists call a habitat that does not allow for a positive equilibrium density a sink habitat (as opposed to a source habitat). Of course, a habitat can be so bad that it is uninhabitable (individuals cannot survive for any reasonable period of time).

'Analyses of spatial strategy games must include the dynamics
in all interconnected populations'

So the heterogeneous landscape at any appropriate scale creates a spatially structured population. Local population sizes differ either because of habitat patch size or quality, or both. But those local populations are rarely isolated and there is a flow of individuals from one population to another.[23] Evolutionary consequences will emerge regardless of whether individuals leave the habitat by chance or actively seek a place to live elsewhere.[24] Active dispersal could be caused by direct resource competition, direct or indirect interactions with predators (high predation risk), or because territoriality, mate acquisition, or any other mechanism yields higher expectations of fitness elsewhere (see also the section on bet-hedging later in this chapter). If the emigration is not directly lethal, then there must be immigration into one or more alternative habitats. If the immigration into a habitat is high enough, the resulting population size can potentially exceed the habitat's carrying capacity. The population growth rate will be negative. Such a habitat is called a pseudosink because it behaves like a sink (has negative population growth rate) but only because its dynamics are 'controlled' by immigration. Attempts to interpret the adaptive landscape of such a population may often be in error unless they simultaneously assess adaptive landscapes in all interconnected habitat patches.

There is, of course, always room for emigration and immigration among sources. If migration rate is marginal compared to the rates of reproduction and survival, the population can be said to be closed. At a sufficiently large scale that can be true, but then spatial extent is so large that there will be heterogeneities within that area, and thus spatial structure and movement (Chapter 4). Realistic population dynamics must include migration and dispersal,[25] and so too must the strategy games assessing density and frequency dependence.

---

[23] A collection of local populations connected by migration of individuals is called a metapopulation (a population of populations). The study of metapopulation dynamics, i.e. the extinction and colonization of local habitat patches, was pioneered by Levins in the 1960s (Levins 1969) and subsequently became a large research field.

[24] Adaptive migration from one habitat to another represents its own evolutionary game.

[25] Spatial population and community dynamics are dealt with at length in, for example, Ranta *et al.* (2007).

Spatial structure plays a crucial role in evolution. Migration and dispersal are gene flow. Adaptation in a local population, or deme,[26] is a response to the local environment that will tend to produce mean strategies and functional traits specific to that environment. If there is immigration from other environments with different characteristics, then there is a chance that the frequency of traits, strategies, and alleles that are appropriate for the local environment will be diluted. If the immigration rate is low, dilution will be small compared to the strength of selection, local adaptation can proceed mostly unimpeded, and yield trait distributions dictated largely by the local environment and the residing population. If, however, immigration is substantial and gene flow large,[27] selection for local adaptation will possibly be opposed by immigrant strategies that are not adapted to the new environment (see also the section dealing with migration in Chapter 2). Local adaptation will slow down or possibly not happen at all (e.g. Kawecki and Holt 2002; Holt *et al.* 2004).[28]

'Niche conservatism eliminates the ability to adapt to novel environments'

Adaptive evolution onto local peaks is closely related to the important concept of niche conservatism, which has been championed by Robert Holt. Niche conservatism is an important concept for our understanding of how organisms can adapt to novel environments, the dynamics of species ranges, the potential for parapatric or allopatric speciation, and the dynamics of invasive species. Let us explore how it might evolve in the context of source–sink dynamics.

On the surface, occupation of a sink environment would appear maladaptive. Recall that the sink is a place where *per capita* growth rate is negative, i.e. the prospects to survive and reproduce successfully are small, as opposed to a source habitat. If migration to the sink nevertheless is high (through passive dispersal,[29] for example) any adaptation to improve performance there would increase the persistence of sink occupants and could allow them to adapt to the sink habitat. Although adaptation to sink habitats can happen, it hinges on a delicate balance. The rate of migration to the sink habitat cannot be too high because then the flow of maladaptive genes from the source would supersede the selection for traits adequate for the sink. But the immigration must be high enough so that the sink population does not go extinct before it can adapt,

---

[26] A somewhat more formal definition of deme than we used in Chapter 4 defines it as a (genetically well-mixed) subpopulation that can import and export alleles.

[27] High immigration yields high gene flow only if the immigrants successfully reproduce and their offspring join the local gene pool.

[28] Immigration of novel strategies can, as Wright first imagined, provide potential mechanisms, including changes in the landscape's height and shape, that allow populations to move from one adaptive peak to another.

[29] The term 'passive' emphasizes that the rate of dispersal is invariant to features of the environment, including changes in population size or composition, and that individuals have no (strong) control of where they are dispersing to.

or at least high enough to maintain sufficient population density for adaptive dynamics to improve the 'sink strategy'. Migration back to the source habitat must not be too high either because then sink-adapted individuals would be lost to the source and the gene pool of suitable sink genes would be drained. If adaptation to the sink (or any alternative habitat other than the currently preferred one) cannot happen, then no niche expansion will take place and the original niche is conserved.

Spatial structure may have a profound influence on the ease or difficulty with which adaptations occur. We have seen examples in previous chapters (e.g. Chapter 3) when, for example, the habitat selection game has been played. It is also, as we have seen in Chapter 5, a problem of scale. We will revisit the spatial heterogeneity problem in our last chapter on adaptation, but for now we turn our attention toward heterogeneity through time.

Bet-hedging

Most organisms live in varying environments. The conditions for reproduction and survival vary from one year to another and long-term fitness is measured as the mean of the yearly fitness contributions. But it is the *geometric mean*, not the arithmetic one, that matters because fitness is multiplicative, not additive, across years. This is easily seen if we start with a simple model for absolute fitness. Recall that $N(t+1)/N(t) = \lambda$, i.e. that the growth rate of a strategy is absolute fitness. In a variable environment, λ depends on time and the long-term growth rate from time 0 to some arbitrary time in the future, t, is given by $N(t)/N(0) = \lambda(t)^t$, i.e. $\lambda(0)\lambda(1)\lambda(2)\ldots\lambda(t)$. Suppose now that the environmental variability is simple, such that we have 'warm' years and 'cold' years. The geometric mean is sensitive to large environmental fluctuations. So a specialist of 'cold' years, say, would fare worse than a generalist that received lower annual fitness (it could not take full advantage of either 'warm' or 'cold' years). The generalist would accrue higher geometric mean fitness because it always achieves some success and avoids the really 'bad' times. This can be appreciated by noting that the product of any two pairs of numbers yielding an equal sum is maximized when the values are similar. The generalist is like a roulette gambler who hedges his bets at the table by playing both red and black. The generalist gets a small reward regardless of the outcome of the ball's rolling, whereas the high-stakes specialist (always playing black or always playing red) gets very much or nothing each turn. There are, in principle, three ways to cope with this problem of reducing variations in fitness. The first is to always play it safe and adopt one single strategy regardless of conditions. The second is the classic 'don't put all eggs in one basket' strategy, and the third is 'adaptive coin-flipping'.

We can see how these alternatives play out by reconsidering the problem of clutch-size evolution, which we addressed in Chapter 3, in terms of bet-hedging. In a bad year, a small clutch might be optimal to ensure offspring survival, but if the year offers ample food and favourable weather, a larger clutch resulting in many surviving young would be better. A strategy that produces an intermediate number of eggs, ensuring some survival regardless of the environmental conditions in any given year, might be the solution. This would exemplify the second option above. Always producing a small clutch; i.e. option one, 'play it safe', would ensure offspring survival in bad years, but would lose out in good ones.

The 'adaptive coin-flipping' strategy (first proposed in Cooper and Kaplan (1982), and developed in Kaplan and Cooper (1984) to account for the trade-off in egg size and number) can also be applied to the clutch-size problem if egg size bears some direct influence on offspring survival. Adaptive coin-flipping mixes two pure strategies (e.g. small clutch versus large clutch) randomly, and the individual 'flips a coin' every year to determine whether to play one or the other strategy. The loading of the coin is assumed to be under selection. A lucid examination of the adaptive coin-flipping version of bet-hedging is given by Olofsson *et al.* (2009). They were able to show in a theoretical exploration of the coin-flipping problem that, unlike most previous conclusions, it is often highly adaptive to produce differently sized eggs (or other propagules) *within* clutches and not only among them. If the environment is unpredictable, and there are no cues about the expected near future that the female can operate on, then diversified clutches in terms of propagule size yield highest fitness.[30] Perhaps this explains why many raptors produce clutches that hatch asynchronously (making the nestling sizes very different; see Newton 1979) and it may explain the seemingly non-adaptive variance in egg size in many arthropods (Fox and Czesak 2000).

Another interesting example of potential bet-hedging comes from partial migration in birds. In many bird species, migration from the breeding areas is the only way to survive the winter (or any adverse season). Other species typically do not migrate at all and spend the entire year in the same area and habitat. An interesting intermediate case is partial migration, i.e. when a segment of the population leaves the breeding grounds in the fall to overwinter elsewhere, and subsequently returns to the breeding grounds the following spring. The remaining segment stays behind and spends the winter on the breeding grounds. There are two principal ways this might have evolved. Either there exists an individual ESS that gives the probability p ($0 < p < 1$) of migrating or the parents of the brood play a game involving bet-hedging making one fraction of the clutch migrants and another fraction residents.[31] This is clearly a frequency-and density-dependent game. The larger the fraction of migrants, the more resources are left for the ones staying behind, and the less resources *per capita* would be available for the migrants at the wintering grounds. So, winter survival is positively frequency-dependent for the residents and negatively so for the migrants (Fig. 6.7). Let us now, for simplicity (and without loss of the principal reasoning), assume that the fitness of the migrants in fact is frequency-independent because the wintering grounds they arrive at in the autumn abound with resources (but migrants pay a cost of travelling, and potentially of reduced reproduction due to later arrival to the breeding grounds; see

---

[30] Forbes' *A natural history of families* (2005) addresses a variety of similar problems.
[31] We encountered a similar problem in Chapter 4 regarding provisioning of young by dung beetles.

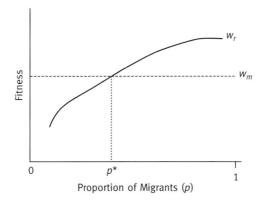

Figure 6.7. The fitness of the two strategies 'migrant' (w_m) and 'resident' (w_r) as functions of the proportion of migrants in the population. For simplicity, it is assumed that the fitness of migrants is frequency-independent, whereas the fitness of residents increases with increasing proportion of migrants. There is an equilibrium proportion of migrants (p^*) where the two fitness functions intersect.

Lundberg 1988). There is thus is the potential for an equilibrium fraction of migrants in the populations.

Let the fitness of migrants w_m be some constant k. Let the fitness of residents w_r be an increasing but decelerating function of p (the fraction of migrants), e.g. $w_r = \frac{ap}{1+bp}$, where a and b are parameters reflecting the strength of the frequency dependence (ultimately determined by average winter conditions on the breeding grounds). The equilibrium (ESS) fraction of migrants (the equilibrium probability of migrating) is found by letting $w_m = w_r$, i.e. $k = \frac{ap}{1+bp}$ and solving for p, $p^* = \frac{k}{a-bk}$, where p^* indicates that this is the ESS solution. Remember that p (and therefore p^*) has to be bound between 0 and 1, and we see that if k (migrant fitness) is large enough, $p^* = 1$, and if it is small enough (in this simplified case actually zero) then $p^* = 0$. So we can see anything, from pure residency to pure migration, depending on the average winter conditions on the breeding grounds.

Now consider a parent playing out this game by bet-hedging. Let the parent control which proportion of the brood should migrate or stay and call that proportion q. The expected fitness of an offspring is now $qw_m + (1-q)w_r$. Replacing the migrant and resident fitnesses with the same expressions as above (and replacing p for q), we get $qk + (1-q)\frac{aq}{1+bq}$. The optimal solution for the parent is to maximize this expression with respect to q, that is calculate the derivative with respect to q, put that equal to zero, and solve for q.[32] This becomes a rather ugly expression.[33] It turns out the optimal

---

[32] This solution follows standard maximization procedures. See, for example, Otto and Day (2007).

[33] $q^* = \dfrac{\left(bk - a + \sqrt{a(1+b)(a-bk)}\right)}{b(a-bk)}$. This expression cannot equal p^* if the environmental parameters a and b, and the constant fitness for migrants k, are reasonably realistic (e.g. greater than 0).

fraction of migrants that would maximize the parent's fitness through bet-hedging cannot be equal to the individual offspring ESS solution (for p or q falling between zero and one). Offspring and parents disagree and engage in potentially intense parent–offspring conflict! Here, the parents lose. The parent solution can always be invaded by offspring deviating from it and the game settles on the offspring solution. Any individual 'mutant' (an offspring not following the parent optimization rule), with a migration strategy p that renders higher fitness than all others following q^*, will be able to invade and eventually the system will settle on p^* rather than q^*. The value q^* is indeed an equilibrium solution, but not an evolutionarily stable one because it can be invaded by alternative strategies.

> '*Bet-hedging can be a successful way of adapting to a variable environment, but the details of the conditions determine the outcome*'

Trophic interactions

The environment in which organisms live is, of course, not only set by its physical and chemical attributes. All organisms consume resources and all provide resources for others, so any specification of an organism's environment must include competition and risks of predation. In order to study such effects, Heino *et al.* (1997) introduced the concept of the evolutionary feedback environment. Suppose an unstructured population lives in a chemostat in which it receives resources at a specific rate so that there is only intraspecific competition for food. The population members interact with only each other in the struggle for resources. The struggle yields adaptation for competitive ability through individuals' resource-exploitation rate, increases the *per capita* growth rate of efficient exploitation strategies, but occurs only in the focal population. The 'dimension' of the evolutionary feedback environment is one. Should the population be age- or stage-structured, say, there is room also for competition among different age- or stage-classes. Depending on the number of classes and to what extent they compete with each other, the number of dimensions would increase. But natural populations do not live in isolation; they are embedded in communities of several interacting species with whom they may or may not interact. Each successive interacting species (e.g. competitors, predators, or mutualists) can potentially increase the number of evolutionary feedback dimensions necessary to do the accounting of evolutionary dynamics. To properly work out the selection gradient for any given trait, the contributions from all relevant dimensions must be understood.

> '*The number of evolutionary feedback dimensions that are relevant to include in a selection gradient for a given trait in a population equals the number of relevant stage-classes and other species it interacts with*'

What is a 'relevant' dimension? One way to answer this question is to focus on the interaction strength between any two interacting populations. The solution is complicated by the rather ambiguous treatment of, and numerous definitions given to, interaction strength in the eco-evolutionary literature. If a predator has the choice of feeding on two prey types, but includes one of them in the diet very infrequently compared to the other, then we would think that the interaction strength is weak between the less preferred prey and the predator, but strong in the other case. The staple food would have large influence on the *per capita* growth rate of the predator, and therefore on traits that are relevant for its capture, digestion, and assimilation. The less preferred prey would have only a marginal effect.

Let us formalize our reasoning a bit and see where it takes us. First, one can capture the concept of interaction strength heuristically by assuming that fitness is a function of various parameters, some of which are under genetic control and so can vary among genotypes. If mutations of small effect arise and change the parameter values, then the likely direction of selection is determined by how a small change in the parameter value alters individual fitness, or *per capita* growth rate.[34] We now say that $\partial w/\partial x$, where x is any population parameter, represents the instantaneous fitness change emerging from a small change in the parameter under genetic control. This is equivalent to the slope of the selection gradient operating at that particular parameter value.

How do we map evolutionary changes onto changes in interaction strength? The quantity

$$\frac{d}{dY}\left(\frac{\partial w}{\partial x}\right) \tag{6.9}$$

describes how the rate of change in fitness with respect to a given parameter in the focal species itself depends upon density (e.g. of an interacting species, Y). In effect this expression determines the density dependence of selection.

One can usually re-order the sequence in which one takes partial derivatives. Hence Expression 6.9 is equivalent to

$$\frac{d}{dx}\left(\frac{\partial w}{\partial Y}\right) \tag{6.10}$$

which now measures the selection gradient on interaction strength because we define interaction strength to be the change in fitness (dw) with changes in the size of the population the organism interacts with (dY). This simple equation represents the mapping of the evolutionary process onto the ecological interaction. Note that

---

[34] Ecologists and evolutionary biologists frequently conduct such 'sensitivity analyses' with computer models that sequentially alter the values of individual parameters.

Expressions 6.9 and 6.10 are mathematically identical but that the biological interpretation shifts between them; ecology influences evolution in 6.9 and evolution influences ecology in 6.10.

'The strength of interaction between two species measures how the presence of the one species affects the fitness of the other'

Let us now build a somewhat more explicit model for a prey population interacting with its predator. We let the dynamics happen in discrete time and we then write

$$N_{t+1} = \frac{\lambda_N N_t}{1 + \alpha_N N_t + \beta_N P_t}$$
$$P_{t+1} = \frac{\lambda_P P_t}{1 + \alpha_P P_t + \beta_P N_t} \tag{6.11}$$

for the dynamics of the two populations. We have N_t and P_t as the prey and predator density, respectively, at some time t. The parameters with corresponding subscripts for prey and predator are the maximum *per capita* population growth rate (λ_i), intraspecific competition coefficient (α_i), and the interaction coefficient between predators and prey (β_i). We could stop here and use β_i as our measure of interaction strength, but it is rather indirect. Obviously, however, the parameters β_i are important components of the interaction strength. Since the model is symmetrical, it is for the present purpose sufficient to keep track of only one of the species. Prey fitness will be defined as that species' realized *per capita* growth rate, i.e.

$$w_N = \frac{\lambda_N}{1 + \alpha_N N_t + \beta_N P_t} \tag{6.12}$$

Note, that w_N is implicitly time-dependent through the population densities N and P.

We follow Laska and Wooton (1998) and let the marginal change in fitness of a focal species as we change the density of the other be our definition of interaction strength. Hence, our definition can be formalized as

$$\frac{\partial w_N}{\partial P} = -\frac{\lambda_N \beta_N}{(1 + \alpha_N N_t + \beta_N P_t)^2} \tag{6.13}$$

i.e. the *per capita* effect that species P has on the fitness of species N. We first note that $\partial w_N / \partial P$ is an increasing function of both N and P. But the right-hand side of Equation 6.13 is negative, so the more abundant the predator or the prey, the less negative is the predator's *per capita* influence on prey fitness (it increases in the mathematical sense from very negative to less negative values, approaching zero). Biologically, this means that the interaction goes from a strongly negative effect of small numbers of predators on few prey (low P and low N; the denominator of the right-hand term is small) towards a neutral interaction (close to zero) when one or the other species is abundant (high N or P). Note also that this function is concave. This means that any variability along the x-axis (i.e. in N or P) by Jensen's inequality results in an average interaction strength that is below the deterministic expectation.[35] That is, the interaction strength increases (becomes more negative) with increasing population variability.

We illustrate how interaction strength, $\partial w_N / \partial P$, varies with the interaction parameter β_N in Fig. 6.8. We hold the density of the focal species (N) constant and plot a family of curves for different P values. As expected, interaction strength generally increases as β_N increases. However, for sufficiently large values of P, interaction strength initially increases, then decreases with increasing β_N. In any case, $\partial w_N / \partial P$ is a convex function of β_N such that any variability in β_N results in a relaxation of the interaction strength.

Assuming now that that the two species reach a dynamic equilibrium (no change in population density from one point in time to another), the equation can be evaluated when $N_t = N_{t+1} = N^*$ (and similarly for species P). Inserting the expression for the equilibrium densities in Equation 6.13,[36] we have

$$\frac{\partial w_N}{\partial P}\Big|_{N^*, P^*} = -\frac{\beta_N}{\lambda_N} \tag{6.14}$$

The interaction strength of species N on P is identical to Equation 6.14 with changed subscripts ($= -\beta_P/\lambda_P$). This symmetry makes it easy to compare the effect of the one species on the other; the effect of species P on N is greater than the reverse if $\lambda_P/\lambda_N > \beta_P/\beta_N$.

Thus, if population parameters are viewed as constants and variability is only manifest through variable population densities (endogenously or exogenously driven), then the interaction strength between the populations is increasing. On the other hand, should life-history parameters such as maximum population growth rate (λ) or the interaction coefficient (β) be intrinsically stochastic, then interaction strength is relaxed.

[35] Jensen's inequality states that the expected value of a non-linear function, $E(f(x))$, does not equal the function value of the expected value of x, $f(E(x))$. For concave functions, as here, the expected value of the function is smaller than the function value of the mean, and for convex functions, the reverse is true (see, for example, Mangel 2006).

[36] Not shown here. They are calculated from Equation 6.11 by replacing all Ns and Ps by N^* and P^*, respectively, then first solving for N^* in the first equation and replacing the P^* that appears there by its solution, followed by some cumbersome rearrangements so that the N and P in Equation 6.13 appear as parameters only.

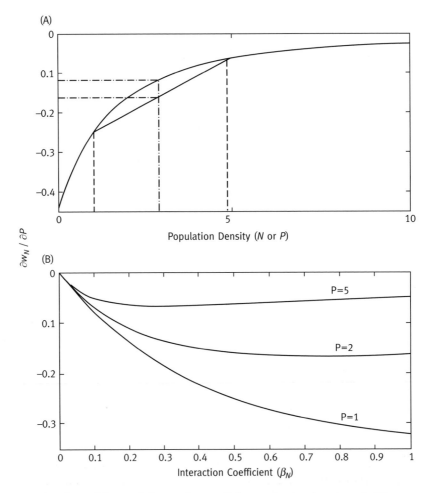

Figure 6.8. The effect of the prey's interaction coefficient on interaction strength. The upper panel shows that as either prey or predator population density increases, the strength of the interaction (of the predator on the prey) decreases (from more negative toward zero). If the population density fluctuates (between the vertical dashed lines), the mean interaction strength increases (becomes more negative). The bottom panel illustrates that interaction strength increases (becomes more negative) as the interaction coefficient increases, but that relationship depends on predator density (from $P = 1$ to $P = 5$).

'Environmental stochasticity can either increase or decrease the ecological interaction strength between two species and thus the evolutionary consequences of their interaction'

Both fitness and interaction strength are obviously non-linear functions of N and P. Now assuming that environmental variability enters directly through changes in population density, and to make a comparison between the effects on fitness and interaction strength, we linearize both functions by using Taylor's expansion of Equation 6.12.[37] This common approach allows us to investigate the behaviour of the population close to its equilibrium. We thus assume, implicitly, that the fluctuating dynamics approach the equilibrium in a linear manner (this assumption becomes less and less crucial as one approaches the equilibrium point). The Taylor expansion involves finding the first, second, third, and so on derivatives of the function at the point (independent variable value) one has chosen. The more of the higher order derivatives that are used, the better the linear approximation. For most problems, it is sufficient to omit the higher-order terms, i.e. the second, third, and higher derivatives, at least as long as we are rather close to the equilibrium point we have chosen. Following this logic, and omitting the second and higher derivatives, we then write down the linear version of Equation 6.12 as

$$
\begin{aligned}
w_N &\approx w_N(N^*, P^*) + \frac{\partial w_N}{\partial N}(N - N^*) + \frac{\partial w_N}{\partial P}(P - P^*) \\
&= 1 - \frac{\alpha_N}{\lambda_N}(N - N^*) - \frac{\beta_N}{\lambda_N}(P - P^*)
\end{aligned}
\tag{6.15}
$$

Note, that w_N is equal to 1 at equilibrium (the equilibrium is defined when there is no change in density, so *per capita* growth rate has to be 1). Careful inspection of Equation 6.15 shows that w_N is a decreasing function of both N and P with slopes $-\alpha_N/\lambda_N$ and $-\beta_N/\lambda_N$, respectively. That is because increasing N values or P values make the terms in parentheses larger, so that the negative influence on fitness (w_N) increases. Following the same procedure for interaction strength, and Taylor expanding Equation 6.13, we have

$$
\frac{\partial w_N}{\partial P} \approx -\frac{\beta_N}{\lambda_N} + \frac{2\alpha_N\beta_N}{\lambda_N^2}(N - N^*) + \frac{2\beta_N^2}{\lambda_N^2}(P - P^*)
\tag{6.16}
$$

Interaction strength is an increasing function of both N and P. Note the negative intercept at the deterministic $-\beta_N/\lambda_N$ (because the second and third terms are equal to zero at equilibrium, i.e. $N - N^* = 0$ and $P - P^* = 0$). Clearly population density has an opposite biological action on the two measures; while fitness is decreasing with increasing density, interaction strength increases.

> *'The evolutionary effects of a species' life history parameters are in turn affected by the life history parameters of the interacting species'*

---

[37] Taylor expansion is a recurrent technique in ecology and evolutionary biology. By Taylor expanding the non-linear function it becomes a linear approximation, and a linear function is often easier to analyse than a nonlinear one. See, for example, Otto and Day (2007).

We can now use our knowledge of interaction strengths to evaluate how adaptive evolution is likely to influence the critical (life-history) parameters in our model (maximum *per capita* growth rate of the prey (λ_N), the coefficient determining intraspecific competition in prey (α_N), and the basic interaction coefficient between the predator and the prey (β_N)). We begin by calculating the selection gradients of those parameters, i.e. $\partial w / \partial x$, where x is one of the three parameters we have for our model (Lande 1982, Caswell 2001). We calculate the partial derivative of fitness (w_N) with respect to the three parameters in turn:

$$\frac{\partial w_N}{\partial \lambda_N} = \frac{1}{\lambda_N}$$

$$\frac{\partial w_N}{\partial \alpha_N} = \frac{\alpha_P(\lambda_N - 1) - \beta_N(\lambda_P - 1)}{\lambda_N(\beta_N \beta_P - \alpha_N \alpha_P)}$$

$$\frac{\partial w_N}{\partial \beta_N} = \frac{\alpha_N(\lambda_P - 1) - \beta_P(\lambda_N - 1)}{\lambda_N(\beta_N \beta_P - \alpha_N \alpha_P)}$$

(6.17)

Equation 6.17 tells us how prey fitness (w_N) changes with small changes in the model's parameters, i.e. along which gradient we would see the most rapid change in fitness. The parameters we have at our disposal are λ_N, the maximum *per capita* population growth rate, α_N, the coefficient of intraspecific density dependence, and β_N, the coefficient determining the interspecific density dependence. All of them are potential targets for adaptive change. Let us now imagine that those parameters are the axes in a multidimensional adaptive landscape.[38] Now we can ask whether evolutionary adjustment of one parameter has a greater or smaller effect on fitness than does adjusting another. That is, we are asking when, for example, a reduction in *per capita* intraspecific competition will yield a greater increase in fitness than will an equal reduction in the *per capita* effect of interspecific competition ($\partial w_N / \partial \alpha_N > \partial w_N / \partial \beta_N$). If we iterate this process for all possible parameters, then we can figure out where the steepest slopes lie in the adaptive landscape. This is equivalent to determining along which axes (parameters) adaptation is most easy or likely to occur. We do so by comparing the right-hand sides of the bottom two expressions in Equation 6.17. After having simplified them we find that this comparison results in

$$\frac{\lambda_N - 1}{\lambda_P - 1} > \frac{\alpha_N + \beta_N}{\alpha_P + \beta_P}$$

(6.18)

---

[38] This is a four-dimensional landscape (!) with the three separate axes for the parameters, and one for fitness, so the word 'imagine' should perhaps not be taken literally (a three-dimensional object can be visualized as the 'shadow' of four dimensions). Luckily, mathematics can, for most problems, handle an arbitrary number of dimensions.

Adjusting the coefficient of intraspecific density dependence has a larger effect on fitness than the adjusting to *inter*specific density if this inequality holds.

If the prey species' maximum *per capita* growth rate is high ($\lambda_N \gg \lambda_P$) and β_N is small, then it is more likely that inequality (6.18) holds and therefore that ($\partial w_N/\partial \alpha_N$) is larger than ($\partial w_N/\partial \beta_N$). This means that selection that reduces α_N (the coefficient of *intra*specific competition) will be greater than selection that reduces β_N (the coefficient of *inter*specific competition).

'Life-history parameters and parameters specifying how populations interact can be used to build an adaptive landscape. Partial derivatives tell us where the hills and valleys are and along which roads adaptations are faster than others'

The above analysis was done under the assumption that an equilibrium is meaningful to calculate. Suppose, instead, that the selection gradients are evaluated without that restriction so that the population densities are still allowed to play a role. Given the fitness expression in Equation 6.12, we then have the following partial derivatives for the same three parameters as before:

$$
\begin{aligned}
\frac{\partial w_N}{\partial \lambda_N} &= \frac{1}{(1 + \alpha_N N + \beta_N P)} \\
\frac{\partial w_N}{\partial \alpha_N} &= -\frac{\lambda_N N}{(1 + \alpha_N N + \beta_N P)^2} \\
\frac{\partial w_N}{\partial \beta_N} &= -\frac{\lambda_N P}{(1 + \alpha_N N + \beta_N P)^2}
\end{aligned}
\tag{6.19}
$$

The selection gradient along the maximum *per capita* growth-rate (λ_N) axis is always positive (the right-hand side of the first equation cannot be negative), but decreasingly so with increasing population size of either N or P (they both occur in the denominator). Conversely, the selection gradients with respect to the parameters determining the density dependence are always negative. However, population size has a dual effect on sensitivity in those cases. For low values of N the selection gradient for intraspecific density dependence (α_N) increases with increasing N (i.e. $\partial w_N/\partial \alpha_N$ becomes more negative, there is thus increased selection for α_N to evolve toward ever smaller values, i.e. less effect of density on fitness), but as population size increases, the marginal change of fitness with changes in α_N decreases (becomes less negative, hence less selection to reduce α_N). The change in selection slope is most pronounced for small values of P. As P increases, the influence of intraspecific density decreases. An identical pattern, but now with N and P reversed, is true for interspecific density dependence (β_N).

What we have done in this somewhat complicated section is to show how the adaptive landscape can be defined and stretched out along axes (parameters) that we believe are relevant for evolutionary change. It is akin to the formulation of the *G*-functions we saw earlier in this chapter, but here we have:

1. let there be *more than one trait* (or strategy) axis.
2. *omitted* frequency dependence.

Without frequency dependence, we cannot play out the full evolutionary dynamics but we can begin to understand what the adaptive landscape looks like. In Chapter 7, we will show an example of how predators and prey coevolve, but along one trait dimension only.

The strength of interaction between populations that we have explored analytically has several ecological and evolutionary consequences. Tightly coupled predator–prey communities, for example, can give rise to unstable dynamics (cycles) and strong links between nodes in food chains may lead to dynamical cascades across trophic levels.[39] This is a huge research field in itself, see, for example, Murdoch *et al.* (2003), Ranta *et al.* (2007), and Loreau (2010). So population and community dynamics are strongly influenced by the degree to which populations interact. But interaction strength is also a measure of the interaction's evolutionary potential. If the interaction is weak, then fitness will only be marginally influenced by the presence of the other population and the interaction will contribute little to the evolutionary feedback environment. But the strength and importance of the interaction varies also with population size. This leads to an important conclusion about the dynamics of adaptation:

> *' The direction and rate of adaptation in an evolutionary feedback environment varies with population density'*

Moreover, the population size may determine which part of the life history or behavioural arsenal is adapting to the interaction. If the population density is high, then perhaps the selection gradient on anti-predator traits is weaker than other traits (the emergent strategy might maximize reproduction), whereas if density is low, then the selection gradients are steep for traits that relate directly to predator protection or evasion. Population dynamics and trophic interactions obviously play important roles in determining the direction and outcome of evolutionary change.

Reflection

The world is ever-changing. Conditions vary from place to place and from time to time. There is dynamics. The conditions for evolutionary change are typically very different

---

[39] A trophic cascade is an effect (on density or fitness) beyond the immediate pairwise interaction such that change at one trophic level influences trophic levels two or more steps away. The loss of top predators may influence plant populations, through other predators and herbivores, despite the fact that top predators and plants do not interact directly.

in a population with rapid growth in comparison with the same population when it has reached its equilibrium density and distribution. The conditions also vary across space, and spatial dynamics can have profound effects on the course of evolution. The mapping of genes through traits, function, fitness, and onto adaptation is ever-changing and is ambiguous except in the light of the dynamics of (often interacting) populations. Although ultimately operating at the level of inheritance (e.g. genes), evolution, as well as ecology, must have the population and its dynamics as the point of departure. The genes that define the individual and its traits have no 'meaning' unless the organism's environment is specified. The obvious and necessary context for this environment is the population to which the individual belongs. Communities are emergent entities, collections of species that potentially influence each others' abundance and distribution, and that are therefore important contributors to both the ecological and evolutionary dynamics of each constituent species. But it is at the population level where the real evolutionary action takes place. Allele frequency is a population-level measure. So are trait distributions. Failing to understand what dictates the dynamics of populations will inevitably give us a poor and incomplete understanding of evolution.

As Darwin understood and evoked so eloquently, evolution is undeniable in animal or plant breeding. The evolving breeds and strains give the illusion that one can ignore population processes, but this holds true only to the extent that animal and plant breeders maintain constant densities (and constant interactions with other species). When we want to understand adaptation in dynamic systems such as those that abound in nature, the density and frequency of individuals, traits, and alleles must be properly characterized.

7
Adaptation

A MAP FOR EVOLUTION

Overview

We learned in earlier chapters that an understanding of adaptive evolution hinges on the five pillars of mechanics, function, structure, scale, and dynamics. But we have not yet seen how they fit together to influence the fit of form and function, the diversity and procession of life, and the distribution and abundance of organisms. If our worldview is correct, then we should be able to use real examples of adaptation to reveal the importance of our underlying models.

We begin by reviewing knowledge gleaned from one of Earth's great adaptive radiations, the *Anolis* lizards of the Caribbean. Like Darwin's famous trip to the Galapagos, we will find through our virtual journey that the West Indies are a crucible not just for biodiversity, but for understanding adaptive evolution. Wonderful studies by Jonathon Losos and his collaborators reveal the underlying processes linking microevolutionary change of populations to local conditions to the macroevolutionary map of their phylogenetic relationships. We will also see that even curious forms of *Anolis* lizards are nearly perfect fits with the functions that they perform.

We then return to Levins' fitness sets for an explanation of how continuous change in character states can lead to discontinuities among species and higher taxa. We will learn that only a subset of what is possible for evolution is feasible for adaptation, and of that, a much smaller portion is probable.

Many characters are not adaptive, and numerous 'traits' that appear adaptive may simply be epiphenomena hitchhiking on the backs of correlated adaptive traits or misinterpreted in terms of their adaptive significance. More problematical still is the potential existence of maladaptive 'traits' that hinder adaptive evolution. We demonstrate that most of these difficulties disappear under a worldview based on the five pillars and a definition of fitness that imagines maladapted phenotypes as those with negative growth rates.

Introduction: explanations for life

The 400 or more different species of lizards belonging to the New World genus *Anolis* represent one of life's spectacular radiations. In the Caribbean Islands alone, nearly 150 species share common ancestors with as few as two colonizing species. It is not just their diversity that piques evolutionary biologists' interest and curiosity in these small, brightly coloured, arboreal predators. Different species occupy different habitats but in a remarkable pattern repeated from island to island.

Many small islands in the Lesser Antilles are occupied by only one or two distantly related species whose ancestors colonized the island chain with separate invasions from north and south (Losos and Thorpe 2004).[1] Anoles living on two-species islands at opposite ends of the archipelago are represented, typically, by one large-bodied and one small-bodied species (Fig. 7.1). Islands near the middle often have only a single species, of intermediate body size. The body-size pattern suggests that species with similar body sizes are incapable of coexisting with one another.

Anolis diversity is much higher in the Greater Antilles where more than 40 species can live on a single island (Losos 1992).[2] The lizards sort into local communities composed of different species but in which the same ecomorphs re-occur time and again (Fig. 7.2). The ecomorphology of these predators represents a body plan associated with each species' sit-and-wait foraging strategy. Different ecomorphs perch, waiting for insect prey, in different structural habitats. In communities with two species, a generalist that occupies many microhabitats coexists with a short-legged, slow-moving 'twig specialist'. Where three species coexist, the generalist is replaced by a large, long-legged, mobile species that forages on the ground as well as on the trunks of trees and shrubs, and by a second species that uses numerous subdigital lamellae on its foot pads to help it forage in the forest crown.[3] The most diverse communities include tiny lizards specialized to forage in small shrubs and grass.

Among the many ecologists and evolutionary biologists who have studied the *Anolis* system, teams led by Harvard University's Jonathan Losos have been particularly interested in the evolutionary roots of its remarkably convergent ecotypic variation. The Losos teams used a variety of molecular and phylogenetic tools to reconstruct the evolutionary history of West Indian anoles, and to link the phylogeny with ecomorphology. These models demonstrate, for the diverse communities of the Greater Antilles,

---

[1] The Lesser Antilles spread in a 1000-km arc between Puerto Rico and the coast of Venezuela.

[2] The Greater Antilles are composed of the four largest Caribbean Islands (Cuba, Hispaniola, Puerto Rico, and Jamaica).

[3] The lamellae can be thought of as a sophisticated biological analogue of 'velcro' that increases adhesion and allows the lizards to climb on surfaces in a way that would otherwise appear to defy gravity.

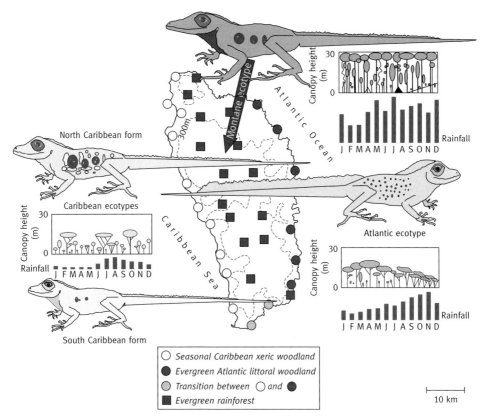

Figure 7.1. An example of the striking ecomorphs of *Anolis oculatus* that inhabit different habitats on the Lesser Antillean island of Dominica. The ecomorphs differ in scalation, body form, and colour pattern. The association of the different ecomorphs with different habitats is strong but circumstantial evidence of an insipient intraspecific radiation. From Losos and Thorpe (2004) © International Institute for Applied Systems Analysis, 2004, published by Cambridge University Press, reproduced with permission.

that the simple two-species community diversifies into the more complex ones through adaptive radiation of the original colonists (Fig. 7.2).

> *'The adaptive radiation of Anolis lizards demonstrates a superb fit between form and function'*

The *Anolis* radiation yields a powerful hypothesis on evolution. If *Anolis* lizards have diversified through adaptive evolution, then we should be able to reveal how their radiation has matched form with function, created diversity through common descent, and produced repeated patterns in the distribution and abundance of Caribbean lizards. All three predictions have been confirmed.

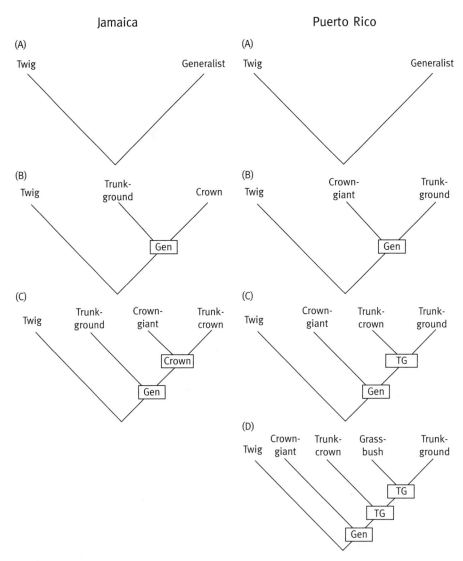

Figure 7.2. A comparison of convergent ecotypes of *Anolis* lizards living in two-, three-, four-, and five-species communities (A–D, respectively) in Jamaica and Puerto Rico. From Losos (1992), reproduced with permission from Oxford University Press.

Much of *Anolis* morphology can be summarized by two composite variables that account for the common variance in different morphometric measurements.[4] One of

---

[4] A variety of multivariate statistical procedures can be used to reduce correlated variables to represent a composite that is often more informative than the original data structure. The summary variables displayed in Fig. 7.3 were generated by principal components analysis (also see footnote 5).

these components corresponds to a cline of large, long-legged lizards at one end to small, short-limbed animals at the other. The second component describes a body form ranging from long-tailed animals with dense lamellae on their toe pads to short-tailed animals with few lamellae (Losos 1992). When these 'new' variables are graphed against one another, they describe the relative specializations of *Anolis* lizards (Fig. 7.3). Losos reasoned that if we associate the morphology with our understanding of lizard phylogeny, we can reconstruct the ancestral communities.

One of the most interesting features of both extant and reconstructed communities on Jamaica and Puerto Rico is that the small, short-limbed, short-tailed, slender twig specialist is distinct from the other ecomorphs. The implication is that the twig-specialist's niche (Box 7.1) is also distinct, and we can speculate that there are no intervening adaptive peaks allowing the evolution and persistence of intermediate forms. But it is not clear whether this intriguing adaptive diastema corresponds to the architecture of shrubs and trees or whether some other mechanism is depressing the adaptive landscape between the twig specialists and all other adaptive morphologies. A more thorough examination of the twig specialist's niche would appear to be fertile ground for those interested in adaptive evolution.

'Adaptations can be understood only through their ecological context'

Are the different morphologies adaptive? Indeed, it appears that they are. Long-legged lizards can run faster and jump higher and farther than short-limbed forms. Both traits are likely to increase the ability to catch prey and evade predators. So what advantage does the short-limbed form possess over its more stocky and quick cousin? It turns out that speed depends on substrate: whereas the long-limbed forms can outperform short-legged lizards on broad substrates (such as the trunks of trees occupied by the long-legged ecomorphs), they cannot run faster than short-limbed species on narrow substrates (such as twigs), and are far less agile. These observations, however, can only infer adaptation in the light of their ecological context. Long-legged, fast species use their speed to escape from predators (Irschick and Losos 1998). The short-limbed, sure-footed lizards use stealth and crypsis to minimize detection by predators. So it is not just the performance of the trait that is important; its function can be understood only with reference to ecology.

Bieke Vanhooydonck and Duncan Irschick (2002) tested the correlation between morphology and ecological context directly. They followed Jonathan Losos' lead and summarized morphology of 46 old-world lizard species and 46 *Anolis* species with principal components analysis.[5] Then they did the same for a series of variables representing performance (measures of speed, endurance, and manoeuvrability) and habitat use. Next, they examined ecomorphological significance by searching for

---

[5] Principal components reduce the shared variation amongst a set of independent variables into a much smaller descriptive subset that reveals how the variables correlate with one another.

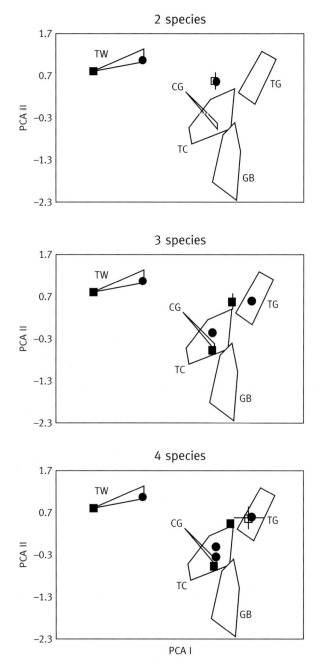

Figure 7.3. The location of current and hypothetical ancestral communities of *Anolis* lizards along two principal components representing the ecomorphology of these mostly arboreal species. The pattern can be further refined by additional principal components. Filled circles represent Anole communities in Jamaica, filled squares represent Puerto Rico. From Losos (1992), reproduced with permission from Oxford University Press.

Box 7.1. How do niches evolve?

Niche evolution is a response to the presence or absence, and relative abundances, of other species in the environment. So it is actually best to think of niches co-evolving. Interactions among species, whether competitors, predators, prey, or mutualists, dictate the range of resources that can be exploited and the habitats used for survival and reproduction. Jörgen Ripa, Joel Brown, and their co-workers explored a rather elaborate evolutionary dynamics model focused explicitly on the co-evolution of niches in a predator-prey community (Ripa *et al.* 2009). Traditionally, niche size and location were viewed as outcomes of ecological processes associated with the limiting similarity of competing species and assembly from the local community. Few considered explicitly the combined effects of ecological and evolutionary dynamics (but see, for example, Kisdi and Geritz, 2003 and Morris 2003a). Ripa's team decided not to fix the number of species in the community, but instead to let that number evolve through adaptive speciation. Answers to classical questions such as 'How many niches does a community have?', 'Are communities saturated?', or 'Is there room for more species than the current ones?' emerged from evolutionary dynamics.

Ripa *et al.* (2009) used the *G*-function approach that we explored in Chapter 6 to let the model community evolve from an initial composition of just one consumer species living on a single resource species. The evolutionary dynamics of the model took a given set of species to a convergent stable set of strategies in trait space called the niche archetypes.[6] When a strategy converged on a local minimum, the model allowed either adaptive speciation or invasion by introducing a new species with a strategy near to the 'parent' strategy. This iterative process increased the diversity of the community and led to additional co-evolution. Eventually, however, addition of new species stalled the dynamics and the system locked onto a set of locally stable maxima (each representing a different niche archetype), but failed to establish a global ESS for the feasible community because species with 'distant' strategies could invade those of the extant species.

As the community co-evolves, it will initially lie far from the ESS. These unstable incipient communities tend to produce a rugose adaptive landscape with steep selection gradients that allow new 'mutant species' to invade with high fitness. The invasion causes immediate ecological and evolutionary changes in the rest of the community. At the new ecological equilibrium, a new adaptive landscape may unfold. An invading species can thus increase opportunity for further invasions. Similarly, an adaptive speciation at one trophic level makes possible further speciation at lower or higher trophic levels.

continues

---

[6] A niche archetype is the expected outcome of gradual, directional co-evolution, and is either a local minimum or a local maximum in the adaptive landscape.

Box 7.1. (Continued)

A key point emerging from these models is that adaptive evolution combines chance with necessity. Evolutionary branching points create opportunities for speciation through disruptive selection, but opportunity alone does not necessarily lead to speciation. Gradual co-evolution stops for a community lying at ecological equilibria on the peaks of local fitness maxima, even though the community is unstable to invasion from distant strategies. But invasion of current non-members of the community can create opportunities for further radiation. In this sense communities can indeed include 'empty niches' such that even if the door for further membership seems ecologically locked, invasion can open it. In a similar vein, co-evolved communities also harbour 'dead zones' where mutant strategies with low fitness are eliminated, but nevertheless influence ecological and evolutionary dynamics on their road to extinction.[7] The pace of adaptive radiation and biodiversity, such as that exemplified by Caribbean anoles, is very much subject to the rate of invasion.[8] The probability of invasion depends, in turn, on the underlying scale and structure of the evolutionary process. Invasion in the evolutionary game varies with the contingencies of history and biogeography, and with their interactions among mechanisms responsible for genetic diversity, phenotypic plasticity, mutation, covariance among traits and strategies, dispersal, and population dynamics. Despite the time required for these various interactions and contingencies to unfold, repeated patterns in model and lizard communities teach us that ecological and evolutionary dynamics frequently run fast enough to produce quasi-stable adaptive landscapes occupied by apparently stable, yet ephemeral, communities.

---

correlations among the different sets of component variables. None of the correlations (after appropriate statistical control) was significant for the old world lizards. But as we might expect, there were strong correlations between morphology and performance by *Anolis*.

An Australian team led by Brett Goodman compared performance indicators (sprinting, climbing, clinging, jumping) among 18 species of tropical skinks (Goodman *et al.* 2007). Contrary to our usual biomechanical interpretation that form fits function, all traits were positively correlated with each other.[9] A skink species that can climb quickly

---

[7] Strategies with low fitness may persist in source–sink systems and thereby have an effect on community evolution that is disproportionate to their function and fitness.

[8] We predict that the evolutionary dynamics of invading species will be fertile ground for further explorations of adaptive radiations, the 'evolution' of extinction, and the conservation of biodiversity.

[9] The skinks belong to the highly variable sub-family Lyosominae. Body mass varied from the tiny 0.55-g *Cryptoblepharus virgatus* to the 30-g *Eulamprus quoyii*. Performance traits corrected for body size differences among species were positively correlated with one another (five out of six comparisons). All six pairwise correlations were positive when the data were simultaneously corrected for body size and phylogeny (independent contrasts). Three of the positive correlations were statistically significant.

can also jump long distances. And the correlations exist amongst species that vary dramatically in body size and morphology. The results mimic those from research at the University of Antwerp that documented a positive correlation between sprint speed and climbing capacity in rock-climbing lacterid lizards (Vanhooydonck and Van Damme 2001). The ability of skink and lacterid species to perform different locomotory tasks equally well is disquieting to those whose view of evolution demands trade-offs in traits and performance. But trade-offs must be interpreted in the context of the organisms being compared. Generalized species, by definition, should perform many different tasks well, but perhaps not as well as specialists. And tasks performed by one group of organisms may have different fitness consequences than the same sets of tasks performed by another group (different fitness-mapping functions). So we should not necessarily expect the same trade-off pattern amongst organisms that make their living in dramatically different ways. Semi-arboreal anoles are not built on the same body plan as rock-hugging skinks, and have evolved in an ecological context where different locomotory skills are related directly to anti-predator behaviour. It will be interesting to learn whether differences in the ecological settings of the skinks relative to those of anoles can explain the importance of these performance trade-offs in anoles, and their absence in skinks.[10]

'Secondary sexual traits also fit form with function'

Given our accumulating evidence of the fit of form and function for ecological traits, it is reasonable to ask questions about the functional significance of secondary sexual traits. Have such traits evolved to maximize competitive potential to procure matings or are they simply useful indicators of mating potential? Simon Lailvaux and colleagues (2005) tested this general idea on the horned dung beetle *Euoniticellus intermedius*. Female *E. intermedius* lay their eggs in tunnels that they dig under dung pats. Males guard the tunnels and use their curved horns in battles with intruders to maintain access to females. But does the horn itself reflect the ability of males to win contests with rivals?

Lailvaux *et al.* (2005) tested this idea with an ingenious experiment. First, they constructed simple beetle-size tunnels from plaster of Paris. They attached a thread to one of a male beetle's two elytra, allowed the male to enter a horizontal tunnel, then measured the force required to pull him out.[11] They measured endurance by the distance that males walked around a specially designed beetle race track until they could walk no farther. Both traits can be expected to covary with body size. So Lailvaux

---

[10] Readers should not interpret the ability to perform one set of tasks equally well as evidence that trade-offs do not exist in skinks. Skink plasticity is imprisoned by similar mechanical, morphological, physiological, developmental, and historical constraints as are other organisms.

[11] Measurement of extraction force was accomplished by the clever solution of passing the thread over a 'pulley' and slowly filling a dangling plastic pot with water. The weight of the pot and water measured the extraction force, which was converted easily into newtons.

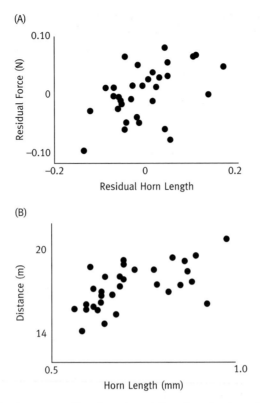

Figure 7.4. Relationships between pulling force (panel A) and maximal exertion (panel B) with horn length in the dung beetle *Euoniticellus intermedius*. After Lailvaux *et al.* (2005).

and colleagues measured horn length and body size, then included both effects in their statistical model in a way that allowed them to assess each variable's independent contribution to each estimate of performance.[12] Horn size was a reliable indicator of both performance measures (Fig. 7.4). So in this species, even secondary sexual characters possess a splendid, though indirect, fit between form and function.

> *'But sexual adaptations involve a wide array of traits, including many that*
> *may be influenced by complicated genotype × environment interactions'*

It is easy to be seduced into thinking that secondary sexual adornments and armatures evolve directly from their contributions to mating success. Mate choice and victory over rivals will often involve a wide variety of ancillary traits that either enhance the expression or effectiveness of secondary traits or contribute directly to success in sexual

---

[12] The independent effects were evaluated by calculating partial correlation coefficients when both variables were entered into a multiple regression model.

contests. Healthy individuals in good 'condition' will normally possess more vigour and stamina,[13] and thus be more capable at promoting their attractiveness, or dominance, than sickly competitors. Health and condition are not traits under direct genetic control, but instead emerge from the grand panoply of possible interactions among genes, development, function, and environment that are responsible for the numerous unavoidable detours on the road from genes to fitness. Canadian evolutionary biologists Michael Whitlock and Aneil Agrawal (2009) use similar reasoning to argue that sexual adaptation (normally called sexual selection) should often act synergistically with viability and fecundity on most, if not all, of the genome.[14] But because health and condition are better considered 'states' that wax and wane throughout an organism's lifetime,[15] rather than phenotypic traits or characters that 'identify' the individual, it is unclear how dilute their effects may be on overall adaptation.

Expression of many sexually adapted traits will, however, covary with condition and early development. Experiments at the University of Toronto by Kevin Judge and colleagues (Judge *et al.* 2008) demonstrated that hatchling fall field crickets (*Gryllus pennsylvanicus*), fed a high (if rather peculiar) ratio of sieved rabbit food and white bran, called more frequently as mid-old-aged adults and lived longer than did hatchlings raised on a lower ratio of the rabbit-food–bran mixture. All adults received the same diet, so the effect of condition was carried over from juvenile exposure to diet.

Much of the interest in so-called condition dependence and sexual adaptation is directed toward their synergistic roles in general adaptation. In their review, Whitlock and Agrawal (2009) pay particular attention to the ability of sexual adaptation to purify the genome of deleterious mutations that otherwise reduce mean fitness. The basic assumption is that deleterious alleles will reduce the 'condition' of their bearers, and that selection against such alleles is more intense for one sex than for the other. If, for example, 'condition' influences mating probabilities either through mate choice or intra-sexual competition, and if we assume that females are the choosier sex,[16] then selection on males should exceed that on females. Females have a greater probability of mating with those males that express the fewest deleterious alleles.[17]

---

[13] Although a variety of indexes have been developed to quantify 'condition', it remains an elusive property of organisms. For many ecologists, concepts such as 'well conditioned' or 'healthy' organisms typically make sense only in the context of unhealthy or poorly conditioned individuals whose vitality or vigour is clearly compromised relative to the norm. Quantitative geneticists often have a different perspective, where adaptation can act directly on the genetic covariance between condition and the traits that it helps to express.

[14] We made the same point in Chapter 5 with reference to fitness correlates and habitat selection.

[15] University of Toronto evolutionary biologist Locke Rowe defines condition as representing the resources that an individual can allocate to adaptive traits other than those related to mating success (we direct interested readers to publications by Rowe and Houle (1996), Lorch *et al.* (2003), Kotiaho *et al.* (2007), and Judge *et al.* (2008)).

[16] This argument would be reversed in species where males provide the bulk of parental care.

[17] The purge of deleterious mutations by condition-dependent mate choice may also provide much of the advantage of sexual selection. Interested readers may wish to read simultaneous independent discoveries of this effect by Agrawal (2001) and Siller (2001).

*'Genotype × environment interactions in sexual ornaments increase
the likelihood of sympatric speciation'*

Condition is not simply the property of genotypes but emerges from the differential ability of genotypes to secure resources from heterogeneous environments. Locally adapted genotypes that are more likely to achieve high condition will also be most likely to express expensive secondary sexual characters. Gerrit Sander van Doorn and colleagues (2009) used this knowledge to demonstrate how condition-dependent sexual characters can enhance the rate of speciation. They began by imagining an environment composed of several habitats. A different specialized phenotype was most efficient at extracting resources from each habitat. Thus, stabilizing selection occurred within each habitat and disruptive selection occurred among them. Intermediate phenotypes had low fitness. If the habitats were dramatically different from one another and if gene flow was low, then populations could diverge to form incipient species, but in most simulations of this model, gene flow overpowered selection. Disruptive selection removed intermediate low-fitness phenotypes, but gene flow and recombination recreated them each generation.

The van Doorn team then imagined that the favoured specialists would secure more resources than less specialized individuals and would thereby achieve higher condition. Increased condition allowed the specialists to produce more attractive secondary sexual characters that advertised their true quality in the habitat to potential mates. When choosy partners maximized their fitness by selecting the highest-quality mates for the local environment, sexual selection reinforced local adaptation and greatly magnified the potential for sympatric speciation.[18]

*'The adaptive fit between form and function influences, and depends on,
the distribution, abundance, and diversity of species'*

It thus seems appropriate to ask whether the often superb adaptive fit between form and function can also explain the diversity and procession of life, and the distribution and abundance of species. Again, we can turn to *Anolis* lizards in the Caribbean for answers. Two processes can account for the local diversity of these island-dwelling species. Species may have radiated in isolation from one another, then entered communities according to the local rules of community assembly. Alternatively, lizard communities could have originated through repeated disruptive adaptation, which created the different body forms and habitat preferences, enabling species' coexistence within communities. The same process operating on different islands or in different areas on the same island could nevertheless cause the remarkable convergence of the overall pattern of coexistence among communities.

---

[18] We anticipate that new insights into the potential for sympatric speciation will emerge when scientists link condition-dependent sexual selection with theories of habitat selection (e.g. Chapter 5).

'Ecological dynamics are crucial in the assembly of species into communities, regardless of whether the available pool of species is driven by biogeographical sorting or direct adaptive evolution'

There is strong evidence for both models. Community assembly in the northern islands of the Lesser Antilles typically involves two distantly related species. But among islands, the two lineages represent sister taxa belonging, respectively, to a large-bodied group of *Anolis bimaculatus* 'species' and a smaller *A. wattsi* group of species. A research team led by the University of Wales' Roger Thorpe used over 1000 base pairs of mitochondrial DNA, as well as alleles from nuclear microsatellite loci, to reconstruct the phylogeny and colonization pathway of the *A. bimaculatus* species (Stenson *et al.* 2004, Losos and Thorpe 2004; Fig. 7.5). The general pattern is a southward migration 'down' the archipelago, which is also loosely tied to the relative ages of islands in this chain.[19] The directional and time-dependent colonization, and the associated pattern of coexisting species in separate taxa, suggest that assembly within islands was driven primarily by ecological processes. The large and small-bodied species were assorted on the basis of their respective ecological superiority and each restricted the potential for disruptive adaptation of the second species.

A very different pattern emerges from the Greater Antilles. Here, on these four species-rich islands, *Anolis* species sort into repeated assemblies of up to six different habitat-related ecomorphs. Each ecomorph is named after the habitat that it occupies. Four of the ecomorphs (crown giant, trunk-crown, trunk-ground, and twig) are common to all islands. If community assembly is caused by ecological sorting alone, then we should observe a strong correlation between the phylogeny of the species and their ecomorphology. In the extreme case, each ecomorph would represent a different monophyletic grouping of species, but if assembly occurs through ecological speciation, then it would be possible for a single lineage to give rise to different ecomorphs on different islands.

Jonathan Losos' team (Losos *et al.* 1998) contrasted the two hypotheses. First, they classified species on each island into their respective eocomorph class, then measured six morphometric characters on each individual. They standardized the morphometry by body size, then confirmed that the different ecomorphs really did cluster together in morphology. Next, they evaluated the similarity among sequences of mitochondrial DNA to build the most parsimonious lizard phylogeny. Once this was complete they asked whether the common ecomorphs on the different islands arose from common or different ancestors (Fig. 7.6). When all islands were considered, there was poor congruence between ancestry and ecomorphology. Thus, for example, the basal species on Jamaica and Puerto Rico is a twig specialist, but on Cuba it is a crown giant. And despite the similarity in the basal ancestor on Jamaica and Puerto Rico, the twig specialist is most closely related to the trunk-ground ecomorph on Jamaica and to the crown-giant on Puerto Rico.

---

[19] The outer arc of islands (St Martin, Barbuda, Antigua, Grande Terre) formed earlier than did the inner arc (St Eustasius, St Kitts, Nevis, Montserrat, Dominica).

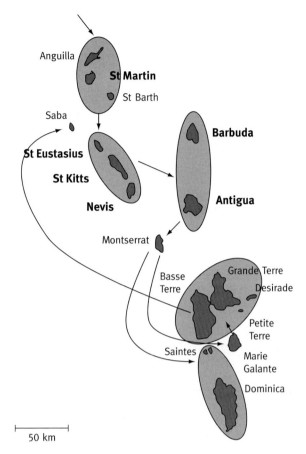

Figure 7.5. An illustration of the reconstructed colonization pathway of the *Anolis bimaculatus* group of species throughout the northern islands in the Lesser Antilles. The exceptional long-distance northward migration from Basse Terre to Saba may have been caused by serendipitous rafting in association with a north-bound hurricane in the Caribbean. From Losos and Thorpe (2004) © International Institute for Applied Systems Analysis, 2004, published by Cambridge University Press, reproduced with permission.

So for the four common ecomorphs in the Greater Antilles, the evidence overwhelmingly supports an important role for ecological speciation. *Anolis* lizards coexist because they inhabit different niches. The niches are not fixed properties of separate lizard lineages.

Does the same general rule also apply to *Anolis* communities with more than four species? To answer this question, the Losos team (Losos *et al.* 2003) assessed congruence between phylogeny and niche characteristics of the richest known *Anolis* community, comprising 11 different sympatric species in western Cuba. They determined each species' position in niche space by measuring variables representing the three resource axes along which lizard species coexist (structural habitat, thermal habitat,

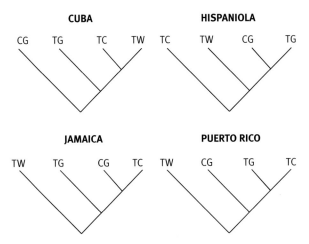

Figure 7.6. A comparison between *Anolis* ecomorphology and phylogeny of the four lizard eco-morphs common to all islands in the Greater Antilles. CG, crown-giant; TC, trunk-crown; TG, trunk-ground; TW, twig. After Losos *et al.* (1998).

prey size), and found very little correspondence with phylogeny. Put another way, the closest competitors in niche space are as likely to be distant relatives as they are to be close ones. Niche divergence is essential for anole coexistence, but it is not closely linked to phylogenetic ancestry of Greater Antillean *Anolis* lizards (Box 7.2).

Box 7.2 The biogeography of niche evolution[20]

Using the adaptive dynamics framework outlined in Chapter 6, and introducing space, we will be able to unfold some of the patterns we see, for example, in the *Anolis* lizard in the Caribbean. First, we define a *G*-function (see Equation 6.7). Depending on the relative magnitudes of the width of the resource distribution σ_K^2 and the niche width parameter σ_a^2, almost any number of species can evolve in this competitive community (Box 7.1; Ripa *et al.* 2009). Let us now extend this scenario to allow evolutionary dynamics in more than one spatial location ('habitat' or 'island'). We let there be five such habitats, which, for simplicity, are identical. We also let there be a small probability that inhabitants of any given habitat disperse to neighbouring habitats so dispersal will be in a stepping-stone fashion. In effect, the habitats ('islands') are linearly arranged and only the nearest island can be reached. When this model is simulated, starting at one end of the chain of islands, a rather striking pattern emerges (Fig. B7.2.1).

continues

---

[20] Jörgen Ripa and Mikael Pontarp at Lund University have made significant contributions to the model presented here.

Box 7.2. (Continued)

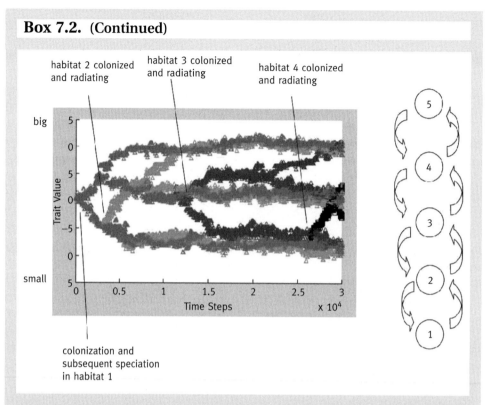

Figure B7.2.1. The evolution of species diversity and body size on a chain of islands with nearest-neighbour dispersal (schematically illustrated to the right). Niche co-evolution and spatial distribution was simulated using a model similar to the one presented in Box 7.1. The trait values on the ordinate have arbitrary meaning (zero corresponds to the maximum of the resource distribution; equal on all islands), but here we let them represent body size. Island 1 is first colonized by a body size close to the optimal one (if the species is alone), but because the niche width is rather large in relation to the width of the resource distribution, there is disruptive selection and the original species splits into two. After some time, Island 2 is colonized (here by the smaller, i.e. smaller trait value) of the two species. Almost immediately (in phylogenetic terms) it radiates into two species: one smaller and one bigger than the ancestral colonist. As adaptation towards bigger size proceeds, the species splits again and the island will be inhabited by three species, just as on Island 1. The pattern repeats itself over and over, finally leading to a situation with all islands occupied by three species (not shown here), the size distribution being more or less identical across islands.

First, the species on the 'source' island radiates into two, one 'big', and one 'small'.[21] After some time, the bigger species splits into an even bigger one and a species of intermediate size. At the end of the simulation we have three species sorted out along the size (trait value) axis. Island 2 is colonized by the smaller of the species on Island 1. It rapidly radiates into two, then three, all roughly the same size as the three species on Island 1. Island 3 is colonized by the species of intermediate size on Island 2. It rapidly radiates into a bigger and smaller one, and after some time into three species, all the same size as the ones on Islands 1 and 2. Eventually, Island 4 is colonized by the small species on Island 3, evolving towards intermediate size and then radiating. And so the story goes on. We see a sequence of colonizations and radiations, with a final pattern of (i) all islands colonized, (ii) all islands having three species, one big, one small, and one intermediate in size. The phylogeny of body sizes is not obvious and straightforward. The big species on Island 2 originates from a small species on Island 1. The small species on Island 3 originates from an intermediate species on Island 2. The intermediately sized species on Island 3 is more closely related to a big species on Island 1, whereas the intermediate species on Island 4 is more closely related to a small one from Island 3. The patterns thus generated from this model are similar to the patterns we see on real islands, including the *Anolis* lizards in the Caribbean.

The model illustrates aspects of all of our pillars of evolution. The *mechanics* of evolution is hidden in the assumptions about mutations and inheritance (the model assumes asexual reproduction, that strategies breed true (with some noise), and that there is no limit to mutation). The strategies' *functions* are revealed in the mappings from traits (e.g. niche width here) to competitive ability and competitive exclusion. *Structure* is encapsulated in the *G*-function formulation, and the *scale* is quite clear from the temporal and spatial dimensions. *Dynamics* drives the ecological play (density-and frequency-dependent competition) in the evolutionary theatre, with the resulting *adaptations* to the available resources on the islands modified by the absence or presence of other species and conspecific individuals. If we want to understand the ecological and evolutionary dynamics of the island problem, we need all six pillars.

'The degree of community convergence depends on underlying variation in body plans as well as differences in adaptive environments'

Should we always expect the incredible community and adaptive convergence represented by *Anolis* lizards? In a word, no. A clear example comes from analyses of convergent adaptation in two genera of North American damselflies by teams led by Dartmouth College's Mark McPeek. Damselflies are smaller and more elegant cousins of their better known odonate predators, the dragonflies. The larvae, if detected, are

---

[21] The trait values have completely arbitrary meaning, but can here be interpreted as body size.

easy targets for fast-swimming insectivorous fish. They can, however, out-swim slower predatory dragonfly larvae. Even so, damselfly larvae reduce activity in habitats with predators and growth rates are thus depressed.

The genus *Enallagma* arose approximately 10–15 million years ago from ancestors living in permanent lakes harbouring fish as top predators. Most extant species are restricted to fish-inhabiting lakes, but at least three species now occupy permanent lakes where dragonflies are the top predators (Fig. 7.7; Stoks and McPeek 2006). Species belonging to a second genus, *Lestes*, evolved somewhat more recently (6–8 million years ago) from ancestors living in temporary ponds with dragonflies. A few *Lestes* species now occupy permanent ponds and lakes (where either dragonflies or fish are top predators), and at least one occupies very small temporary ponds without predators.

The life histories of both groups of univoltine species reflect the habitats that they live in. *Enallagma* species' eggs hatch into larvae during their first summer and emerge as adults in spring. Most *Lestes* species, like those of *Enallagma*, lay their eggs in summer. Their diapausing eggs are dormant over winter and do not hatch until the following spring. The three species that occupy permanent water bodies, however, hatch during their first summer and overwinter as larvae.

Let us focus on adaptive convergence of predator-mediated traits between the *Lestes* species occupying permanent ponds and lakes, and the *Enallagma* species living in ponds lacking fish. We can predict that *Lestes*, as a group, possess adaptations to increase swimming speed because they have a long evolutionary exposure to dragonfly

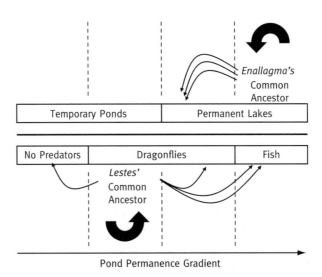

Figure 7.7. A summary of the origin and adaptive evolution of two species of North American damselflies living in temporary or permanent ponds and lakes with fish or dragonflies as top predators. Arrows indicate adaptive evolution within (broad) or among (narrow) habitats (after Stoks and McPeek 2006, with permission from the University of Chicago Press).

predators. *Enallagma* species occupying 'dragonfly lakes' should converge on these traits. Similarly, we can predict that *Lestes* species converging on *Enallagma* in lakes with fish should become less active.

Our predictions, in general, are supported by data (Fig. 7.8). Experiments on captive animals forced to swim away from a virtual predator (metal spatula) revealed that the body-size corrected swimming speeds of *Enallagma* and *Lestes* were not different from one another in dragonfly lakes. *Enallagma* living in 'fish lakes' swam more slowly. And these differences were also expressed in two traits associated with swimming ability. Lamella (gill) size and abdominal muscle mass were larger for *Enallagma* species living in dragonfly lakes than for those living in fish lakes. Similarly, species living in lakes with dragonflies moved less in laboratory experiments that exposed larvae to nearby dragonflies than when dragonflies were absent,[22] and fish-lake species were inactive for longer periods than dragonfly-lake species when fish were present (Stoks and McPeek 2006).

'Adaptive evolution proceeds at different rates for different traits'

But there were also some rather significant differences. Although *Lestes* were less active in fish lakes, they lost none of their swimming ability. The important lesson here is that adaptation to changed environments proceeds at different rates for different traits. A shift from dragonfly to fish lakes reduces activity because less active larvae survive better than active ones. But the same shift from dragonfly to fish lakes has negligible effect on swimming ability. The lack of an apparently adaptive response could have several causes, such as a shallow adaptive gradient (low cost associated with maintaining swimming speed), low additive genetic variance, trade-offs with associated pleiotropic genes, or any of the numerous mechanisms that constrain adaptation. Constraints are particularly interesting because they help us identify the limits of bauplans, and thus the likelihood that a population will reach its predicted evolutionary stability.

Adaptation in such divergent fauna as *Anolis* lizards and damselflies, in concert with historical biogeography, thus appears sufficient to explain their high diversity, as well as their overall patterns of distribution and abundance. Ecological processes operating within and among communities and within and among islands and lakes can account for the two radiations. Such adaptive radiations have much to teach us about the fourth major biological pattern, the procession of life.

'The procession of life occurs through the sequential replacement of each bauplan by others with novel adaptations'

Organisms belonging to a single bauplan should be able, with time and opportunity, to evolve any of its potential strategies. We have strong evidence for this prediction from

---

[22] Movements of damselfly larvae were observed in a safe plexiglass enclosure surrounded on all sides by a larger enclosure with, or without, predators.

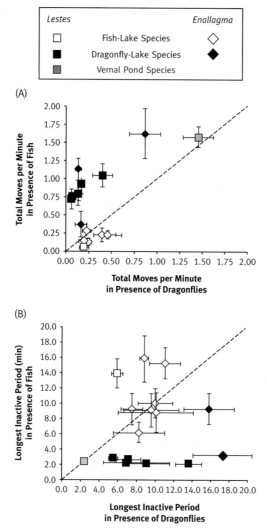

Figure 7.8. An example of convergent behavioural adaptation between two genera of North American damselfies. Panel A illustrates that species living in dragonfly lakes move much less in the presence of dragonflies than in the presence of fish. Panel B illustrates that species living in fish-lakes are much less active in the presence of fish than in the presence of dragonflies (and vice versa for dragonfly-lake species). Note that the single species living in vernal-ponds without either dragonflies or fish is more active than all others, and shows no recognition for either type of predator. The straight line represents a 1:1 correspondence between the two measurements. From Stoks and McPeek (2006), reproduced from The American Naturalist with permission of the University of Chicago Press, © 2006 by The University of Chicago. All rights reserved.

Losos' observation that anole lizards belonging to different phylogenetic lines can nevertheless crossover to inhabit different and complementary niches. But with sufficiently long periods of time, taxa do diverge from one another and become ever more distantly related. At some point, their available strategies also diverge: they break the shackles of their adaptive constraints and escape to a new and different bauplan. If successful, the new taxon will radiate. Repeated radiations yield the macroevolutionary history and procession of life from some sets of body plans and strategies to others. If this view of life is correct, we should be able to observe the clash of body plans where new and innovative strategies supplant successful strategies of the past.

We draw our favourite example from an ingenious model of macroevolution by the University of Arizona's Michael Rosenzweig (Rosenzweig and McCord 1991).[23] The model assumes that incumbent species are well adapted to their environment but, lacking a new and improved adaptation, they are susceptible to invasion and replacement. We can gain an appreciation for this process of incumbent replacement by considering Rosenzweig and McCord's interpretation of the invasion of New World crotaline snakes (pit vipers) into south-east Asia.

Crotalines, such as rattlesnakes, possess remarkable pit-like sensory organs on either side of their head that allow them to use infra-red radiation to detect, identify, and attack prey. Many other snakes also have heat receptors, but none are as well developed as the directional pits of the crotaline vipers. The crotalines originated in the New World, where they appear to have driven other vipers to extinction, then crossed the Bering Strait. One might expect that their superb bauplan would allow them to quickly supplant their non-pit relatives in Asia and beyond. But sensory ability is only one of many different adaptations that spell success for snakes. Both pit and non-pit vipers vary, for example, in colouration, body size, climbing ability, and habitat preference. Their difference is nevertheless profound. The pit vipers possess a novel weapon in their evolutionary arsenal that the other vipers lack.

We can thus imagine a scenario where the new and improved pit viper adapted to foraging in open country encounters an incumbent arboreal viper that climbs easily through the trees. As long as the incumbent is abundant, its crotaline foe cannot invade the forest and it thus is incapable of adapting to the forest habitat. But should the incumbent's population falter, the pit viper on its doorstep can invade and begin to adapt to life in the trees. As it does so, it becomes ever more efficient, eventually replacing the incumbent, which has no ability to match the pit-viper's heat-detecting skill. We thus predict that the pit vipers' advance throughout Asia and Europe will continue, that their successful adaptation will allow them to diversify, and, gradually but inexorably, replace the non-pit vipers.

When new successful bauplans emerge, they leave their evolutionary mark through adaptive radiation. Given an evolutionary foothold, they can squeeze other previously

---

[23] This system is also a favourite of Joel Brown (Brown 2001) and Thomas Vincent (Vincent and Brown 2005).

successful body plans out of existence and on to the midden of extinction. The midden's shattered fossil record allows us, through its broken history of life, to occasionally reconstruct one bauplan's demise while another rises to replace it. If we know enough about the new body plan's strategy set, we may be able to predict alternative possible routes for subsequent evolution. But we are unlikely to foresee the future sequence of constraint-breaking adaptations. And as anyone who has turned the pages of Dougal Dixon's *After man: a Zoology of the Future* (1998) knows, there is a rather stunning difference between what is imaginable or even probable in evolution, and what is possible and feasible in life on Earth.

The possible, the ephemeral, and the feasible

Earlier, we discussed the differences between gene- and development-centred views of what is possible versus feasible in adaptive evolution (Chapter 2). We defined possible trait values as those that emerged from genetics, development, and their interactions with environment. Feasible trait values were those that yielded positive fitness at low population size, values whose carriers possessed positive fitness. We learned (Chapters 5 and 6) that a trait or strategy's adaptive success varies with its ecological and evolutionary dynamics. So we need another way to display and differentiate what is possible and ephemeral in evolution versus what is feasible for adaptive eco-evolutionary stability.

Levins' fitness sets provide the solution (Fig. 7.9). For species that use their environment in a fine-grained manner, the optimal phenotype, at any density, lies along the outer 'active edge' of the convex fitness set where it lies tangential to the adaptive function at that density (see Chapter 5). All possible trait values for the current bauplan lie inside the fitness set. Any point in or along the edge of the fitness set that has negative growth rate at low density is maladapted and cannot increase in that environment when rare. Conversely, any point within the portion of the fitness set with positive fitness is a candidate for adaptive evolution, but cannot be evolutionarily stable because it can always be invaded by those individuals with trait values (phenotypes), the fitness of which lies along the outward active edge of the fitness set.

We illustrate two scenarios. In Fig. 7.9A we assume that the environment is fine grained, as displayed in Fig. 7.10A. Recall that if individuals use the two habitats in the proportions in which they occur, the adaptive function is a simple linear average of the separate contributions to fitness achieved in each habitat. The adaptive function is hyperbola-like if individuals spend their entire lifetime in one habitat or another. In the fine-grained environment displayed in Fig. 7.9A, both types of adaptive function can intercept the active edge at any point along it. Thus all trait values within this range are feasible candidates for eco-evolutionary stability regardless of the grain at which individuals exploit the environment.

Fig. 7.9B (and Fig. 7.10B) illustrate the possible solutions in a coarse-grained environment, where the fitness functions lie more distant from one another. The range of

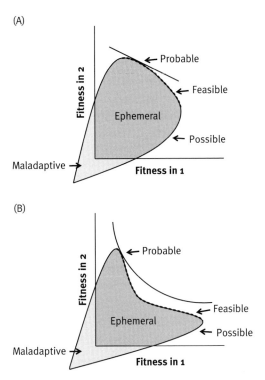

Figure 7.9. Fitness sets generated in two environments or habitats that illustrate what is possible, emphemeral, feasible, and probable in adaptive evolution. Dotted lines along the outside 'adaptive edge' specify the set of feasible solutions for adaptive evolution towards the evolutionarily stable solution. Only a subset of these solutions will remain as probable candidates for future evolution following adaptation to the adaptive function (light line) Panel A shows a concave fitness set emerging from a fine-grained environment and one of many possible linear adaptive functions. Panel B shows a convex fitness set expected when the environmental grain is coarse. The single concave curve represents one of many possible adaptive functions that might apply to individuals exploiting the two environments in a coarse-grained manner. See the text for a full explanation.

feasible strategies in this example depends critically on the shape of the adaptive function and thus the grain of exploitation. Differently shaped adaptive functions intercept the active edge at different possible points. Fine-grained exploitation and its associated linear adaptive functions can intercept the convex fitness set only along the short negatively sloped sections, where specialization on one or the other environment yields greatest fitness. So with fine-grained exploitation in a coarse-grained environment, the set of feasible evolutionarily stable strategies (ESS) consist only of extreme specialists. Coarse-grained exploitation with its associated curved adaptive functions can yield a much greater range of possible intermediate (and occasionally binary) solutions.

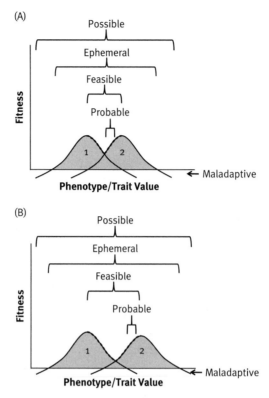

Figure 7.10. Examples of trait–fitness (phenotype–fitness) distributions that could create the abstract fitness sets illustrated in Fig. 7.9. Feasible evolutionarily stable trait values lie along the dotted lines between the modes of the two curves. In Panel A the trait–fitness distributions lie close to one another and produce a concave fitness set (Fig. 7.9A). In Panel B the trait–fitness distributions lie farther apart and produce a convex fitness set (e.g. Fig. 7.9B). Numbers identify the trait–fitness distributions in the two environments.

    Points lying along the positively sloped outward edges of concave fitness sets are particularly intriguing. These points correspond to the best possible phenotypes in that particular trait space, and can never attain evolutionary stability because the fitness set always contains other phenotypes with higher fitness. None of the phenotypes in this region can approach evolutionary equilibrium, hence each point represents what Stefan Geritz and colleagues call an evolutionary repellor (Geritz *et al.* 1998). Similar evolutionary repulsion zones exist along the boundaries of the 'cups' within convex fitness sets, where the boundary can never lie tangential to the system's adaptive function. The terms 'repellor' and 'repulsion' are a bit misleading. Any phenotype lying along a repulsion zone can exist ephemerally but other possible phenotypes always possess higher fitness. Thus, trait distributions are always attracted away from these low-fitness marginal phenotypes so that their elusive niches are unattainable by adaptive evolution.

These abstractions are necessary to grasp what is possible and impossible through evolution. We have, of course, made numerous assumptions. We assume implicitly that we are dealing only with heritable characters (traits), that we have been able to infer the traits' functions, and that we know how those functions are translated into fitness at different densities in variable environments. But it is crucially important to ask whether all feasible outcomes are equally probable. The answer to this question is clearly 'No'. Adaptation in the past will have winnowed out the losers. If trait values converge on their ESS, the genetic and developmental flexibility necessary for creation of different 'possible' trait values will often be limited. The population is likely to consist only of those values near the ESS.

Epiphenomena: where are the trees?

Anolis lizards possess a superb fit between form and function. Anoles with long hind limbs can run faster to escape predators than lizards with shorter legs. But short-limbed lizards do not rely only on sprint speed to evade predation. Instead, they tend to live in dense habitats such as brushland and forest canopies, where they use their enlarged toe pads to cling, inconspicuously, to branches and twigs. The elongated bodies of anoles with short legs distribute their weight longitudinally and let them perch on the smallest twigs in the safety of camouflaging foliage.

All naturalists can relate equally spectacular examples of superbly engineered organisms that fit the tasks they perform. The incredible 30-cm long tongue of Madagascar's giant hawkmoth is a favourite of many evolutionary biologists. The hawkmoth is a specialized pollinator of the Madagascar star orchid, which otherwise inexplicably 'hides' its reward of nectar at the end of a 30-cm long spurred floral tube.[24] Who among us has not marvelled at dandelion seeds wafting about on their silken parachutes in a warm summer breeze? Did you bid them a safe journey when they whisked aloft on the rising currents of a gentle, swirling wind, surfing the aeolian ocean like Aladdin in search of untold adventures? Perhaps, walking through an old field on a cool autumn day, you sidestepped the protective thorns protruding ominously from the twisted mass of stems in a thick scrum of brambles. Maybe you brushed, ever so lightly, against a beggartick's ripened seeds, then spent the afternoon dispersing them, one 'pitchfork' after another, from your new fleece jacket.

If you hike through native prairie grasses in the northern great plains of western North America during the early summer you will likely pause to absorb the shimmering

---

[24] The long floral tube (spur) of *Anagraecum sequepedale* was not a mystery for Charles Darwin who, on examining the white, fragrant, flower, predicted the hawkmoth's existence more than 40 years before it was finally discovered in 1903. The prediction is immortalized in the hawkmoth's scientific name, *Xanthopan morgani praedicta*.

beauty of 'needle and thread' grass wearing a glistening coat of dew in the morning sun.[25] If you return in midsummer you will find the warped corkscrew awns of detached seeds lying horizontal on the ground. What purpose could there be to maintaining the long awn after the seed is ripe? Wait a moment for a breeze and you will see the corkscrew rise up and turn with the wind, auguring the hardened tip of its pointed seed into rich prairie soil. Later that same day chances are that you will be painfully annoyed to discover that the weave of your socks gives a tangled knot of spiralled awns purchase to drive their sharpened spears deep into tender ankles.

' Despite overwhelming evidence on the often striking fit between form and function, many traits with apparent adaptive significance are epiphenomena of other traits and strategies under more direct adaptive control'

Casual naturalists can spin countless similar fables on the splendid fit between form and function; on the adaptive significance of myriad traits. They might captivate you with stories on the evolution of long-necked giraffes outreaching competitors by foraging higher than all coexisting ungulates who skilfully prune the African savannah like a bonsai gardener.[26] They might regale you with monologues on how the giant thorns of the bullhorn acacia protect the Central American plant from browsing mammals. Alas, their fables can be as much myth and wishful invention as reality.[27] In the case of the giraffe, Robert Simmons and Lue Scheepers (1996) developed a convincing alternative hypothesis. They noted that dominant bull giraffes with long necks, the preferred mates of sexually dimorphic females, intimidate shorter-necked rivals. When stature alone fails to resolve dominance, male giraffes courting oestrous females throw their necks and heads about in pitched battles like gladiators brandishing clubs. The winners have longer, more massive necks, and larger, better-armoured skulls than do the losers. Both features are larger, relative to body size and proportion, in males than in females, and larger still in the biggest males. Giraffe necks are also much longer than expected from the allometry of growth in their African forest relative, the okapi. The evolution and maintenance of the giraffe's long neck may thus be related more to its advantages in securing matings than in avoiding competition.

---

[25] Needle and thread grass, *Stipa comata*, is the provincial grass of Saskatchewan.

[26] Elephants forage at similar heights, but cause much more damage to the trees.

[27] We recommend the classic article by Stephen J. Gould and Richard Lewontin (1979) as required reading. Gould and Lewontin provide numerous examples of the risks associated with adaptationist 'story-telling'. Their main parable revolves around false interpretations that the spandrels holding up the dome of St Mark's Cathedral in Venice were designed instead to 'support' the iconography of Christianity painted on the dome's ceiling. The spandrels are a design constraint of the dome's architecture. The primary function that explains their existence is architectural, but they have also been used for a secondary purpose. There is a delightful but somewhat trivial irony in the metaphor. The 'spandrels' of San Marco are actually pendentives, a story told wonderfully by Gould (1997).

Swollen thorns protect acacias from herbivores, but mainly by mutualistic, fiercely aggressive *Pseudomyrmex* ants living in hollowed-out thorn caverns, rather than by the thorns themselves. Why do the ants attack all comers with apparent reckless abandon? The *Acacia* is both home and larder. The ants feed on protein- and lipid-rich Beltian bodies at the tips of the *Acacia*'s leaflets, and on nectar secreted by petiolar glands at the base of the compound leaves.

These observations do not mean that long necks are unimportant at reducing competition for limited forage or that thorns cannot serve multiple functions. It does mean that adaptation can be confirmed only through function. A trait's adaptive story, no matter how obvious or seductive, can easily misinform the unwary naturalist unless she demands experimental support for a specified function. If the long necks of giraffes have evolved primarily as a tool for dominance, then their use to forage at high heights is, at best, secondary to their main function in sexual contests. At worst, it represents a misleading epiphenomenon that bears no relationship to function. Giraffes do browse higher in trees than their smaller ungulate competitors. In South Africa's Kruger National Park, they appear to do so because each bite at shoulder and head height yields more food than one at the knees, where more efficient selective feeding by smaller browsers with narrow muzzles reduces the biomass available to giraffes (Woolnough and du Toit 2001, Cameron and du Toit 2007).[28] Similar patterns have not been reported in other parts of Africa, where much giraffe foraging occurs at heights accessible to competitors (Simmons and Scheepers 1996). So current evidence suggests that long necks are adaptive because they fulfil at least two important and positively correlated functions. The same is likely true for the bullhorn *Acacia* and its ancestors. Thorns do provide physical protection. Yet there can be little doubt that the primary function of today's exaggerated thorns is to provide a home for mutualistic ants.

So we must be forever vigilant if we are to detect 'traits' that are simply fortuitous epiphenomena carried along by adaptation through alternative functions. Traits, like the genes that code for them, are invisible to adaptation. Adaptation emerges only through the trait's function(s), the map of function onto fitness, and the adaptive value afforded by the environment.

> *'Whether or not a trait or strategy is an adaptation can be assessed*
> *only through its function and the function's map onto fitness'*

Tests for adaptation must, therefore, include clear statements on the presumed function of the trait or strategy, unambiguous demonstration that the trait or strategy fulfils the function, knowledge of how the function maps onto fitness, and proof that different

---

[28] Coexistence in the species-rich African ungulate guilds appears to depend on body size. Smaller selectively-feeding species may reduce the quality of forage and displace larger generalists with greater food requirements to new habitats (grazing succession) or force them to use forage unavailable to small species (height-dependent browsing).

values of the trait or strategy are adaptive in the environment(s) in which they are being tested.[29] It is easy to be deceived: recall our earlier discussion on the evolution of an optimum clutch size (Chapter 3). Positive selection differentials for clutch size have been reported in several species. Mean clutch size should thus represent an adaptive trait that, in these populations at least, is increasing through time. Does the conclusion meet our stringent requirements of proof? The trait has an obvious fitness-related function: an optimum degree of procreation maximizes fitness. When tested with controlled experiments, clutch size is heritable. When merged with data on survival, clutch size can be directly associated with fitness. Parents producing clutches larger than average also tend to produce more descendants (positive selection differentials).

The problem is that, in these studies, average clutch size does not tend to increase through time. We listed (in Chapter 3) three general reasons why positive selection differentials could fail to increase mean clutch size. The reasons included temporal and spatial variation in the environment (the adaptive value of clutch size depends on the environment), asymmetrical survival among clutch sizes (the fitness-mapping function is asymmetrically biased against large clutches), and adaptation on correlated traits (the trait's function is subsidiary to other traits such as the ability to maintain high-quality territories). Although many epiphenomena emerge through adaptation operating on correlated characters associated with genetic mechanisms such as pleiotropy and epistasis, the evolution of an optimum clutch size demonstrates that others are related to the dynamics of adaptation itself. An optimum clutch size can evolve as an adaptation that optimizes trade-offs between production and survival. It can also represent an epiphenomenon because we failed to properly identify the correlated traits (such as territoriality) undergoing adaptive evolution.

Maladaptation: lost expectations or promised success?

The existence of evolutionary epiphenomena raises the question of whether such traits and strategies 'maladapt' organisms for their environment. Unfortunately, the term 'maladaptation' has been used in several different contexts (reviewed in Crespi 2000). To us, a 'maladapted strategy' would be one existing below its carrying capacity and exhibiting net negative population growth.[30] Species with such strategies are racing toward extinction.[31] The process of maladaptation would then represent a change in

---

[29] We do not include a test for heritable variation because our definitions of 'trait' and 'strategy' already include a requirement for inheritance.

[30] The carrying capacity assumption is crucial because the definition must include both ecological and evolutionary dynamics. A strategy driven to negative fitness by high population size or other ecological dynamics is not maladapted if it is simply converging on an adaptive peak that yields positive fitness at lower densities.

[31] The fossil and phylogenetic records are filled with two types of extinct strategies. One type became extinct because their negative population growth rates failed to leave descendants. Others became extinct because they were replaced with descendant strategies yielding higher fitness elsewhere in the adaptive landscape.

the adaptive landscape that causes strategies to 'sink' more rapidly than adaptation can increase their fitness.[32] A 'maladapted strategy' could then lie anywhere on the landscape where its fitness is always negative. Maladaptation does not properly refer to the strategy (hence our use of quotation marks), but is instead associated with environments in which the adaptive landscape lies below zero fitness for all trait values.[33]

Simon Fraser University's Bernard Crespi (2000) defined maladaptative strategies differently. To Crespi, maladaptation represents the 'deviation from adaptive peaks'. The two definitions reflect whether one views their evolutionary glass as 'half empty' or 'half full'. In the Crespi definition, any strategy with a positive growth rate undergoing directional adaptation would be classified as 'maladapted'. But a strategy resting on a sinking adaptive peak would not be maladapted. The definition is not reconciled easily within a dynamic view that evolutionarily stable strategies represent ephemeral moving targets in an ongoing and endless process.

'Few traits and strategies are perfectly matched with their underlying adaptive landscape'

Regardless of definition, it is nevertheless important to identify processes that limit adaptation's ability to match trait and strategy values with their expected evolutionarily stable maxima or minima. These processes include all of the usual mechanistic suspects (mutation, drift, inbreeding, pleiotropy, epistasis, heterozygote advantage, genotype × environment interactions), plus developmental, historical, physical, and environmental constraints, environmental grain, time-lagged density-dependent responses, interspecific interactions, rates and magnitude of environmental change, and gene flow. The relative importance of different processes depends, as we have so often seen, on worldview. Predictions of optimal strategies based on models that fail to include dynamics will necessarily be constrained by time-lagged population growth and species interactions. Predictions that assume perfect heritability of strategies will be limited by the mechanics of genetics and development.

Irrespective of worldview, most of these processes are best thought of in terms of their interactions rather than as mutually exclusive, independent constraints. Closely interacting and co-evolving species, for example, often exist as mosaics whose metapopulations exchange genes among dramatically different adaptive zones. Such co-evolutionary mosaics can generate a wide spectrum of adaptive possibilities, which include a stable deviation from fitness peaks, as well as both simple and complex adaptive cycles (Thompson *et al.* 2002). Different populations would, in turn, possess different degrees of adaptation to local conditions and coexisting species, as well as different population and community dynamics, immigration and emigration rates,

---

[32] Changes in the adaptive landscape result from changes in fitness-mapping or adaptive functions, including the dynamics of density and frequency dependence.

[33] We learned earlier (Chapters 3 and 6) that ecologists typically refer to such environments as sink habitats.

mechanistic constraints, and the respective sizes of environmental grain (recall Cohen's similar conclusion in Chapter 5).

Except for simple traits with profound effects on fitness, we are unlikely to ever measure and understand the full complement of interactive processes that constrain adaptation (Chapter 4). It might be more productive to develop procedures that allow us to visualize and quantify adaptation in the context of adaptive landscapes. In principle this should be easy. We simply merge the fitness-mapping function (e.g. via fitness sets) with its corresponding adaptive function, to determine a population or species' evolutionary maximum. Then we evaluate how close the distribution of the trait or strategy matches the predicted value (Fig. 7.11). Indeed, a substantial body of literature is devoted explicitly to measuring the strength of selection on phenotypic traits (Endler 1986, Kingsolver *et al.* 2001, Kingsolver and Pfenning 2007). Most of these

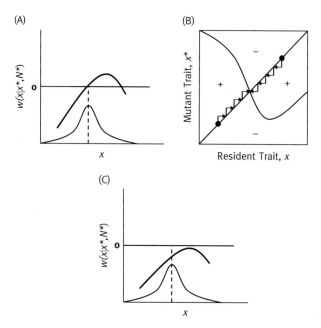

Figure 7.11. Three alternative views of adaptation and maladaptation. Panel A compares the fit of the distribution of trait values with the predicted evolutionary maximum. Evolution yields directional adaptation toward the fitness maximum. Panel B graphs the invasion dynamics (positive versus negative growth rates) of mutant trait values relative to two different initial values of the resident trait on a pairwise invasibility plot (Chapter 6). Adaptation (arrows) produces a single stable strategy. Panel C illustrates a maladaptive environment where all values of the trait posses negative fitness. Even with adaptation toward the fitness maximum, extinction is inevitable. Bold lines in panels A and C represent the adaptive landscape of the mutant's fitness; dashed lines correspond with the mean trait value in the population. After Rice (2004) and Dieckmann and Ferrière (2004).

studies aim to reveal a standardized selection gradient by calculating estimates of fitness for individuals possessing different phenotypes.[34]

A serious problem with this approach is that several mechanisms can cause a mismatch between observed and expected values. The population may not yet have attained the expected value (directional adaptation), is constrained from reaching that value, is chasing a moving target (the adaptive landscape is changing), or the model itself could be either incorrect or mis-specified.

An alternative is to use the selection gradients to query the population about how rapidly it is approaching 'equilibrium' by measuring rates of change in such things as the mean (linear gradient) and variance (quadratic gradient) of the trait value. Knowing these values, the scientist then builds successive models until one comes close to matching the empirical data.

But something rather substantial is missing in these 'tests'. What motivates our interest in measuring the current adaptiveness of the population? Is the objective to actually forecast the evolutionary trajectories of populations? Or are we content to know that we understand enough of the mechanics and dynamics of evolution to appreciate how and why traits and strategies change through time?

*' The effective study of adaptation emphasize ideas
and concepts over patterns and examples '*

The answers to these questions will not only guide our research, they will reflect our worldview. Sewall Wright used the concept of an adaptive landscape mainly as analogy to understand adaptation and evolution. We no longer need to think of adaptive landscapes as analogy. They are real. We can visualize their general outline through the characteristics of the populations and species that evolve within them. We can map their ebb and flow by measuring the growth rates of populations, documenting rates of trait divergence, measuring changes in trait distributions, and summarizing those effects with selection gradients. As we do this we are gaining deep insights into the characteristics of adaptive landscapes leading toward specialist versus generalist strategies, the processes that determine the number of coexisting species, and the rules influencing adaptive radiations.

Reflection: the thread of evolution

Biologists share a collective interest in understanding the processes that explain the fit of form and function, the diversity and procession of life, and the distribution and abundance of organisms. Answers fit comfortably in a worldview where adaptation

---

[34] Most studies calculate both a linear (measures directional selection) and quadratic (measures stabilizing and disruptive selection) gradient. We direct interested readers to Joel Kingsolver and David Pfenning's (2007) lucid review and discussion of phenotypic selection.

responds to the mechanics of procreation, inheritance and development, the dynamics of populations in heterogeneous and changing environments, the functional relationships among traits and fitness, and the constraints and opportunities of structure operating at numerous scales of organization in time and space. This worldview is not about merging genetics, development, and ecology to understand 'evolution'. Its aim is not to describe evolution as pattern or to provide myriad examples documenting adaptation's power to answer the fundamental questions of biology. Rather, it represents a philosophy and research programme aimed at understanding evolutionary processes from first principles. The philosophy is centred on the knowledge that adaptation operates on functions that influence fitness, that it is blind to traits and to their complex mappings to the genome, to function, and across environments. It is also centred on the knowledge that those mappings are crucially important to creating the pattern and structure of nature.

This worldview acknowledges that adaptation towards the ESS eliminates genetic and developmental opportunities for trait diversification. It is this very process that creates the most striking patterns in living nature. The tree of life, as we observe and measure it, is not continuous. The exquisite biodiversity that inspires poets and lovers, that Linnaeus first began to categorize scientifically, and that is now so threatened by human pride and foolishness, occurs through adaptive breaks in trait distributions and strategies. This worldview nevertheless recognizes that it is indeed possible to trace individual evolutionary threads from genes to traits to fitness. But it also recognizes that attempts to do so come at the risk of entangling oneself in the warp and weft of evolution's loom. Instead, the philosophy anchors its separate pillars on a bedrock of first principles then protects them with the capstone of adaptation. From this vantage we can observe each pillar, peer at evolution's maps, and better understand the limits and potential of some perspectives over others. The worldview does not give precedence or prominence to any subdiscipline or approach. Indeed, it forces us to sort among them, to move beyond historical groupings of research interests and search for the fundamental principles underpinning the mechanics, function, structure, scale, and dynamics of evolution. We call this worldview evology.

References

Abrams, P. A. 1986a. Adaptive responses of predators to prey and prey to predators—the failure of the arms race analogy. Evolution 40: 1229–47.

—— 1986b. Is predator prey coevolution an arms race? Trends in Ecology and Evolution 1: 108–10.

—— 2001. Adaptive dynamics: neither F nor G. Evolutionary Ecology Research 3: 369–73.

—— and H. Matsuda. 1994. The evolution of traits that determine ability in competitive contests. Evolutionary Ecology 8: 667–86.

—— H. Matsuda, and Y. Harada. 1993. Evolutionary unstable fitness maxima and stable fitness minima of continuous traits. Evolutionary Ecology Research 7: 465–87.

Abzhanov, A., W. P. Kuo, C. Harmann, B. R. Grant, P. R. Grant, and C. J. Tabin. 2006. The calmodulin pathway and evolution of elongated beak morphology in Darwin's finches. Nature 442: 563–7.

Agrawal, A. F. 2001. Sexual selection and the maintenance of sexual reproduction. Nature 411: 692–5.

—— 2010. Ecological determinants of mutation load and inbreeding depression in subdivided populations. American Naturalist 176: 111–22.

—— and J. R. Stinchcombe. 2009. How much do genetic covariances alter the rate of adaptation? Proceedings of the Royal Society B 276: 1183–91.

Andrade, M. C. B. and M. M. Kasumovic. 2005. Terminal investment strategies and male mate choice: extreme tests of Bateman. Integrative and Comparative Biology 45: 838–47.

—— L. Gu, and J. A. Stoltz. 2005. Novel male trait prolongs survival in suicidal mating. Biology Letters 1: 276–9.

—— 1996. Sexual selection for male sacrifice in the Australian redback spider. Science 271: 70–2.

Anton, J., 2000. Ceratopsian crests as acoustic devices. Sixtieth Annual Meeting of the Society of Vertebrate Paleontology, Journal of Vertebrate Paleontology, 20 (Supp 3): 17A.

Apaloo, J., J. S. Brown, and T. L. Vincent. 2009. Evolutionary game theory: ESS, convergence stability, and NIS. Evolutionary Ecology Research 11: 489–515.

Arnold, S. J. 1981. Behavioral variation in natural populations. I. Phenotypic, genetic and environmental correlations between chemoreceptive responses to prey in the garter snake, *Thamnophis elegans*. Evolution 35: 489–509.

Arnqvist, G. and L. Rowe. 2005. Sexual conflict. Princeton University Press, Princeton, NJ.

Barton, N. H., D. E. G. Briggs, J. A. Eisen, D. B. Goldstein, and N. H. Patel. 2007. Evolution. Cold Spring Harbor Laboratory Press, Cold Spring Harbor, NY.

Bates Smith, T. 1993. Disruptive selection and the genetic basis of bill size polymorphism in the African finch *Pyrenestes*. Nature 363: 618–20.

Bégin, M. and D. A. Roff. 2004. From micro- to macroevolution through quantitative genetic variation: positive evidence from field crickets. Evolution 58: 2287–304.

Bell, G. 2008. Selection: the mechanism of evolution (2nd edition). Oxford University Press, Oxford.

—— 2010. Experimental genomics of fitness in yeast. Proceedings of the Royal Society B 277: 1459–67.

Bergman, A. and M. L. Siegal. 2003. Evolutionary capacitance as a general feature of complex gene networks. Nature 424: 549–52.

Bernatchez, L., A. Chouinard, and G. Lu. 1999. Integrating molecular genetics and ecology in studies of adaptive radiation: whitefish, *Coregonus* sp., as a case study. Biological Journal of the Linnean Society 68: 173–94.

Boag, P. T. and P. R. Grant. 1981. Intense natural selection in a population of Darwin's finches (Geospizinae) in the Galápagos. Science 214: 82–5.

Bondurianeky, R. and T. Day. 2003. The evolution of static allometry in sexually selected traits. Evolution 57: 2450–8.

Bondurianeky, R. and T. Day. 2009. Nongenetic inheritance and its evolutionary implications. Annual Review of Ecology and Systematics 40: 103–25.

Boyce, M. S. and C. M. Perrins. 1987. Optimizing great tit clutch size in a fluctuating environment. Ecology 68:142–53.

Brockelman, W. Y. 1975. Competition, fitness of offspring, and optimal clutch size. American Naturalist 109: 677–99.

Brown, J. S. 1988. Patch use as an indicator of habitat preference, predation risk, and competition. Behavioral Ecology and Sociobiology 22: 37–47.

—— 1998. Game theory and habitat choice. In L. A. Dugatkin and H. K. Reeve, eds. Game theory and animal behaviour. Oxford University Press, Oxford, 188–220.

—— 2001. Fit of form and function, diversity of life, and procession of life as an evolutionary game. In S. Orzack and E. Sober, eds. Adaptationism and optimality. Cambridge University Press, Cambridge, 114–60.

—— and B. P. Kotler. 2004. Hazardous duty pay and the foraging cost of predation. Ecology Letters 7: 999–1014.

—— R. A. Morgan, and B. D. Dow. 1992. Patch use under predation risk II: a test with fox squirrels, *Sciurus niger*. Annales Zoologici Fennici 29: 311–18.

Brown, J. H., P. A. Marquet, and M. L. Taper. 1993. Evolution of body size: consequences of an energetic definition of fitness. American Naturalist 142: 573–84.

—— J. F. Gillooly, A. P. Allen, V. M. Savage, and G. B . West. 2004. Toward a metabolic theory of ecology. Ecology 85: 1771–1789.

Cameron, E. Z. and J. T. du Toit. 2007. Winning by a neck: tall giraffes avoid competing with shorter browsers. American Naturalist 169: 130–5.

Capellini, I., C. Venditti, and R. A. Barton. 2010. Phylogeny and metabolic scaling in mammals. Ecology 91: 2783–93.

Caswell H. 2001. Matrix population models. Sinauer Associates, Inc. Sunderland, MA.

Charnov, E. L. 1976. Optimal foraging: the marginal value theorem. Theoretical Population Biology 9: 129–36.

—— and J. R. Krebs. 1974. On clutch size and fitness. Ibis 116: 217–19.

Civetta, A. and A. G. Clark. 2000. Correlated effects of sperm competition and postmating female mortality. Proceedings of the National Academy of Sciences, USA 97: 13162–5.

Clutton-Brock, T. H., F. E. Guinness, and S. D. Albon. 1982. Red deer: behavior and ecology of two sexes. University of Chicago Press, Chicago, IL.

—— S. D. Albon, and F. E. Guinness. 1984. Maternal dominance, breeding success, and birth sex ratios in red deer. Nature 308: 358–60.

—— —— —— 1986. Great expectations: dominance, breeding success and offspring sex ratios in red deer. Animal Behaviour 34: 460–71.

Cohen, D. 2006. Modeling the evolutionary and ecological consequences of selection and adaptation in heterogeneous environments. Israel Journal of Ecology and Evolution 52: 467–84.

Cohen, Y., T. L. Vincent, and J. S. Brown. 1999. A G-function approach to fitness minima, fitness maxima, evolutionarily stable strategies, and adaptive landscapes. Evolutionary Ecology Research 1: 923–42.

Cooke, F., P. D. Taylor, C. M. Francis, and R. F. Rockwell. 1990. Directional selection and clutch size in birds. American Naturalist 136: 261–7.

Cooper, W. S. and R. H. Kaplan. 1982. Adaptive 'coin-flipping'—a decision-theoretical examination of natural selection for random individual variation. Journal of Theoretical Biology 94: 135–51.

Coulson, T., T. G. Benton, P. Lundberg, S. R. X. Dall, and B. E. Kendall. 2006. Putting evolutionary biology back in the ecological theatre: a demographic framework mapping genes to communities. Evolutionary Ecology Research 8: 1155–71.

Crespi, B. J. 2000. The evolution of maladaptation. Heredity 84: 623–9.

Cronin, H. 2005. Adaptation: 'a critique of some current evolutionary thought'. Quarterly Review of Biology 80: 19–26.

Darwin, C. 1859. The origin of species by means of natural selection, or the preservation of favoured races in the struggle for life. John Murray, London.

Dawkins, R. 1976. The selfish gene. Oxford University Press, Oxford.

—— 1986. The blind watchmaker. W. W. Norton, New York.

—— 1997. Climbing mount improbable. W. W. Norton, New York.

Debat, V. and P. David. 2001. Mapping phenotypes: canalization, plasticity and developmental stability. Trends in Ecology and Evolution 16: 555–61.

Dekinga, A., M. W. Dietz, A. Koolhaas, and T. Piersma. 2001. Time course and reversibility of changes in the gizzards of red knots alternately eating hard and soft food. Journal of Experimental Biology 204: 2167–73.

del Rio, C. M. 2008. Metabolic theory or metabolic models? Trends in Ecology and Evolution 23: 256–60.

Dieckmann, U. and M. Doebeli. 1999. On the origin of species by sympatric speciation. Nature 400: 354–7.

—— and R. Ferrière. 2004. Adaptive dynamics and evolving biodiversity. In R. Ferrière, U. Dieckmann, and D. Couvet, eds. Evolutionary conservation biology. Cambridge University Press, Cambridge, 188–224.

—— and R. Law. 1996. The dynamical theory of coevolution: a derivation from stochastic ecological processes. Journal of Mathematical Biology 34: 579–612.

Dixon, D. 1998. After man: a zoology of the future (New edition). St Martin's Griffin, New York.

Dobzhansky, T., F. J. Ayala, G. L. Stebbins, and J. W. Valentine. 1977. Evolution. W. H. Freeman and Company, San Francisco.

Doebeli, M. and U. Dieckmann. 2000. Evolutionary branching and sympatric speciation caused by different kinds of ecological interactions. American Naturalist 156: S77–S101.

Doncaster, C. P. 2000. Extension of ideal free resource use to breeding populations and metapopulations. Oikos 89: 24–36.

Drake, A. G. and C. P. Klingenberg. 2010. Large-scale diversification of skull shape in domestic dogs: disparity and modularity. American Naturalist 175: 289–301.

Eastman, C. R. (translator and editor) 1902. Text-book of paleontology, volume II. Translated and edited from the original by K. A. Von Zittel. MacMillan and Company, New York (Figure 350, p 244).

Eldridge, N. and S. J. Gould. 1972. Punctuated equilibria: an alternative to phyletic gradualism. In T. J. M. Schopf, ed. Models in paleobiology. Freeman, Cooper & Co., San Francisco, 82–115.

Emlen, D. J., J. Hunt, and L. W. Simmons. 2005a. Evolution of sexual dimorphism and male dimorphism in the expression of beetle horns: phylogenetic evidence for modularity, evolutionary lability, and constraint. American Naturalist 166: S42–S68.

—— J. Marangelo, B. Ball, and C. W. Cunningham. 2005b. Diversity in the weapons of sexual selection: horn evolution in the beetle genus *Onthophagus* (Coleoptera: Scarabaeidae). Evolution 59: 1060–84.

Endler, J. A. 1986. Natural selection in the wild. Princeton University Press, Princeton, NJ.

Fairbairn, D. J. and J. P. Reeve. 2001. Natural selection. In C. W. Fox, D. A. Roff, and D. J. Fairbairn, eds. Evolutionary ecology: concepts and case studies. Oxford University Press, Oxford, 29–43.

Felsenstein, J. 1985. Phylogenies and the comparative method. American Naturalist 125: 1–15.

Fisher R.A. 1930. The genetical theory of natural selection. Clarendon Press, Oxford.

Flatt, T. 2005. The evolutionary genetics of canalization. Quarterly Review of Biology 80: 287–316.

Forbes, S. 2005. A natural history of families. Princeton University Press, Princeton, NJ.

Fox, C. W. and M. E. Czesak. 2000. Evolutionary ecology of progeny size in arthropods. Annual Review of Entomology 45: 341–69.

Frank, S. A. 1995. George Price's contributions to evolutionary genetics. Journal of Theoretical Biology 175: 373–88.

—— 1997. The Price equation, Fisher's fundamental theorem, kin selection, and causal analysis. Evolution 51: 1712–29.

Freeman, S. and J. C. Herron. 2004. Evolutionary analysis (3rd edition). Pearson/Prentice Hall, Upper Saddle River, NJ.

—— —— 2007. Evolutionary analysis (4th edition). Pearson/Prentice Hall, Upper Saddle River, NJ.

Fretwell, S. D. and H. L. Lucas Jr. 1969. On territorial behavior and other factors influencing habitat distribution in birds. Acta Biotheoretica 14: 16–36.

Futuyma, D. J. 1998. Evolutionary biology (3rd edition). Sinauer Associates, Inc. Sunderland, MA.

—— 2005. Evolution. Sinauer Associates Inc. Sunderland, MA.

Gavrilets, S. 1997. Evolution and speciation in holey adaptive landscapes. Trends in Ecology and Evolution 12: 307–12.

Geritz, S. A. H., É. Kisdi, G. Meszéna, and J. A. J. Metz. 1998. Evolutionary singular strategies and the adaptive growth and branching of the evolutionary tree. Evolutionary Ecology 12: 35–57.

Gluckman, P. D., M. A. Hanson, and H. G. Spencer. 2005. Predictive adaptive responses and human evolution. Trends in Ecology and Evolution 20: 527–33.

Gomulkiewicz, R., R. D. Holt, M. Barfield and S. L. Nuismer. 2010. Genetics, adaptation, and invasion in harsh environments. Evolutionary Applications 3: 97–108.

Goodman, B. A., A. K. Krockenberger, and L. Schwarzkopf. 2007. Master of them all: performance specialization does not result in trade-offs in tropical lizards. Evolutionary Ecology Research 9: 527–46.

Gottfred, J. and A. Gottfred. 1995. The life of David Thompson. Northwest Journal ISSN 1206–4203, Vol. V: pp.1–19. http://www.northwestjournal.ca, accessed 17 April 2006.

Gould, S. J. 1973. Positive allometry of antlers in the 'Irish elk', *Megaloceros giganteus*. Nature 244: 375–6.

—— 1997. The exaptive excellence of spandrels as a term and prototype. Proceedings of the National Academy of Sciences, USA 94: 10750–5.

—— and R. C. Lewontin. 1979. The spandrels of San Marco and the Panglossian paradigm: a critique of the adaptationist programme. Proceedings of the Royal Society B 205: 581–98.

Grant, P. R. 1986. Ecology and evolution of Darwin's finches. Princeton University Press, Princeton, NJ.

—— and B. R. Grant. 2006. Evolution of character displacement in Darwin's finches. Science 313: 224–6.

Hamilton, W. D. 1980. Sex versus non-sex versus parasite. Oikos 35: 282–90.

Harvey, P. H. and M. D. Pagel. 1991. The comparative method in evolutionary biology. Oxford University Press, Oxford.

Heino, M., J. A. J. Metz, and V. Kaitala. 1997. Evolution of mixed maturation strategies in semelparous life histories: the crucial role of dimensionality of feedback environment. Philosophical Transactions of the Royal Society B 352: 1647–55.

Heywood, J. S. 2005. An exact form of the breeder's equation for the evolution of a quantitative trait under natural selection. Evolution 59: 2287–98.

Hofbauer, J. and K. Sigmund. 1998. Evolutionary games and population dynamics. Cambridge University Press, Cambridge.

Holmes, R. B., C. Forster, M. Ryan, and K. M. Shepherd. 2001. A new species of *Chasmosaurus* (Dinosauria: Ceratopsia) from the Dinosaur Park formation of southern Alberta. Canadian Journal of Earth Sciences 38: 1423–38.

Holt, R. D. 2003. On the evolutionary ecology of species' ranges. Evolutionary Ecology Research 5: 159–78.

—— 2007. IJEE Soapbox: In ecology and evolution, when I say 'I', should I mean 'we'? Israel Journal of Ecology and Evolution 53: 1–7.

—— T. M. Knight, and M. Barfield. 2004. Allee effects, immigration, and the evolution of species niches. American Naturalist 163: 253–63.

Houle, D. 1991. Genetic covariance of fitness correlates: what genetic correlations are made of and why it matters. Evolution 45: 630–48.

Houston, A. I. and J. M. McNamara. 1999. Models of adaptive behaviour: an approach based on state. Cambridge University Press, Cambridge.

Irschick, D. J. and J. B. Losos. 1998. A comparative analysis of the ecological significance of maximal locomotor performance in Caribbean *Anolis* lizards. Evolution 52: 219–26.

Judge, K. A., J. J. Ting, and D. T. Gwynne. 2008. Condition dependence of male life span and calling effort in a field cricket. Evolution 62: 868–78.

Kacelnik, A., J. R. Krebs, and C. Bernstein. 1992. The ideal free distribution and predator-prey populations. Trends in Ecology and Evolution 7: 50–5.

Kaplan, R. H. and W. S. Cooper. 1984. The evolution of developmental plasticity in reproductive characteristics: an application of the 'adaptive coin-flipping' principle. American Naturalist 123: 393–410.

Kawecki, T. 2004. Genetic theories of sympatric speciation. In U. Dieckmann, M. Doebeli, J. A. J. Metz, and D. Tautz, eds. Adaptive speciation. Cambridge University Press, Cambridge, 36–53.

Kawecki, T. J. and R. D. Holt. 2002. Evolutionary consequences of asymmetric dispersal rates. American Naturalist 160: 333–47.

Kennedy, M. and R. D. Gray. 1993. Can ecological theory predict the distribution of foraging animals? A critical analysis of experiments on the ideal free distribution. Oikos 68: 158–66.

Kilfoil, M. L., P. Lasko, and E. Abouheif. 2009. Stochastic variation: from single cell to superorganisms. HFSP Journal 3: 379–85.

Kimbrell, T. 2010. Canalization and adaptation in a landscape of sources and sinks. Evolutionary Ecology 24: 891–909.

—— and R. D. Holt. 2007. Canalization breakdown and evolution in a source-sink system. American Naturalist 169: 370–82.

Kingsolver, J. G. and D. W. Pfenning. 2007. Patterns and power of phenotypic selection in nature. Bioscience 57: 561–72.

Kingsolver, J. G., H. E. Hoekstra, J. M. Hoekstra, D. Berrigan, S. N. Vignieri, C. E. Hill, A. Hoang, P. Gilbert, and P. Beerli. 2001. The strength of phenotypic selection in natural populations. American Naturalist 157: 245–61.

Kisdi, É. and S. A. H. Geritz. 2003. Competition-colonization trade-off between perennial plants: exclusion of the rare species, hysteresis effects and the robustness of coexistence under replacement competition. Evolutionary Ecology Research 5: 529–48.

Klingenberg, C. P. 1998. Heterochrony and allometry: the analysis of evolutionary change in ontogeny. Biological Reviews 73: 79–123.

—— 2010. Evolution and development of shape: integrating quantitative approaches. Nature Reviews Genetics 11: 623–35.

Kodric-Brown, A., R. M. Sibly, and J. H. Brown. 2006. The allometry of ornaments and weapons. Proceedings of the National Academy of Sciences USA 103: 8733–8.

Kotiaho, J. S., N. R. LeBas, M. Puurtinen, and J. L. Tomkins. 2007. On the resolution of the lek paradox. Trends in Ecology and Evolution 23: 1–3.

Lack, D. 1947. The significance of clutch size. I. Intraspecific variation. Ibis 89:302–52.

—— 1948. The significance of litter size. Journal of Animal Ecology 17: 45–50.

Lailvaux, S. P., J. Hathway, J. Pomfret, and R. J. Knell. 2005. Horn size predicts physical performance in the beetle *Euoniticellus intermedius* (Coleoptera: Scarabaeidae). Functional Ecology 19: 632–9.

Lande, R. 1976. Natural selection and random genetic drift in phenotypic evolution. Evolution 30: 314–34.

—— 1979. Quantitative genetic analysis of multivariate evolution applied to brain-body size allometry. Evolution 33: 402–16.

—— 1980. The genetic covariance between characters maintained by pleiotropic mutations. Genetics 94: 203–15.

—— 1982. A quantitative theory of life-history evolution. Ecology 63: 607–15.

—— and S. J. Arnold. 1983. The measurement of selection on correlated characters. Evolution 37: 1210–26.

Laska, M. S. and J. T. Wooton. 1998. Theoretical concepts and empirical approaches to measure interaction strength. Ecology 79: 461–76.

Law, R. 1979. Optimal life histories under age-specific predation. American Naturalist 114: 399–417.

Levins, R. 1962. Theory of fitness in a heterogeneous environment, I. The fitness set and adaptive function. American Naturalist 96: 361–78.

Levins, R. 1968. Evolution in changing environments. Princeton University Press, Princeton, NJ.

—— 1969. Some demographic and genetic consequence of environmental heterogeneity for biological control. Bulletin of the Entomological Society of America 15: 237–40.

Li, B-L., V. G. Gorshkov, and A. M. Makarieva. 2004. Energy partitioning between different-sized organisms and ecosystem stability. Ecology 85: 1811–13.

Lively, C. M. 2010. A review of Red Queen models for the persistence of obligate sexual reproduction. Journal of Heredity 101: S13-S20.

Lorch, P. D., S. Proux, L. Rowe, and T. Day. 2003. Condition-dependent sexual selection can accelerate adaptation. Evolutionary Ecology Research 5: 867–81.

Loreau, M. 2010. From populations to ecosystems. Princeton University Press, Princeton, NJ.

Losos, J. B. 1992. The evolution of convergent structure in Caribbean *Anolis* communities. Systematic Biology 41: 403–20.

—— and R. S. Thorpe. 2004. Evolutionary diversification of Caribbean *Anolis* lizards. In U. Dieckmann, M. Doebeli, J. A. J. Metz, and D. Tautz, eds. Adaptive speciation. Cambridge University Press, Cambridge, 322–44.

—— T. R. Jackman, A. Larson, K. de Queiroz, L. Rodríguez-Schettino. 1998. Contingency and determinism in replicated adaptive radiations of island lizards. Science 279: 2115–18.

—— M. Leal, R. E. Glor, K. de Queiroz, P. E. Hertz, L. Rodríguez-Schettino, A. C. Lara, T. R. Jackman, and A. Larson. 2003. Niche lability in the evolution of a Caribbean lizard community. Nature 424: 542–5.

Lu, G. and L. Bernatchez. 1998. Experimental evidence for reduced hybrid viability between dwarf and normal ecotypes of lake whitefish (*Coregonus clupeaformis* Mitchill). Proceedings of the Royal Society B 265: 1025–30.

Lundberg, P. 1988. The evolution of partial migration in birds. Trends in Ecology and Evolution 3: 172–5.

Lynch, M. and J. B. Walsh. 1998. Genetics and analysis of quantitative traits. Sinauer Associates Inc., Sunderland, MA.

Mangel, M. 2006. The theoretical biologist's toolbox. Cambridge University Press, Cambridge.

Mayer, A. L. and G. N. Cameron. 2003. Consideration of grain and extent in landscape studies of terrestrial vertebrate ecology. Landscape and Urban Planning 65: 201–17.

Mazer, S. J. and J. Damuth. 2001. Evolutionary significance of variation. In C. W. Fox, D. A. Roff, and D. J. Fairbairn. Evolutionary ecology: concepts and case studies. Oxford University Press, Oxford, 16–28.

—— and C. T. Schick. 1991. Constancy of population parameters for life-history and floral traits in *Raphanus sativus* L.: 1. Norms of reaction and the nature of genotype by environment interactions. Heredity 67: 143–56.

Medawar, P. B. 1952. The uniqueness of the individual. Dover, New York.

Messina, F. J. and C. W. Fox. 2001. Offspring size and number. In C. W. Fox, D. A. Roff, and D. J. Fairbairn. Evolutionary ecology: concepts and case studies. Oxford University Press, Oxford, 113–27.

Metz, J. A. J., R. M. Nisbet, and S. A. H. Geritz. 1992. How should we define 'fitness' for general ecological scenaros? Trends in Ecology and Evolution 7: 198–202.

—— S. A. H. Geritz, G. Meszéna, F. J. A. Jacobs, and J.S. Van Heerwaarden. 1996. Adaptive dynamics: a geometrical study of the consequences of nearly faithful reproduction. In van Strien, S. J. and S. M. Verduyn Lunel (eds) Stochastic and spatial structures of dynamics systems. Proceedings of the Royal Dutch Academy of Sciences, Dordrecht, 183–231.

Mitchell, W. A. and T. J. Valone. 1990. The optimization research program: studying adaptations by their function. Quarterly Review of Biology 65: 43–52.

Moczek, A. P. 2006a. A matter of measurements: challenges and approaches in the comparative analysis of static allometries. American Naturalist 167: 606–11.

—— 2006b. Pupal remodeling and the development and evolution of sexual dimorphism in horned beetles. American Naturalist 168: 711–29.

—— and D. J. Emlen. 2000. Male horn dimorphism in the scarab beetle, *Onthophagus taurus*: do alternative reproductive tactics favour alternative phenotypes? Animal Behaviour 59: 459–66.

—— C. A. Brühl, and F-T. Krell. 2004. Linear and threshold-dependent expression of secondary sexual traits in the same individual: insights from a horned beetle (Coleoptera: Scarabaeidae). Biological Journal of the Linnean Society 83: 473–80.

Morris, D. W. 1985. Natural selection for reproductive optima. Oikos 45: 290–2.

—— 1988. Habitat-dependent population regulation and community structure. Evolutionary Ecology 2: 253–69.

—— 1992. Optimum brood size: tests of alternative hypotheses. Evolution 46: 1848–1861.

—— 1994. Habitat matching: alternatives and implications to populations and communities. Evolutionary Ecology 8: 387–406.

—— 1998. State-dependent optimization of litter size. Oikos 83: 518–28.

—— 2003a. Toward an ecological synthesis: a case for habitat selection. Oecologia 136: 1–13.

—— 2003b. How can we apply theories of habitat selection to wildlife conservation and management? Wildlife Research 30: 303–19.

—— P. Lundberg, and J. Ripa. 2001. Hamilton's rule confronts ideal free habitat selection. Proceedings of the Royal Society B 268: 921–4

Mountford, M. D. 1968. The significance of litter size. Journal of Animal Ecology 37: 363–7.

Murdoch, W. W., C. J. Briggs, and R. M. Nisbet. 2003. Consumer-resource dynamics. Princeton University Press, Princeton.

Myers, R. A. and B. Worm. 2003. Rapid worldwide depletion of predatory fish communities. Nature 423: 280–3.

—— and B. Worm. 2005. Extinction, survival, or recovery of large predatory fishes. Proceedings of the Royal Society B 360: 13–20.

Næsje, T. F., J. A. Vuorinen, and O. T. Sandlund. 2004. Genetic and morphometric differentiation among spawing sympatric spawning stocks of whitefish (*Coregonus lavaretus* L.) in Lake Femund, Norway. Journal of Limnology 63: 233–43.

Newton, I. 1979. Population ecology of raptors. Buteo Books, Vermillion, SD.

Nunney, L. 2001. Population structure. In C. W. Fox, D. A. Roff, and D. J. Fairbairn. Evolutionary ecology: concepts and case studies. Oxford University Press, Oxford, 70–83.

Nygrén, T., J. Pusenius, R. Tiilikainen, and J. Korpelainen. 2007. Moose antler polymorphism: age and weight dependent phenotypes and phenotype frequencies in space and time. Annales Zoologici Fennici 44: 445–61.

Odling-Smee, F. J., K. N. Laland, and M. W. Feldman. 2003. Niche construction: the neglected process in evolution. Princeton University Press, Princeton, NJ.

Olofsson, H. and P. Lundberg. 2007. The twofold cost of sex unfolded. Evolutionary Ecology Research 9: 1119–29.

—— J. Ripa, and N. Jonzén. 2009. Bet-hedging as an evolutionary game: the trade-off between egg size and number. Proceedings of the Royal Society B. 276: 2963–9.

Ostrom, J. H. 1964. A functional analysis of the jaw mechanics in the dinosaur *Triceratops*. Postilla 88: 1–35.

Otto, S. P. and T. Day. 2007. A biologist's guide to mathematical modeling in ecology and evolutionary biology. Princeton University Press, Princeton, NJ.

Parker, G. A. and W. J. Sutherland. 1986. Ideal free distributions when individuals differ in competitive ability: phenotype-limited ideal free models. Animal Behaviour 34: 1222–42.

Paley, W. 1802. Natural theology: or, evidences of the existence and attributes of the deity, collected from the appearances of Nature. Faulder, London.

Pfennig, D. W., M. A. Wund, E. C. Snell-Rood, T. Cruickshank, C. D. Schlichting, and A. P. Moczek. 2010. Phenotypic plasticity's impacts on diversification and speciation. Trends in Ecology and Evolution 25: 459–67.

Piersma, T. and J. Drent. 2003. Phenotypic flexibility and the evolution of organismal design. Trends in Ecology and Evolution 18: 228–33.

Pigliucci, M. 2001. Phenotypic plasticity. In C. W. Fox, D. A. Roff, and D. J. Fairbairn. Evolutionary ecology: concepts and case studies. Oxford University Press, Oxford, 58–69.

Pigliucci, M. 2005. Evolution of phenotypic plasticity: where are we going now? Trends in Ecology and Evolution 20: 481–6.

Price, G. R. 1970. Selection and covariance. Nature 227: 520–1.

—— 1972. Extension of covariance selection mathematics. Annals of Human Genetics 35: 485–90.

Price, T. and L. Liou. 1989. Selection on clutch size in birds. American Naturalist 134: 950–9.

Price, C. A., J. F. Gilooly, A. P. Allen, J. S. Weitz, and K. J. Niklas. 2010. The metabolic theory of ecology: prospects and challenges for plant biology. New Phytologist 188:696–720. doi: 10.1111/j.1469-8137.2010.03442.x

Ranta, E., P. Lundberg, and V. Kaitala. 2007. Ecology of populations. Cambridge University Press, Cambridge.

Ravigné, V., I. Olivieri, and U. Dieckmann. 2004. Implications of habitat choice for protected polymorphisms. Evolutionary Ecology Research 6: 125–45.

Rice, W. R. 2000. Dangerous liasons. Proceedings of the National Academy of Sciences, USA, 97: 12953–5.

Rice, S. H. 2004. Evolutionary theory: mathematical and conceptual foundations. Sinauer Associates Inc., Sunderland, MA.

Ridley, M. 1993. Evolution. Blackwell Scientific Publications, Osney Mead, Oxford.

Ripa, J., L. Storlind, P. Lundberg, and J. S. Brown. 2009. Niche co-evolution in resource-consumer communities. Evolutionary Ecology Research 11: 305–23.

Robinson, B. W. and K. J. Parsons. 2002. Changing times, spaces, and faces: tests and implications of adaptive morphological plasticity in the fishes of northern postglacial lakes. Canadian Journal of Fisheries and Aquatic Sciences 59: 1819–33.

Rockwell, R. F., C. S. Findlay, and F. Cooke. 1987. Is there an optimal clutch size in snow geese? American Naturalist 130: 839–63.

Rosenzweig, M. L. 1987. Habitat selection as a source of biological diversity. Evolutionary Ecology 1: 315–30.

—— 1991. Habitat selection and population interactions. American Naturalist 137: S5-S28.

—— 1995. Species diversity in space and time. Cambridge University Press, Cambridge.

—— and McCord, R. D. 1991. Incumbent replacement: evidence for long-term evolutionary progress. Paleobiology 17: 202–13.

Rowe, L. and D. Houle. 1996. The lek paradox and the capture of genetic variance by condition dependent traits. Proceedings of the Royal Society B. 263: 1415–21.

Ruse, M. 2003. Darwin and design: does evolution have a purpose? Harvard University Press, Cambridge, MA.

Ryan, M. J., A. P. Russell, D. A. Eberth, and P. J. Currie. 2001. The taphonomy of a Centrosaurus (Ornithischia: Certopsidae) bone bed from the Dinosaur Park Formation (Upper Campanian), Alberta, Canada, with comments on cranial ontogeny. Palaios 16: 482–506.

Saint-Laurent, R., M. Legault, and L. Bernatchez. 2003. Divergent selection maintains adaptive differentiation despite high gene flow between sympatric rainbow smelt ecotypes (*Osmerus mordax* Mitchill). Molecular Ecology 12: 315–30.

Schluter, D. 1993. Adaptive radiation in sticklebacks: size, shape, and habitat use efficiency. Ecology 74: 699–709.

—— 1996. Ecological speciation in fishes. Philosophical Transactions of the Royal Society B 351: 807–14.

Siegal, M. L. and A. Bergman. 2002. Waddington's canalization revisited: developmental stability and evolution. Proceedings of the National Academy of Sciences, USA 99: 10528–32.

Sih, A., A. Bell, and J. Chadwick Johnson. 2004. Behavioral syndromes: an ecological and evolutionary overview. Trends in Ecology and Evolution 19: 372–8.

Siller, S. 2001. Sexual selection and the maintenance of sex. Nature 411: 689–92.

Simmons, R. E. and L. Scheepers. 1996. Winning by a neck: sexual selection in the evolution of girafffe. Amercian Naturalist 148: 771–86.

Smith, C. C. and S. D. Fretwell. 1974. The optimal balance between size and number of offspring. American Naturalist 108: 499–506.

Starck, J. M. 1999. Phenotypic flexibility of the avian gizzard: rapid, reversible and repeated changes of organ size in response to changes in dietary fibre content. Journal of Experimental Biology 202: 3171–9.

Stearns, S. C. and R. F. Hoekstra. 2000. Evolution: an introduction. Oxford University Press, Oxford.

Stearns, S., G. de Jong, and B. Newman. 1991. The effects of phenotypic plasticity on genetic correlations. Trends in Ecology and Evolution 6: 122–6.

Stenson, A. G., R. S. Thorpe, and A. Malhorta. 2004. Evolutionary differentiation of *bimaculatus* group anoles based on analyses of mtDNA and microsatellite data. Molecular Phylogenetics and Evolution 32: 1–10.

Stoks, R. and M. A. McPeek. 2006. A tale of two diversifications: reciprocal habitat shifts to fill ecological space along the pond permanence gradient. American Naturalist 168: S50–S72.

Tatar, M. 2001. Senescence. In C. W. Fox, D. A. Roff, and D. J. Fairbairn. Evolutionary ecology: concepts and case studies. Oxford University Press, Oxford, 128–41.

Thompson, J. N., S. L. Nuismer, and R. Gomulkiewicz. 2002. Coevolution and maladaptation. Integrative and Comparative Biology 42: 381–7.

Tomkins, J. L., J. S. Kotiaho, and N. R. LeBas. 2005. Matters of scale: positive allometry and the evolution of male dimorphisms. American Naturalist 165: 389–402.

—— —— —— 2006. Major differences in minor allometries: a reply to Moczek. American Naturalist 167: 612–18.

Trivers, R. L. and D. E. Willard. 1973. Natural selection of parental ability to vary the sex ratio of offspring. Science 179: 90–2.

van Doorn, G. S., U. Dieckmann, and F. J. Weissing. 2004. Sympatric speciation by sexual selelection: a critical re-evaluation. American Naturalist 63: 709–25.

—— —— —— 2006. The long-term evolution of multilocus traits under frequency-dependent disruptive selection. Evolution 60: 2226–38.

—— —— —— and P. Edelar. 2009. On the origin of species by natural and sexual selection. Science 326: 1704–7.

Vanhooydonck, B. and D. J. Irschick. 2002. Is evolution predictable? Evolutionary relationships of divergence in ecology, performance and morphology in old and new world lizard radiations. In P. Aerts, K. D'Août, A. Herrel, and R. Van Damme, eds. Topics in functional and ecological vertebrate morphology, Shaker Publishing, Maastricht, 191–204.

—— and R. Van Damme. 2001. Evolutionary trade-offs in locomotor capacities in lacterid lizards: are splendid sprinters clumsy climbers? Journal of Evolutionary Biology 14: 46–54.

van Noordwijk, A. J., J. H. van Balen, and W. Scharloo. 1981. Genetic and environmental variation in clutch size of the great tit (*Parus major*). Netherlands Journal of Zoology 31: 342–72.

van Valen, L. 1973. A new evolutionary law. Evolutionary Theory 1: 1–30.

Vincent, T. L. and J. S. Brown. 1984. Stability in an evolutionary game. Theoretical Population Biology 26: 408–27.

—— —— 2005. Evolutionary game theory, natural selection, and darwinian dynamics. Cambridge University Press, Cambridge.

Vincent, T. L., Cohen, Y., and Brown, J. S. 1993. Evolution via strategy dynamics. Theoretical Population Biology 44: 149–76.

Waddington, C. H. 1942. Canalization of development and the inheritance of acquired characters. Nature 150: 563–5.

—— 1957. The strategy of the genes. George Allen and Unwin, London.

Warrick, D. R., B. W. Tobalske, and D. R. Powers. 2005. Aerodynamics of the hovering hummingbird. Nature 435: 1094–7.

Wasik, B. R., D. J. Rose, and A. P. Moczek. 2010. Beetle horns are regulated by the *Hox* gene, *Sex combs reduced*, in a species- and sex-specific manner. Evolution & Development 12: 353–62.

West, G. B., J. H. Brown, and B. J. Enquist. 1997. A general model for the origin of allometric scaling laws in biology. Science 276: 122–6.

West-Eberhard, M. J. 2003. Developmental plasticity and evolution. Oxford University Press, Oxford.

—— 2005. Developmental plasticity and the origin of species differences. Proceedings of the National Academy of Sciences, USA 102: 6543–9.

Whitlock, M. C. 2002. Selection, load and inbreeding depression in a large metapopulation. Genetics 160: 1191–1202.

—— and A. F. Agrawal. 2009. Purging the genome with sexual selection: reducing mutation load through selection on males. Evolution 63: 569–82.

Williams, G. C. 1957. Pleiotropy, natural selection, and the evolution of senescence. Evolution 11: 398–411.

—— 1966. Adaptation and natural selection: a critique of some current evolutionary thought. Princeton University Press, Princeton, NJ.

Wilson, D. S. 1975. A theory of group selection. Proceedings of the National Academy of Science, USA 72: 143–6.

—— 2001. Cooperation and altruism. In C. W. Fox, D. A. Roff, and D. J. Fairbairn, eds. Evolutionary ecology: concepts and case studies. Oxford University Press, Oxford, 222–31.

—— 2002. Darwin's cathedral: evolution, religion, and the nature of society. University of Chicago Press, Chicago, IL.

—— and E. O. Wilson. 2007. Rethinking the theoretical foundation of sociobiology. Quarterly Review of Biology 82: 327–48.

—— —— 2008. Evolution 'for the good of the group'. American Scientist 96: 380–9.

Woolnough, A. P. and J. T. du Toit. 2001. Vertical zonation of browse quality in tree canopies exposed to a size-structured guild of African browsing ungulates. Oecologia 129: 585–90.

Worm, B., E. B. Barbier, N. Beaumont, J. E. Duffy, C. Folke, B. S. Halpern, J. B. C. Jackson, H. K. Lotze, F. Micheli, S. R. Palumbi, E. Sala, K. A. Selkoe, J. J. Stachowicz, and R. Watson. 2006. Impacts of biodiversity loss on ocean ecosystem services. Science 314: 787–90.

Worm, B., R. Hilborn, J. K. Baum, T. A. Branch, J. S. Collie, C. Costello, M. J. Fogarty, E. A. Fulton, J. A. Hutchings, S. Jennings, O. P. Jensen, H. K. Lotze, P. M. Mace, T. R. McClanahan, C. Minto, S. R. Palumbi, A. M. Parma, D. Ricard, A. A. Rosenberg, R. Watson, and D. Zeller. 2009. Rebuilding global fisheries. Science 325: 578–85.

Wright, S. 1931. Evolution in mendelian populations. Genetics 16: 97–159.

—— 1932. The roles of mutation, inbreeding, cross-breeding and selection in evolution. Proceedings of the 6th International Congress of Genetics 1: 356–66.

—— 1969. Evolution and genetics of populations, Vol. 2. University of Chicago Press, Chicago.

Index

Note: page numbers in *italics* refer to Figures and Tables.